Christina Wink

W9-COW-839

Lost Childhoods

The Plight of
the Parentified Child

Gregory J. Jurkovic, Ph.D.

 BRUNNER/MAZEL, *Publishers* • New York
A member of the Taylor & Francis Group

Library of Congress Cataloging-in-Publication Data

Jurkovic, Gregory J.
    Lost childhoods : the plight of the parentified child / Gregory J.
Jurkovic.
        p.   cm.
    Includes bibliographical references (p.   ) and index.
    ISBN 0-87630-825-6 (hard)
    1. Parental influences.   2. Stress in children.   3. Problem
families.   4. Helping behavior in children.   5. Role playing in
children.   I. Title.
RJ507.P35J87   1997
618.92'89071—dc21   96-54241
                                                                  CIP

Copyright © 1997 by Brunner/Mazel, Inc.

All rights reserved. No part of this book may be reproduced
by any process whatsoever without the written
permission of the copyright owner.

Published by
BRUNNER/MAZEL, INC.
19 Union Square West
New York, New York 10003

Manufactured in the United States of America

10 9 8 7 6 5 4 3 2 1

CONTENTS

iv   Contents

ACKNOWLEDGMENTS

Many people have contributed to this work—both directly and indirectly. I am indebted to my mentor, Norman Prentice, Ph.D., who introduced me to the excitement and relevance of clinical research and practice when I was a graduate student at the University of Texas at Austin. His example as a consummate clinician and articulate contributor to the literature in clinical child and family psychology continues to inspire my work.

My subsequent collaboration with Robert Selman, Ph.D., on the Harvard-Judge Baker Social Reasoning Project further instilled in me a commitment to test theory and research against the exigencies of clinical practice. I am grateful to have worked with a scientist-practitioner of Bob's caliber. Ernest Bergel, M.D., also at the Judge Baker Child Guidance Center, deserves credit as well. In addition to modeling the essence of a compassionate, intelligent, and ethical professional, he encouraged my early work in the area of parentification and my interest in integrative clinical approaches.

I am also intellectually indebted to a number of investigators and theoreticians whose ideas and observations have greatly enriched my understanding and treatment of destructive parentification: Ivan Boszormenyi-Nagi, M.D., Mark Karpel, Ph.D., Urie Bronfenbrenner, Ph.D., Salvador Minuchin, M.D., John Bowlby, M.D., Murray Bowen, M.D., Alice Miller, M.D., L. Alan Sroufe, Ph.D., Carolyn Zahn-Waxler, Ph.D., and their collaborators. Unfortunately, Mark Karpel's major writing in this area exists only in the form of an unpublished doctoral dissertation. Serious students of parentification would be well advised to obtain this work through University Microfilms.

Numerous graduate and undergraduate students have contributed in various ways to this project. They have worked with me on master's theses, doctoral dissertations, tutorials, and special projects on parentification, participated in my proseminars and research groups in the area, reviewed drafts of different chapters, and served as my co-therapists with parentified children and their families. The enthusiastic and helpful collaboration of these associates merits special recognition: Donna Ulrici, Ph.D., Ed Jessee, Ph.D., Michael Sessions, Ph.D., Linda Goglia, Ph.D., Clare Rubin, Ph.D., Robert Godsall, Ph.D., Joan Wolkin, Ph.D., Afton Burt, Ph.D., Kim Deffebach, M.A., Claire McLauchlin, M.A., Alan Schuererman, M.A., Joseph Cullen, M.A., Graham Jelley, M.A., Marion Latham, Ph.D., Amy Erskine, B.S., Lisa Bell, B.S., Robert Casey, M.A., Alison Thirkield, M.A., Marcella Maguire, M.A., Hamid Mirsalimi, M.A., Johannes Naudè, M.A., Samantha Levy, M.A., Nadya Khatchikian, B.S., and Jenny Bell, M.A.

I am particularly thankful to Alison Thirkield and Robert Casey for their reading of the entire manuscript. Their perceptive comments and insightful questions greatly improved the book. The help of many of my colleagues, Lauren Adamson, Ph.D., Ronald Berlin, Ph.D., Martha Foster, Ph.D., Ted Ayllon, Ph.D., Lou L'Abate, Ph.D., James Dabbs, Ph.D., and Mary Morris, Ph.D., who read various parts of the book and contributed in other significant ways, is also appreciated. I wish to extend my thanks as well to Walter Daves, Ph.D., and Robin Morris, Ph.D., the chairmen of the Psychology Department at Georgia State University during the writing of this book. By providing release time and encouraging (or, should I say, urging) me to finish, they contributed significantly.

Richard Sauber, Ph.D., editor of the *American Journal of Family Therapy* and series editor for Brunner/Mazel, suggested that I undertake this project. I am grateful to him for his recommendation and ongoing encouragement. I am also greatly appreciative of the support, guidance, and patience of Natalie Gilman, editorial vice president of Brunner/Mazel. Her astute and frank reviews were instrumental in transforming this work into a clearer and more direct statement of my perspective on destructive parentification and its treatment. The input and support of Suzi

Tucker and Maggie Kennedy, editors at Brunner/Mazel, are greatly appreciated as well.

I owe thanks to the many clients and research participants who have taught me about the parentification process. Indeed, they have provided much of the foundation for this book. Many of their experiences are presented here; to protect their confidence, I have changed certain identifying data and, in some instances, integrated similar cases.

I am indebted to my children, Erika, Nicole, and Misha, for their understanding and endurance. Erika's artistic contribution and her presence at key times these past few years have meant a great deal to me. Nicole's interest in my work, including her reading of a number of chapters, has touched me as well. I owe a great debt in particular to Misha for waiting so patiently to play together until my break times. I know he tired of hearing, "Just 10 more minutes." I also appreciated the loving and generous encouragement of my mother, father, and sisters, Diane and Kathy.

My dear wife, Lori Jurkovic, M.A., was my chief collaborator and humorist on this project. Her levity and wit provided much needed comic relief. Although her invited critiques of the manuscript were not always sources of personal happiness, I invariably found them helpful. Moreover, through our work together as cotherapists, some of which is presented here, our many discussions of clinical issues, and her example of love and justice in our family, I have learned invaluable lessons. To the extent that this book successfully articulates the dynamics and needs of destructively parentified children, Lori deserves a great deal of credit.

In loving memory of my mother, Dorothy Jones Jurkovic, who held an unwavering image of my intrinsic worth, even when I could not. In return, she asked only that I do the same for my own children.

INTRODUCTION

Unlike other children who frequented the clinic, Jenny sat unusually still in the waiting room. She looked lifeless with her chin resting in her hand and her almond-shaped eyes focused somewhere in space. Brought to the clinic by her mother, Jenny had been acting oddly at home in recent months. She often retreated to her darkened room for long periods of time or huddled in the corner of the bathroom, wearing her hooded jacket backward to cover her face. Oblique comments about not wanting to live anymore finally galvanized Jenny's mother to seek help.

After meeting with Jenny and her mother together, during which time Jenny volunteered little information, I met with her alone. Furtively making eye contact and speaking with minimal affect, other than sighing frequently, she provided a remarkably detailed account of her family situation. Several times during the session I had to remind myself that this little girl was 7, not 37 years old. Her parents had divorced four years earlier. Jenny's mother, Barbara, was raised by "poor dirt farmers" of Germanic descent. Throughout Barbara's childhood, her father expressed regret that she had not been born a boy who could have better fulfilled the role of a much needed farmhand.

In a subsequent session, Barbara talked about her loneliness and alienation as a child and her identification with the disenfranchised, minority members of her classes in school. She also recalled that her many contributions to the family—cooking, cleaning, placating her father to "keep the peace"—went unnoticed. Feelings of not being "good enough" haunted Barbara throughout her childhood.

Her knight in shining armor was a man who—much to her sur-prise—took an interest in her as a late adolescent. He was climbing the corporate ladder, ready for a long-term relationship, and un-daunted by the differences in their family backgrounds. They married. Quickly adopting her rescuer's upwardly mobile values, Barbara enrolled in college with aspirations of becoming a teacher. Barbara's social ascendancy, however, contributed to mounting ten-sions in her marriage. Her husband left her shortly before Jenny's third birthday and soon married another woman, who forbade him to have any contact with his former family. Devastated by the divorce, Barbara quit school, worked sporadically, and bore a child out of wedlock. She also became involved in a long-term abusive relationship.

At the time I began seeing Jenny, she was still painfully cut off from her father. Jenny consoled herself, in part, by rereading daily the last birthday card her father had sent her more than three years ago. Her feelings of loss were submerged beneath her mother's pre-potent needs. Any hint of Jenny's missing him threatened Barbara, prompting her to question her daughter's loyalty and to affirm her emotional dependence on Jenny. "I don't know what I'd do with-out you," Barbara frequently reminded her. Seldom asking her mother for help, Jenny kept "things inside." "She's got enough problems," Jenny reasoned, "I need to help her." Indeed, she did, serving as her mother's confidante, dutiful helper, and primary source of support. She often advised her about relationships, fi-nances, and major purchases. Jenny also assumed considerable re-sponsibility for her half-brother's care. It seemed that until recently she could successfully regulate her mother's moods. Something had changed, but Jenny would not elaborate.

Empathizing with Jenny, I said, "No wonder you're upset. Is there anything I can do to help?" "No," she replied stoically, then proceeded to minimize her difficulties. I inquired about her wish to die. She merely shrugged her shoulders. Shifting the focus from other family members to Jenny appeared discomforting for her. She did intimate that school was stressful, because worrisome thoughts about her mother and brother frequently distracted her. Later in therapy, Jenny complained of social isolation. She had trouble relating to her classmates, whom she regarded as "child-ish." None shared her aspirations of achieving perfect marks and one day attending medical school. She wanted to become a pedia-trician "to help sick children."

Returning to her feelings of depression, I wondered aloud about the effect of her suicidal comments on her mother. My question energized her. "She gets upset and asks why I'd want to do something like that," Jenny blurted out. "She says, 'Don't you know I'd never leave you! Why would you want to leave me?'" Jenny hinted that there was more, but unless I promised to treat the information confidentially, she would not continue. I explained the limits of confidentiality, as I normally do with children, and also expressed my hope that Jenny could trust me to handle her secret in a sensitive manner; if not, I would understand.

After a long delay, Jenny nervously reported that her mother had been threatening to abandon the family. She often talked about not being able to "handle it anymore" on her way out of the house, leaving Jenny alone with her younger brother. Jenny was panicked that her mother would not return. She also added, with embarrassment, that there was little food at home and she worried that her brother was hungry much of the time. "So it must be a huge weight off your shoulders when your mother tells you she'd never leave you," I suggested. Jenny vigorously nodded her head in agreement.

Only later did Jenny help me appreciate that her crisis stemmed as much from being unable to help her family and her concern that she was the cause of her mother's burdens as from her fears of abandonment. It also became increasingly clear early in therapy that she was willing to make tremendous sacrifices, including perhaps hurting herself, to protect family members. As we were about to leave the office after that first session, to rejoin her mother, Jenny looked at me with tears in her eyes and gave me permission to talk openly to her mother. To obtain help for her family and, perhaps on a less conscious level, for herself, she appeared willing to breach her overweening filial loyalty.

PARENTIFICATION: AN OVERVIEW

Theoretical Background

Theoreticians observed some time ago that family dynamics may overburden children such as Jenny with the responsibility of protecting and sustaining parents, siblings, and the family as a whole. In 1948, Schmideberg, for example, postulated from a psychoanalytic perspective that early interpersonal deprivation unconsciously disposes individuals to regard their children as parental figures. In their discussion of complementary unconscious motivations of family members, Mahler and Rabinovitch (1956) further observed that the child may assume various roles (e.g., buffer, pawn, confidante) to strengthen tenuous family ties, especially in the marital relationship. Along these lines, Anna Freud (1965) speculated that divorce often creates a role vacuum in the family that is filled by a child.

Minuchin, Montalvo, Guerney, Rosman, and Schumer (1967) observed a similar phenomenon in their work with delinquent-producing families living in the ghettos of New York City. They described youngsters, referred to as "parental children," whose parents and/or siblings implicitly or explicitly charged them with child-rearing and other executive functions in the family. The families in their study were marked by the absence or underfunctioning of the father, leaving the mother with the responsibility of both nurturing and guiding the children. Although the mother may have been capable of the former, her anxiety and helplessness contributed to her relinquishing authority to the parental child.

In subsequent years, Minuchin and his colleagues noted the presence of parental children in other families as well. In the language of structural family therapy that evolved from Minuchin's early research of delinquency, this role reflects possible violation of subsystem boundaries. Parental children may become inappropriately involved in the parental subsystem, although not fully accepted by parental figures, and be excluded from the sibling subsystem (Minuchin, 1974; Minuchin & Fishman, 1981).

In the development of their intergenerational, contextual approach to family therapy, Boszormenyi-Nagy (1987) and his cohorts (e.g., Framo, 1965) recognized a related dynamic. While conducting intensive individual and family therapy at the Eastern Pennsylvania Psychiatric Institute in the late 1950s, they observed that parents of disturbed children tended to ascribe parentlike qualities to them. Fixated on the loss of a parent of their own, these parents unconsciously regarded their marital partner and, subsequently, their child as a replacement figure.

Boszormenyi-Nagy and Spark (1973) later speculated that "parentification," the term Boszormenyi-Nagy (1965) coined to describe such a process, is not confined to family dysfunction but is seen in family life in general. Indeed, they posited that parentification is a constituent, albeit regressive, aspect of intimate relating. Whether a natural tendency to parentify one's partner or children is problematic, however, depends on its dynamic meaning within the balance of give-and-take in the family. For example, parentification may vary from mere wishful fantasizing to overt behavior, in which another family member is unfairly induced to assume a guilt-laden, caretaking role to fulfill unmet needs.

When parentification assumes pathological proportions, parents are often unwittingly replaying painful and abusive scripts from their own childhood and setting the stage for succeeding generations to do the same. In the process, their children's intrinsic loyalty, concern, and trust are exploited, often egregiously. Thus, parentification is a multivalent construct that has individual, transactional, and existential-ethical referents (Boszormenyi-Nagy & Krasner, 1986).

Clinical Picture

At a young age, Jenny found herself in the role of caretaker not only for her brother but also for her mother. Had she been an adult caring for her sickly or aging parent, few questions would be raised about the reversal in their roles. Nor would it seem abnormal had they occasionally transposed roles playfully. Parent-child roles also frequently become less well defined on a temporary basis during periods of stress and crisis in the family. In the disruptive months following her mother's divorce, for example, Jenny's caretaking behaviors were adaptive. Cultural prescription and other factors, such as large families, single-parent households, parental illness, and poverty, often contribute to children's functioning in the parental role. Certainly, Barbara's social isolation and financial problems increased her reliance on her daughter.

As a result of enacting a parental role, youngsters may learn invaluable lessons in responsibility and giving, which can contribute to healthy identity formation and self-esteem. They also gain trustworthiness and satisfy their need to express caring and affection. In addition to allowing parents and children to meet outside the confines of their conventionally defined positions, the occasional reversal of their roles provides youngsters with an opportunity to master socialization skills and to rehearse future role activities (see Boszormenyi-Nagy & Krasner, 1986; Boszormenyi-Nagy & Spark, 1973; Minuchin, Montalvo, Guerney, Rosman, & Schumer, 1967).

Yet, in many instances parental role behavior by children can severely compromise their development, both in the short and long term, especially if they chronically respond to overt or implicit demands by their families that are confusing, age inappropriate, burdensome, unsupervised, captivating, or unacknowledged. Parental blame of the child's efforts to caretake is also a common feature of parentification in its most crippling and exploitative form (see Bossard & Boll, 1956; Boszormenyi-Nagy & Spark, 1973; Boszormenyi-Nagy & Krasner, 1986; Jurkovic, Jessee, & Goglia, 1991; Karpel, 1976; Minuchin, Montalvo, Guerney, Rosman, & Schumer, 1967).

As with Jenny, parentified children often suffer from depression, suicidal feelings, shame, excessive guilt, unrelenting worry, social isolation, and other internalizing symptoms, such as psychosomatic problems. Conduct disturbances may also be part of the clinical picture of parentification. These problems are frequently overlooked by teachers, parents, and other adults or seen as incongruous with other features of the child's presentation, such as his or her pseudomaturity and extreme helpfulness. The net result is that the childhood of destructively parentified children is lost.

Their adulthood may be affected as well. Parentification during a youngster's formative years is often the prologue to an adult life characterized by interpersonal distrust, ambivalence about extrafamilial ties, involvement in unfair and harmful relationships, a destructive sense of entitlement, an inability to function independently, and—perpetuating the cycle—a tendency to misuse parental authority.

Historical Perspective

The history of family life, particularly in northern Europe, reveals that parents have long demanded adultlike services and behaviors of children. In the Middle Ages, for example, distinctions between servants and children were ambiguous. The word *valet* denoted both a young boy and a servant in medieval England. As a youngster, Louis XIII would affectionately talk about desiring to be "Papa's little valet" (Aries, 1962, p. 367). It is well documented that failure to appreciate childhood as a separate stage of life led to various abuses of children, including parents' unfair exploitation of them to meet their own needs (Aries, 1962; Kessen, 1965; Zigler & Hall, 1989).

Child labor and abuse laws and other more recent legislative, legal, medical, educational, social service, mental health, and scientific developments reflect growing contemporary concern with the needs and rights of children. Nevertheless, children continue to be maltreated in our society at an alarming rate (National Center on Child Abuse and Neglect, 1996). One insidious form of such maltreatment is reflected in the case of Jenny.

Media and Popular References

Although not labeled as such, parentification and related processes are occasionally highlighted in the media and popular literature. For example, writing about her renowned mother in the book, *Marlene Dietrich*, Maria Riva (1993) vividly describes her parentification as a child. She includes a revealing entry from her mother's diary that illustrates the parentifying adult's desperate dependence on his or her offspring:

> Nobody understands that I am so attached to the child because nobody knows that apart from that, I have nothing. I, myself, experience nothing as a woman—nothing as a person.... (p. 54)

News from Chicago of a couple who left their two children, aged 5 and 11, home alone while vacationing in Mexico also drew national attention to irresponsible parental practices, involving neglect and parentification, and to the role of sociopolitical factors (e.g., rising child-care costs) in child maltreatment (McRoberts, 1993). Public exposure of the misuse of parental authority often evokes painful memories. For example, reacting to news coverage in Atlanta of an infant girl brutally killed by her father, a local resident empathized with the man. He recalled that after his own abusive father left home when he was 12, he assumed responsibility for raising his younger siblings. His mother, an alcoholic, stayed in bed when not working. In response to her locking the kitchen cabinets, he resourcefully played on the pity of the neighbors to feed his young charges. As a parent, he found himself mistreating his children in much the same way he was mistreated, and his realization prompted him to seek help (Hansen, 1992).

Aspects of this man's experience were echoed in a *New York Times* story (Wilkerson, 1993) about a 10-year-old boy, Nicholas, growing up in an impoverished, violent section of Chicago. Described as "all boy" in some respects but also as prematurely grownup in others (" ... his walk is the stiff slog of a worried father behind on the rent"), he was the oldest of four half-siblings for whom he had considerable responsibility. Nicholas's mother, a recovering crack addict, was pursuing a nursing degree and, consequently, relied heavily on her oldest son. The article further reported:

> He is nanny, referee, housekeeper, handyman. Some nights he is up past midnight, mopping the floors, putting the children to bed and washing their school clothes in the bathtub. (p. 1Y)

When his grades suffered as a result of his onerous duties, he was beaten.

Pictures from Somalia and the Balkans in recent years (e.g., Morrow, 1992; Nelan, 1992) of gun-toting children also grimly portray the degree to which the younger generation's blind loyalty and allegiance to familial and tribal forces can be wantonly manipulated. Such an heteronomous orientation on the part of children leaves them extremely vulnerable to various abuses and privations, including destructive parentification.

Another news story about a Muslim refugee family from Bosnia reveals the willingness of children, even young ones, to help their parents (Kurylo, 1993). Forced to leave their extended family with whom they were living in a rural village near Prijedor, the family resettled in the United States. Although helped by a refugee relief program, they experienced immense pain and frustration at being unemployed, unable to speak English, penniless, and torn from their loved ones, many of whom are missing or were killed in the fighting. The response of the children, four and five years of age, to their family's situation was moving. Their mother reported:

When my children want something, usually I have to say
no. I have no money. Then the children say I will find a
job and I will make some money and I will give it to you.
Then I cry. (p. 10A)

An article in the *Atlantic Monthly* (Maeder, 1989b) considers
the possibility that the career choices of many helping professionals, particularly psychotherapists and ministers, stem from their
role as caretakers in their families of origin. Continuing such a role
in adulthood as professional helpers, they perhaps harbor fantasies of finally curing their parents either directly or symbolically
through those they counsel. Maeder cited a case of a psychiatric
resident whose plans to pursue child psychiatry and to help
doctors' families were disrupted by the stress of caring for his
emotionally dysfunctional mother and dependent father, a psychia-
trist (see also Maeder, 1989a).

NEED FOR FURTHER STUDY

My own interest in parentification[1] grew directly out of the problems that Jenny and her family presented more than a decade ago.
In the course of Jenny's therapy, my student cotherapist[2] and I negotiated a maze of intrapsychic, family, sociocultural, and existential-ethical dynamics, which at the time were still being treated in
much of the clinical and developmental literature in isolation. I
was interested in how various levels of analysis might be productively integrated in the conceptualization, treatment, and research
of problems posed by Jenny in particular and by other children
and families generally (Jurkovic, 1980, 1984; Jurkovic & Berger,
1984; Jurkovic & Ulrici, 1982, 1985; Levy, Jurkovic, & Spirito,
1995).

At that time a small number of investigators were writing theoretically about the interdigitating relation of different analytic lev-

---

[1]Throughout this book, the terms "parentification" and "parentified"
children rather than "parental" children are used, as the former stem
from a theoretical framework (i.e., Boszormenyi-Nagy's) that has played
a central role in my studies in this area.
[2]Donna Ulrici, Ph.D.

els.[3] Even fewer, however, were empirically studying such relationships. To do so involves identifying a content domain or problem that lends itself to examination and to operationalization from a multilevel perspective. Clearly, any number of clinical problems potentially fill the bill. Those of Jenny and her family seemed particularly well suited to theoretical, clinical, and empirical analyses that traverse the boundaries of most conventional individual- and family-level approaches (circa 1980 and earlier).

Despite the idiosyncrasies of Jenny's case, the clinical picture that emerged seemed illustrative of a widely generalizable process. She and her family became the first participants in an ongoing program of research by my students and me to define, understand, treat, and prevent destructive parentification. Although questions of a metatheoretical nature spawned and continue to be a focus of my work, growing concern about the hidden and often tragic plight of parentified children and their families has sustained my interest in this area.

Our work has been increasingly guided over the years by the differing but complementary insights of Boszormenyi-Nagy (1987), Bronfenbrenner (1977, 1979), and their colleagues (Belsky, 1980; Boszormenyi-Nagy & Krasner, 1986; Boszormenyi-Nagy & Ulrich, 1981; Garbarino, 1981; Garbarino & Abramowitz, 1992). Although our definition of parentification is more circumscribed than Boszormenyi-Nagy's (see Chapter 1), we have drawn significantly from his theoretical and treatment approach. Specifically, his emphasis on "relational ethics," a sui generis realm, challenged our early focus, from a classical systemic perspective, on the transactional and structural properties (e.g., communication, hierarchies, triangles, circularity) of families of parentified children. We came to embrace the existential reality of justice and trust as essential ingredients in healthy family relationships. Indeed, as discussed later, whether or not parentification assumes destructive proportions turns on qualities at an ethical level.

---

[3]See, for example, Belsky (1980), Boszormenyi-Nagy & Ulrich (1981), Bronfenbrenner (1979), Cicchetti & Rizley (1981), Clark, Zalis, & Saccho (1982), Garbarino (1980a, b), Henggeler (1982), Hoffman (1981), Keeney (1979), Sameroff & Chandler (1975), Santostefano (1978), and Scheflen (1980). In recent years, many other investigators (e.g., Achenbach, 1990; Bentovim & Kinston, 1991; Kirschner & Kirschner, 1986; Rosman, 1986; Schwartzman, 1985) have also proffered multilevel, metatheoretical frameworks.

Yet, like Boszormenyi-Nagy, we were unwilling to abandon systemic models of human behavior, particularly the ecological-developmental framework of Bronfenbrenner. A developmentalist who has explicated the multiple nested systems within which children live and grow, Bronfenbrenner oriented us to the peer, community, and sociocultural contexts of parentification. A danger of attending only to less molar levels of analysis is that parents are portrayed as solely responsible for a destructive process whose determinants (such as deteriorating neighborhoods, racism, poverty) extend beyond their capabilities.

Although strange bedfellows philosophically, existential-ethical and ecological-systemic perspectives can jointly contribute to a comprehensive understanding of parentification. Building on the earlier integrative efforts of Boszormenyi-Nagy and Bronfenbrenner, ways of productively combining their work are discussed in Chapter 1. The resulting ecological-ethical orientation has proven to be an invaluable heuristic.

Basic and applied investigation of parentification is in an inchoate stage. One important goal of this book is to stimulate further investigative activity. References to parentification and related constructs (e.g., role reversal) are scattered throughout the clinical, developmental, sociological, and cultural anthropological literature. Unfortunately, authors within and across disciplines, writing at different levels of analysis, seldom cite one another. By acquainting them with one another's work, and by highlighting the full context of parentification, the benefits of cross-disciplinary dialogue and collaboration will, it is hoped, become clear.

Also noteworthy in the literature is the limited attention that parentification has received in areas of study and practice directly concerned with parent-child relationships. For example, the work of Boszormenyi-Nagy, Minuchin, and their colleagues notwithstanding, the family therapy literature has been surprisingly silent about the unique problems of parentified children and their families.

The socialization literature has also ignored child or sibling caretaking (Weisner & Gallimore, 1977). The focus has been, and continues to be, almost exclusively on caretaking by parental figures (mothers in particular). On the basis of ratings from ethnographic descriptions of 186 societies, Barry and Paxson (1971) discovered that female children were principal companions and caretakers of infants in 16.7 percent of the sampled societies. In 11.6 percent of the societies, youngsters of both sexes served in this capacity with younger children. Despite the legitimacy and adaptiveness of such behavior in various social groups in this country and others, it is likely that many child or sibling caretakers are at risk of being destructively parentified.

Curiously, the child maltreatment literature also contains limited discussion of parentification. Typically referred to as "role reversal" by investigators in this area (e.g., Morris & Gould, 1963, 1979), the phenomenon has been seen as an associated feature of physical abuse and neglect. Indeed, a significant proportion of the estimated 1,012,000 children in the United States who were identified as having been abused or neglected in 1994 (National Center on Child Abuse and Neglect, 1996) were probably parentified as well.

It is my thesis, however, that pathological parentification is a discriminable category of maltreatment in its own right. In addition to being part of the spectrum of problems subsumed under the label "child maltreatment," severe forms of parentification may have specific etiologies, sequelae, intergenerational transmission patterns, and treatment responses. This book represents one of the first attempts to explore this possibility.

Just as systematic investigation in this area is still at a rudimentary level, so is our knowledge of how to help pathologically parentified youngsters. A small but disconnected therapy literature does exist. Much of it, however, approaches parentification from a unitary perspective and does not sufficiently address the moral dilemmas and inequities that inhere in the destructively parentified child's interactions with family members (cf. Doherty, 1995). Specific guidelines and models for evaluating, treating, and preventing destructive parentification of children and adolescents within an ecological-ethical framework are presented in the pages that follow.

This book is divided into two parts: (I) Understanding and (II) Treatment and Prevention. Separate chapters of Part I define and conceptualize destructive parentification from an ecological-ethical perspective (Chapter 1) and consider causes and consequences of parentification (Chapters 2 and 3, respectively). Applications of material discussed in the first section of the book are taken up in Part II. Specifically, clinical manifestations of destructive parentification and their identification (Chapter 4), treatment within family, couple, and community contexts (Chapters 5 through 7), and prevention (Chapter 9) are addressed. In Chapter 8, the special professional, ethical, and personal challenges facing therapists with a history of pathological parentification are discussed.

Part I

UNDERSTANDING

CHAPTER 1

Mapping the Territory

Although the term *parentification* has only recently secured a place in the argot of clinicians, many of the characteristics and dynamics it denotes have long been recognized by theorists, practitioners, and researchers of various orientations. This soon became apparent to us in our efforts to understand Jenny and her family from a traditional academic perspective. Our literature search uncovered a multiplicity of interrelated constructs (see Appendix A).

Yet, not unlike the proverbial blind men who each uniquely described the same elephant from diverse vantage points, investigators in this area have highlighted different processes and role behaviors. Are they referring to the same phenomenon? What are the parameters of parentification? How might this process be theoretically framed to capture its complex psychosocial and ethical nature? The answers to these questions are important at this juncture because they will provide benchmarks for discussion of theory, research, and practice in the rest of this book.

PARENTIFICATION AND KINDRED CONSTRUCTS

The spawning beds of various constructs that relate to parentification include individual and family psychodynamic approaches (e.g., false self, symbiotic therapist, symbiotic survival pattern, delegation), family systems theory (e.g., family healer, parental child, over- and underfunctioning relational patterns), sociological and anthropological observations (unfulfilled role functions, junior partner), addiction models (e.g., co-dependence, family hero), and perspectives from developmental psychology, including attachment theory (e.g., spousification, hurried child, compulsive caregiving).[1]

Of note is that investigators from differing theoretical traditions, disciplines, and research settings have drawn attention to children who either directly or indirectly perform caregiving functions in the family and fulfill parental needs and fantasies, often at the expense of their own development and self-realization. Thus, descriptively, at least, there appears to be a high degree of face validity for the parentification construct.

Conceptually, complementary unconscious processes, role assignments, functional interdependencies, boundary issues, exploitation, caring and therapeutic tendencies, attachment patterns, and co-dependency refer to phenomena that are constituent parts of parentification. Indeed, parentification can be seen as a central organizing construct for individual psychodynamic, sociofamilial, and existential-ethical perspectives on parent-child relationships. It is an emphasis on the latter that distinguishes Boszormenyi-Nagy's theorizing in this area. He assumes that deeper, covert, or "invisible" existential-ethical processes structure psychological adaptations and family functioning across the generations (Boszormenyi-Nagy & Krasner, 1986).

Specifically, the existential interdependence of family members raises questions about mutual concern, accountabilities, responsibilities, and loyalties. Are expectations and needs balanced in the family? How do children repay their parents for giving them nurturance, structure, and life itself? What can parents reasonably expect in light of the existential fact that their offspring depend initially on receiving more than they give? Is the power differential

---

[1]See Appendix A for further discussion of these and other constructs.

between the generations, even if marked by boundaries, qualified by responsible concern and fairness on the part of parental figures? Do socially legitimate arrangements in the home mask exploitation of family members? These queries are ethical in nature, the answers to which are evaluated within Boszormenyi-Nagy's framework on an intergenerational scale of give-and-take (see Boszormenyi-Nagy & Krasner, 1986).

In ethical family relationships, parents are sensitive to asymmetries vis-à-vis their children. Although they enjoy their children's loyalty, concern, and growth and increasingly alternate subject and object roles with them in developmentally appropriate ways, they accept the fact that their contributions outweigh those of their offspring. They do not expect equal reciprocity in their relationships with their children, as they do in the spousal relationship. Yet, just as they reciprocated their own parents' care giving by responsibly and lovingly caring for their own children, they expect the same of the next generation.

Giving to children also ethically earns parents "constructive entitlement," according to Boszormenyi-Nagy and his colleagues (Boszormenyi-Nagy & Krasner, 1986). That is, they acquire merit and ethical self-worth as a result of their continuing contributions. In the event that such parents parentify their children at various times, they explicitly rather than manipulatively recruit them and acknowledge their availability. By crediting their children's contributions to the family, responsibly responding to their needs, and caring about a fair distribution of relational benefits and burdens, they maintain their trustworthiness.

Unethical parenting, on the other hand, involves a breakdown in the dialogic relation between parents and their offspring, a process that often has its roots in the miscarriage of just and trustworthy relating in the parent's family of origin. The end result is the misapplication of parental authority. Boszormenyi-Nagy observes that deprivation and abuses in the parents' past leave them "destructively entitled." That is, the parent-to-be derives a just but unsettled claim for caring and protection to which he or she expects innocent third parties to respond. In pathological forms of parentification, children are often expected to meet these claims. They are induced to accept assignments that exploitatively fashion their loyalty and concern into a personally meaningful, albeit an often highly captivating, obligation to serve parental and familial interests. Children's distrust of their interpersonal world is one of the most destructive consequences of such a process (Boszormenyi-Nagy, 1965; Boszormenyi-Nagy & Spark, 1973; Boszormenyi-Nagy & Krasner, 1986).

Issues of an ethical genre (e.g., reciprocity and responsibility) are acknowledged by functionally oriented structural and strategic theorists, such as Minuchin and Madanes, just as power and function are included in Boszormenyi-Nagy's framework, especially in his recent multidimensional characterization of relational reality (Boszormenyi-Nagy & Krasner, 1986). The former, however, have not fully explored the significance of the ethical dimension as a primary determinant of family functioning. Nor have other theorists who describe parent-child relationships in terms of filial devotion (Searles, 1975), loyalty (Stierlin, 1974, 1977), and exploitation (Elkind, 1981), although they have paid greater attention to the existential-ethical substrate of individual and family process.

DELIMITING THE CONSTRUCT

Destructive parentification is broadly characterized within Boszormenyi-Nagy's approach as involving the unilateral and self-serving use of children by parental figures to satisfy possessive, dependent, aggressive, and sexual needs. This type of parentification is not confined to manifest caretaking roles and executive functioning à la Minuchin's "parental child." Rather, it may include a variety of (1) roles (e.g., sacrificial, bad, scapegoat, well sibling), (2) behavior patterns (e.g., delinquency, psychosis, addiction, infantilization, idealization), and (3) interactional processes (e.g., go-between, split loyalty, triangulation) that overtly or covertly serve to protect or gratify the needs of family members and to stabilize the family as a whole.

Both the depth and scope of Boszormenyi-Nagy's account of parentification challenge practitioners and investigators alike to translate his usage of this construct into clinically and empirically relevant terms (cf. Karpel, 1976). It is clear, for example, that youngsters like Jenny, who assume direct responsibility for their family's needs, are parentified. But what about a preadolescent who has consistently underachieved in school over the years? He knows his parents will eventually rescue him by striking bargains with teachers, reading his assignments aloud to him, and, if all else fails, actually doing his homework. In light of the fact that the parents' marriage is stagnant, it could be inferred that their son is self-destructively but loyally colluding with them to gratify their unfulfilled needs for relatedness. If so, then from Boszormenyi-Nagy's perspective, this adolescent's behavior is symptomatic of parentification.

The level of inference required to subsume the variety of children, such as the infantilized one just described or others whose role behavior ranges from rebel to scapegoat, under the rubric of parentification is problematic. Sacrificed in the process are both the specificity and measurability of the construct. Like codependence, parentification will remain a tantalizing and protean conception unless better delineated and objectified.

Toward this end, the following parameters of parentification are proffered: (1) overtness, (2) type of role assignments, (3) extent of responsibility, (4) object of caretaking, (5) age appropriateness, (6) internalization, (7) family boundaries, (8) social legitimacy, and (9) ethicality. The first four refer to properties of the parentified role per se, whereas the rest characterize important dimensions of its developmental, psychological, sociofamilial, and existential-ethical context.

Overtness

One of the most important distinctions to make in defining parentification is whether or not the child's object role entails *overtly* protective, caretaking, and responsible behaviors. In his descriptive and theoretical study of this role pattern, Karpel (1976) used the term "loyal object" to differentiate destructively parentified children from those who are excessively loyal in the face of various privations, abuses, and injustices but do not engage in overt caretaking.

Pathologically parentified children are a member of the class of loyal objects, in that they are bound out of loyalty and concern to importunate parental figures who unilaterally exploit them. These children differ at an observable, functional level. Although children as loyal objects may caretake indirectly (e.g., by detouring conflicts between parents through their misbehavior), in the absence of direct evidence of overresponsible and adultlike behavior on their part, they are not seen to be parentified.

In the event that indirect caretaking in children occurs sans overt parentification, it is likely that the dynamics of this general loyal–object process differ from those of direct caretaking. Empirical verification of this hunch would further underscore the import of the distinctions drawn here. We have found that restricting usage of the term *parentified* to behavioral patterns that overtly reflect overresponsibility and caretaking has greatly reduced ambiguity in this area, facilitating research and the development of evaluation and intervention strategies.

Type of Role Assignments

A variety of situations and stressors that impinge on the caregiving system in families may either reverse or level parent-child roles. These impingements range from primarily physicalistic claims to emotionally or psychologically oriented demands. In contrast to the former, which may relate, for example, to a parent's health status, financial stress, or family size, the latter pertain to emotional, homeostatic, and intergenerational processes in the family, including such variables as parental neediness and marital conflict.

Drawing on the early work of Parsons and Bales (1955), we have labeled these different demands and the role behaviors they occasion in children as "instrumental" and "expressive" (Jurkovic, Jessee, & Goglia, 1991).[2] Instrumental role assignments require children to assume responsibility for concrete functional tasks that are necessary for the physical maintenance and support of the family, such as child care, grocery shopping, cooking, nursing an ill or disabled parent, and earning income. These assignments are at the core of Minuchin's (1974) concept of the "parental child."

In the performance of expressive tasks, youngsters minister to the family's socioemotional needs through such activities as protecting family members, serving as a confidant, companion, or matelike figure, mediating family conflicts, and providing support,

---

[2]An analogous distinction can be found in Karpel's (1976) differentiation between "physical" and "emotional" caretaking functions and Stierlin's (1974) discussion of "simple helping or supporting" and more "complex ego-support" missions.

nurturance, and comfort (cf. Main, Kaplan, & Cassidy, 1985; Main & Goldwyn, 1984). Although perhaps not as apparent as instrumental functioning, expressive parentification also involves overt behavioral displays of caretaking.

The line demarcating different classes of parentified behavior is not always clear. Instrumental behaviors are not without a psychological-expressive component, just as expressive caretaking activities may have instrumental properties. Moreover, children such as Jenny often perform both instrumental and expressive tasks in the family.

It should be noted as well that demands to ensure the emotional well being of parental figures or the family as a whole are often subtly imposed and accompanied by guilt inducement; thus, on balance, expressive tasks are probably more stressful and stultifying than instrumental ones (Boszormenyi-Nagy & Spark, 1973; Boszormenyi-Nagy & Krasner, 1986). Yet, depending on other characteristics, as discussed later (e.g., their chronicity and relational significance within the family), instrumental demands may also deleteriously affect the child.

Extent of Responsibility

Both the degree and duration of a child's expressive and instrumental role responsibilities must be considered as well. Excessive caretaking that extends beyond a situational adaptation to become a chronic process depletes children both emotionally and physically. On the other hand, too little parental expectation of responsible role behavior is also unhealthy.

Object of Caretaking

Another distinguishing property of the role of parentified children is the object of their caretaking. They may overfunction primarily in relation to their mother, father, or one or more of their siblings. Many parentified children, of course, assume responsibility for several family members, the marital subsystem, and/or the family as a whole (Karpel, 1976). As discussed in Chapter 3, the effects of destructive parentification possibly vary as a function of the primary object of concern and the child's gender. For example, same-gender parentification between parent and child (mother-daughter, father-son) may differ from cross-gender parentification (mother-son, father-daughter).

Age Appropriateness

A defining contextual feature of parentification is the child's developmental stage. The earlier and the more age inappropriate the caretaking charge (e.g., assigning unsupervised sibling caretaking responsibilities to a 6-year-old), the more destructive the consequences for the child. Young children simply do not have as many internal or external resources to cope with caretaking assignments as do their older counterparts, especially those in adolescence. Moreover, disruptions in their negotiation of early stage-salient tasks (e.g., formation of a secure attachment to a primary caregiver, exploration of the environment) because of excessive demands to accommodate to parental figures affect their mastery of subsequent tasks.

Internalization

A less obvious but nonetheless important parameter of the parentified role is the degree to which it has been internalized as an organizing part of the child's identity and interpersonal style. At one extreme, he or she identifies fully with the role, assuming a compulsive caregiving stance (Bowlby, 1979). At the other extreme, the child experiences the various demands as external expectations that are to be fulfilled for functional or pragmatic reasons.

Family Boundaries

At a family level, parentification is defined not only by overt role characteristics but also by underlying transactional processes, particularly by self-other and subsystem boundaries. Parentification can occur within a familial context with either healthy or unhealthy boundaries. In the worst instances, children have excessive caretaking responsibilities that are neither supervised nor shared with other family members. They are also triangulated by and enmeshed with (or perhaps cut off from) undifferentiated parental figures, having become a defining aspect of their identities (cf. Bowen, 1978; Boszormenyi-Nagy & Krasner, 1986; Minuchin, 1974).

Social Legitimacy

Broader cultural considerations point to social legitimacy as yet another defining property of parentification. In many sociocultural contexts, this role pattern, particularly as evidenced by extensive sibling caretaking, is an adaptive, legitimate response to normative expectations, which mitigates its destructive potential (see, e.g., Harrison, Wilson, Pine, Chan, & Buriel, 1990). Yet many customary role behaviors, such as those supported by traditional gender socialization in our culture, reflect adaptations to self-limiting and dehumanizing social conditions and mores. Thus, whether parentification is destructive or healthy cannot depend solely on an evaluation of its social legitimacy.

Ethicality

As discussed previously, the definition of parentification ultimately rests on ethical grounds. The balance of fairness between children and their care givers over the generations, including the larger sociocultural contexts in which they live, always qualifies the other defining properties. Imbalances in this realm underlie the destructive parentification of children. Their exploitation exists at an ethical level, whether or not recognized by the children themselves, their parents, or others, including society and the therapeutic community.

From Destructive Parentification to Infantilization

Based on the various parameters of parentification, at least four major prototypes of children's caretaking activities in familial settings are identifiable. The first, *destructive parentification*, refers to youngsters who assume overtly expressive and/or instrumental responsibilities that are excessive and developmentally inappropriate, represent a primary source of identity, violate personal and family subsystem boundaries, and are neither culturally prescribed nor fairly assigned and maintained. As implied earlier, however, if the child's parentification is supported by sociocultural norms that either foster unethical parent-child relating or are exploited by parental figures, then the process is likely to have the same destructive result.

The second type, *adaptive parentification,* also refers to children whose caretaking activities are overtly expressive and/or instrumental as well as excessive. For many, the parentification process is transient; for others, however, it is of longer term. Regardless of duration, nondestructively parentified youngsters are those who are typically not captivated by their role and receive support and fair treatment from their families and the larger sociocultural community of which they are a part.

The third, healthy *non-parentification,* includes youngsters who are expected to engage in a moderate level of overtly instrumental and expressive caretaking relative to their culture and developmental stage. Their caretaking efforts are acknowledged, reciprocated, and supervised. As a result, the child's identity is not unduly shaped by his or her caretaking activities, boundaries are maintained, and fairness is observed.

Finally, a fourth prototypal pattern, *infantilization,* refers to children who are expected to engage in minimal, if any, overtly instrumental and expressive caretaking. Thus they are underchallenged developmentally by parents who excessively meet their needs. Rather than defining themselves as overfunctioners, these youngsters are at risk of identifying with an underfunctioning role in life. Like their destructively parentified cohorts, however, they experience boundary violations and are drawn into a loyal–object process that is unjust.

TOWARD AN ECOLOGICAL-ETHICAL PERSPECTIVE

The parameters of parentification span multiple levels of analysis. Of course, this multilevel perspective is not adventitious, inasmuch as a guiding assumption of my work is that parentification reflects not only individual parent and child issues but also larger familial, sociocultural, and existential-ethical concerns. Most theoretical approaches to parentification and related constructs, however, are too reductionistic to accommodate the full spectrum of processes in this area. Yet, even more comprehensive theories are not without their limitations, pointing to the need for further refinements in the higher-order integration of different levels and types of analysis.

Conceptual Foundations

As noted in the Introduction, a number of integrative frameworks have been proffered over the years. Two of them form the matrix for our ecological-ethical orientation to parentification. The first is Boszormenyi-Nagy's "contextual" view (see Boszormenyi-Nagy & Krasner, 1986). He has identified four basic dimensions of relational reality: (1) *factual* (e.g., preexisting biosocial factors), (2) *individual psychological* (e.g., unconscious defenses), (3) *family systemic* (e.g., patterns of manifest transactions), and (4) *ethical* (e.g., fair balance of give-and-take).

The contextual model integrates a number of critical causal factors in family relationships generally and in the parentification process particularly. Most important, it highlights the existential-ethical significance of family members' life circumstances, psychological makeup, and transactions with one another. However, it contains a number of lacunae. Specifically, settings, institutions, and processes (other than the immediate family) that directly or indirectly impinge on child development and possibly contribute to or prevent destructive forms of parentification are either not mentioned or treated cursorily. These include, for example, peers, school, parents' social networks, health and welfare services, national policies on children and families, and the institutional structures and ideological patterns of different cultures.

Such variables are systematically included in Bronfenbrenner's (1977, 1979) ecological account of human development, the other major approach that has informed our work. It has been employed in various forms in the literature on child maltreatment, health psychology, and adolescent delinquency and treatment (e.g., Belsky, 1980; Belsky & Vondra, 1989; Garbarino, 1977; Henggeler, 1982; Henggeler, Rodick, Borduin, Hanson, Watson, & Urey, 1986; Kazak, 1989; Willis, Holden, & Rosenberg, 1992).

In brief, reacting to severe limitations in the ecological validity of developmental research, most of which had been conducted in laboratory settings, Bronfenbrenner called for an approach that examines the progressive interplay between the developing child and the changing contexts in which he or she lives. These different contexts include the (1) immediate settings (*microsystems*) containing the developing person (family, peer group, school), (2) the transactions between these settings (*mesosystem*), (3) other formal and informal social structures (e.g., parents' social network and workplace) that do not include the developing person but which affect and encompass his or her immediate environment (*exosystem*), and (4) general patterns of the culture or subculture that are manifested formally in recorded laws, rules, and regulations and informally in the ideologies, customs, and everyday practices of society's members at the micro- , meso- , and exosystemic levels (*macrosystem*).

Along with characterizing person-environment interactions in terms that are familiar to family systems theorists (e.g., bidirectional or reciprocal causality, N + 3 systems, ecological transitions), an ecological approach provides a general framework for systematically ordering and linking divergent conceptualizations and data sets in a given area of study. For example, investigators have productively coupled individual-developmental and social-ecological perspectives in their multilevel examination of child maltreatment (Belsky, 1980, Belsky & Vondra, 1989; Willis, Holden, & Rosenberg, 1992).

Significantly missing from their analyses, however, are existential and ontological considerations. For example, a parent's abuse as a child not only affects her psychosocially but also represents an injustice existentially that has unavoidable consequences for her children and for humankind. It is not surprising that questions about such effects on society at large are seldom considered in the child development literature. Like other scientific endeavors, developmental and ecological research is fundamentally grounded in a logical positivistic epistemology that does not recognize the larger existential frame of person-environment relations across time (Vandenberg, 1991).

Human development is more than the "person's evolving conception of the ecological environment, and his relation to it, as well the person's growing capacity to discover, sustain, or alter its properties" (Brofenbrenner, 1979, p. 9). It is also an ontological matter that includes grappling with the predicament of existing in an uncertain and ultimately unknowable world, inhabited by other beings with whom we share the experience (Vandenberg, 1991).

Processes characterizing person-environment transactions from an ecological-developmental perspective (e.g., bidirectionality) are qualitatively different from those intrinsic to the existential domain. Co-being has ethical implications. As Boszormenyi-Nagy and Krasner (1986) observe, the consequences of one's behavior in relationships affect not only others in the present but also posterity and, thus, the "chain of transgenerational survival." In other words, the livelihood of the newborn and ultimately the viability of the human community depend on responsible and ethical intergenerational relating (Boszormenyi-Nagy & Krasner, 1986; Sampson, 1986).[3] From an existential-ethical perspective, then, the dynamic of interest in person-environment transactions is the just balancing of different claims from past, present, and future generations.

On this point, I suspect that Bronfenbrenner would agree. Indeed, implicit in his view of culture as a blueprint for society is a moral prescription: Societally shared agreements, policies, values, and priorities concerning parenting may have to be changed to serve the best interests of children and unborn generations (Garbarino & Abramowitz, 1992). Thus, concern about fair exchange from an ecosystemic perspective is not limited to parent-child relating. It applies to relationships at both proximal and distal points in the ecologies of children—for example, between

---

[3]Of note is that Sampson, a social psychologist concerned with the fundamental basis of justice in human affairs, has drawn many of the same conclusions as Boszormenyi-Nagy. Both, however, can be faulted on philosophic grounds for committing the logical fallacy of confusing facts with ethics, that is, of equating in this case the adaptive significance of adequate parenting with its moral relevance. Although quality of the younger generation's care has objective consequences for humanity, whether parental caregiving *should* be valued in society is an ethical matter (see Kagan, 1989, pp. 19–31). On the other hand, following Bateson (1972) and others (e.g., Sperry, 1977), it is arguable that factual-epistemological and ethical-ontological discourses are reciprocally related. Ethical decisions and priorities have factual implications, which, in turn, inform society's moral stance in various areas. Consequently, although separable philosophically, facts and ethics are intertwined from a naturalistic perspective and merit joint consideration in theoretical accounts purporting to be comprehensive in nature.

teachers and students, employers and employees, politicians and constituents, and society and its members. Decisions and actions within each of these ecosystemic spheres can either place our children at risk for unhealthy forms of parentification and other problems or expand their opportunities to develop optimally.

An Ecological-Ethical Perspective

The foregoing existentially oriented observations in conjunction with those from an ecological-epistemological tradition have been adumbrated to lay the groundwork for the following integrative proposition: *Individual developmental, immediate environmental, and larger sociocultural variables not only transact with one another but also influence and are influenced by existential-ethical processes.* Therefore, neither the ecology of parentification nor its ethical context can be understood fully without reference to the other.

CONCLUSIONS

The kind of role pattern exhibited by Jenny and other children has captured the attention of a theoretically diverse group of investigators. Notwithstanding the richness of their observations, conceptual boundaries in this area have been roughly hewn. Thus, a set of parameters has been proposed to help delimit the properties and contextual dimensions of the parentified role. An overarching perspective has also been introduced to integrate ecological-developmental and existential-ethical levels of parentification. The heuristic and clinical significance of this perspective will become increasingly apparent in subsequent chapters. Indeed, greater clarity in the definition and conceptualization of parentification promises to improve our efforts to understand, identify, treat, and prevent destructive instances of this phenomenon.

CHAPTER **2**

Causation:
An Integrative Framework

Having presented a metatheoretical orientation to direct the conceptual approach to parentification, this book now deals with the more specific problem of causation. This problem raises two interrelated questions: What variables are important? And how do they function, either in isolation or together, to cause destructive parentification? Unlike the first question, which pertains to correlates and predictors of this phenomenon, the second concerns explanation. Consideration must be given to both in the development of a comprehensive framework for understanding destructive parentification.

Such a framework can only be as good as the variables it contains. However, to discover which of them have potential descriptive, predictive, and explanatory significance is a time-consuming and labor-intensive process. Theories suggest promising places to look. I am reminded of the fellow who was searching in vain one night for his key under a street lamp. When asked why he did not look elsewhere, he replied, "Because it's light here." Narrowly conceived theories greatly restrict our search for causal agents, whereas an integrative theoretical framework can illuminate an expansive conceptual terrain.

As suggested by an ecologically oriented ethical approach, consideration is given in this chapter to factors ranging from molecular to molar levels of analysis. For example, extrapolating from recent developmental research of the intra- and interpersonal functioning of infants, processes are discussed that may explain surprisingly young children's active participation in their own destructive parentification. Also considered at the other end of the continuum is the parentifying role of broader contextual dimensions such as acculturative stressors. The objective of this chapter is to draw attention to these and other factors and to organize them according to different levels of analysis, thereby providing helping agents and investigators a scheme to guide their conceptualization of and response to pathologically parentified children and their families.

AN INTEGRATIVE FRAMEWORK

In light of the multivariate nature of causality in this area, no single variable or causal pathway can fully explain the pathogenesis of destructive forms of parentification. Nor are independent and dependent variables fixed as they transact with and transform one another over time (Lewis, 1990). Consequently, the model proposed in Table 1 refers to different risk and protective factors, familial patterns, intervening variables, and transgenerational transmission processes that contribute to and are affected by destructive parentification. Each of the variable classes shown in the table and their interrelationships are explicated in the following sections of this chapter.

INDIVIDUAL DEVELOPMENT

Parents

Important etiological factors can be found in the parents' developmental histories and personalities, which leave them with pressing

TABLE 1
Levels of Analysis of Parentification

Individual Development (Ontogeny)	Proximal Settings (Microsystem)	Interrelation of Settings (Mesosystem)	Distal Settings (Exosystem)	Cultural Consistencies (Macrosystem)	Ethical Context (Co-Being)
Parents	Family	Home–School	Neighborhood	Societal Attitudes	Balance of Fairness
Privation	Stressors	Parent–Peer	Employment	Social Legitimacy	Entitlement
Attachment	Role Induction		Social Services	Gender Roles	
Self-Differentiation	Boundaries				
Cognitive Schema					
	Peers				
Children	School				
Temperament					
Capacity to Care					
Attachment					

Note: The various settings are viewed from the perspective of the child.

needs for nurturance, support, and recognition from others, including their children.

Privation

The quality of the parent-child relationship is rooted in the parent's
parenting by his or her own parents. Although further empirical
investigation of transgenerational transmission patterns is needed,
the operative factor in the histories of many parents of destructively parentified children appears to be the presence of some type
of marked privation, exploitation, or boundary disturbance such
as sexual abuse, neglect, pathological parentification, or overprotection (see, e.g., Burkett, 1991; Jacobvitz, Morgan, Kretchmar, &
Morgan, 1991; Karpel, 1976; Sroufe & Ward, 1980; Sroufe,
Jacobvitz, Mangelsdorf, DeAngelo, & Ward, 1985; Zeanah &
Klitzke, 1991).[1]

Jenny's mother, for example, grew up feeling neither accepted
nor acceptable. Another parentifying parent recalled her own protracted sexual abuse as a child, a fact that she had closely guarded
over the years to protect her family's name. A 14-year-old in her
third trimester of pregnancy refused to consider adoption as an
option for her youngster; she was convinced that the baby would
give her the "love" withheld from her as a child.[2]

Attachment

The early history of many parentifying parents suggests that their
attachment to primary caretakers may have been disrupted. Drawing
from attachment theory and research, Alexander (1992) recently

---

[1]Interestingly, Jacobvitz and colleagues (1991) discovered different manifestations of boundary dissolution across three generations: intrusive caring by mothers of their infants, role reversal in the mothers' relationships
with their mothers, and overprotectiveness in the childhood of the mothers' mothers. These finding suggest that the organization of parent-child
relationships rather than particular behaviors, such as role reversal, are
transmitted from generation to generation (Sroufe & Fleeson, 1986).
[2]Hanson (1990) found that in comparison to pregnant adolescents who
decided to keep their babies, those who opted for placement showed less
evidence of role reversal on a parenting inventory.

speculated that sexual abuse involves the intergenerational transmission of an insecure attachment. It is probable that the same dynamic often exists for parentification. Thus, role reversals may occur in parent-child relationships because of the unavailability of secure attachment figures in the lives of the parents (Bowlby, 1973, 1980).

Self-Differentiation

We have also observed that as a result of early emotional impoverishment, the primary narcissistic needs of many parentifying parents for recognition and empathy were frustrated. They were not provided the interpersonal foundation for developing a core sense of themselves (Miller, 1979/1981). Or, in Bowenian terms, remaining undifferentiated (i.e., emotionally fused with or reactively cut off from their families of origin), they failed to acquire a "solid self" that allowed them to think, feel, and act for themselves. The undifferentiated and narcissistically injured parent is prone to fuse with, neglect, and exploit his or her children.

Cognitive Schema

Cognitive processes are also centrally involved in the transgenerational transmission of dysfunctional parent-child relationships. Bowlby (1979) assumes that, based on their early attachments to primary caretakers, children construct "internal working models" of relationships that reflect qualities of (1) their role (e.g., overgiving) and (2) the other's role (e.g., exploitative). These models mediate their interpersonal perceptions, emotional experiences, memories, and behaviors both as children and as adults (Dean, Malik, Richards, & Stringer, 1986; Jurkovic, Jessee, & Goglia, 1991; Zeanah & Zeanah, 1989).

For example, later in the development of parentified youngsters, they may assimilate members of their families of procreation into their internal models of relationships. For example, the parent with a history of destructive parentification may invert roles with his or her children or continue to assume an overnurturing and protective posture (Bowlby, 1979; Jurkovic, Jessee, & Goglia, 1991; West & Keller, 1991). In the latter case, rather than parentify their children, they are at risk of infantilizing them, which entraps them in the role of loyal object. These parents often marry needy and dependent individuals who themselves are at risk of parentifying their future children and/or maltreating them in other ways.

It is important to note that mothers and fathers with a history of parentification are frequently quite responsive to their offspring's needs, indicating that both appropriate and inappropriate representational models of relationships are to be found in the repertoires of such parents. Inappropriate responding on their part, however, tends to be activated as anxiety increases. For example, children who are required to grow up quickly may later, particularly when they are feeling needy, envy the attention that their offspring receive and, hence, vacillate between being attentively caring and emotionally distant as parents (Weiss, 1979).

Internal representations of self-other relations are also influenced by cognitive-developmental processes. Deprived parents, for example, may have difficulty conceptualizing children and the child-rearing process in terms that extend beyond their own perspective. The ability to conceptualize and to coordinate the various perspectives of self and other progresses through a series of predictable stages (see, e.g., Selman, 1980). Interested in the development of this process within the specific content domain of parenting, Newberger and her co-workers have identified different levels in parents' understanding of children as people, the parent-child relationship, and the parental role. The levels range from an immature, egoistic perspective to a psychologically complex, process-oriented view (see Cook, 1979; Newberger, 1977, 1980; Newberger & White, 1989).

It is probable that higher-level thinking serves as a protective factor in parentification, whereas reasoning at lower levels represents a clear risk. For example, consider the following exchange between Newberger and one of the parents she interviewed:

> *What do you feel is the most important goal of raising a child?*
>
> I think to grow up into the image of what you wanted to be, or what you wanted them to be, what you wanted to be yourself. (Newberger, 1977, p. 225)

Characteristic of egoistic thinking, of greatest concern to this parent is that her child fulfill her expectations. The child's preferences and needs are not considered. This orientation, which also frequently surfaces in our work with parentifying parents, reflects a severe disruption in the self-other dialectic, most likely occasioned by early deprivation and exploitation.

The extent to which some parentifying parents egoistically view their children as objects can be shocking. A father who was tragically abused as a child said to his severely parentified adolescent daughter in therapy: "I brought you into the world, and I can take you out." His disturbing sense of ownership of his daughter, which had not been clear in previous sessions, helped to explain his abusively parentifying attitudes and behaviors.

We have also worked with many parentifying parents who, although cognitively capable, did not consistently exercise their higher-level perspective-taking skills. In addition, some of these parents either were insensitive to or overidentified with their children's affective states. In view of evidence that empathic behavior is a multifaceted cognitive, affective, and motivational process (see e.g., Feshbach, 1989; Hoffman, 1982; Zahn-Waxler & Robinson, 1995), different aspects of empathy may be implicated in the parentification process.

It is important to consider environmental influences as well. Parental understanding and empathy are often compromised by severe anxiety and problems of survival related to little disposable income, single parenting, or congenital disabilities and intercurrent illnesses in the children, as well as other stressors, as reviewed earlier (Newberger, 1977).

Children

Are there primary determining features in the individual development of children that increase their susceptibility to exploitative parentification and their proclivity to engage actively in the process? The answer to this question points to at least three variables: (1) temperament, (2) capacity to care, and (3) attachment behavior.

Temperament

Just as constitution has been implicated in the physical abuse of children, so may it play a role in parentification. Rather than having a disabling condition, an illness, or a difficult disposition that contributes to parental stress, many parentified children are temperamentally shy and slow to warm up, although interpersonally sensitive (Kagan, Reznick, & Snidman, 1990; Plomin & Dunn, 1986; Thomas & Chess, 1977). Inhibited in their movement into extrafamilial relationships, these children seek interpersonal gratification within their immediate home environments. As a result, they are not only vulnerable to parentification but also inclined to reinforce the parentifying behaviors of family members.[3]

We have also treated many parentified youngsters who are temperamentally easy. Their regularity and adaptability appear to encourage parents, especially those who rely on their children for protection and nurturance, to overestimate their developmental capacities and thus to neglect their stage-related needs. One mother of a destructively parentified youngster commented early in therapy that she often had to remind herself of her daughter's needs, because she was so "easy going."

Capacity to Care

A more ubiquitous developmental process that also places children at risk for exploitative parentification is their biologically based propensity to empathize and growing capacity to care for others (Sagi & Hoffman, 1976; Zahn-Waxler & Robinson, 1995). Clinical observers have long postulated that this process begins at an early age, perhaps within the first 12 months. Searles (1973), for example, has drawn attention to parental exploitation of young children's "innate therapeutic strivings." Similarly, Winnicott (1965) has hypothesized that infants may become prematurely "attuned" to the unconscious needs of their parents.

Speculation about the concern, therapeutic strivings, and attunement of young children, particularly infants, implicitly assumes that they have some sense of self and of other. This assumption challenges generally accepted theories (e.g., Mahler, 1968) of early development, which describe a normal state of fusion or sym-

---

[3]As discussed later, however, social inhibition is often an effect of parentification. Although an inhibited style appears in many cases to have had independent origins, thus representing a potential causal factor in the parentification process, our clinical observations have yet to be examined empirically.

biosis with the primary caretaker for most of the first year of life. Self-other distinctions are said to emerge from this primarily un-differentiated state. Stern (1985), a psychoanalyst and developmental investigator, has presented more recent data, from both his own research and that of others, indicating a radically different order of events. His findings suggest that within two months after birth infants actively begin creating their interpersonal worlds by forming a core self and core others. A watershed in developmental psychology, Stern's work points to the primarily social nature of infants' development and experience. Their "core relatedness," built on the physical and sensory distinction of self and other, is the "existential bedrock of interpersonal relations" (Stern, 1985, p. 125).

Between the seventh and ninth months of life, the domain of "intersubjective relatedness" is added to that of core relatedness, reflecting the infant's developing realization that inner subjective experiences can be shared with others (Stern, 1985). A phenomenon referred to as "social referencing" (Campos & Stenberg, 1981) is one important source of data documenting the emergence of this domain. When infants are enticed to crawl across an apparent "visual cliff," they characteristically hesitate and look to their mothers. If their mothers smile as so directed by the experimenter, infants happily negotiate the cliff. If their mothers exhibit fear, however, the infants become upset and retreat.

The implication is that infants recognize not only that their mothers have affects but also that maternal emotional displays have referential significance. They are thus able to enter into a prelinguistic form of communication with their mothers that influences their own affective state and behavior.[4] *The early development of intersubjective relatedness helps explain young children's uncanny capacity to sense and to accommodate to the subtle demands and needs of others, a capacity which places them at risk of*

---

[4]Research of nine-month-old infants' responses to their mothers' expressions of joy and sadness further support this conclusion (e.g., Termine & Izard, 1988). Termine and Izard also note that while the social referencing effect is typically explained in terms of the infant's observation of maternal affect, their data point to the capacity of nine-month-old children to experience vicariously the emotional states of maternal figures (see also Boccia & Campos, 1989).

contributing directly to their own parentification. It appears that as early as the seventh month of life, normal children begin to resonate with and respond to the affects, intentions, and projections of their primary caretaker. Consistent with Winnicott's (1965) concept of the "false self," infants' spontaneity and self-development may be sacrificed as they increasingly become what parental figures need them to be.

Karpel (1976), however, argues that parents typically do not demand excessively responsible behavior of children until their third or fourth year, that is, until they have developed the sensitivity, autonomy, and skills to discharge their assigned tasks. To the extent that parents attempt to parentify their children earlier, it is assumed that developmental limitations prevent such children from responding in any meaningful way.

Indeed, it appears that most parents in this country and in other cultures do not expect children to contribute significantly to the household and family, at least instrumentally, before the age of three (see reviews by Goodnow, 1988; Weisner & Gallimore, 1977). I am not suggesting, however, that infants' responses to parental needs are well differentiated and overtly expressed in a consistent and organized manner. Rather, it is possible that their prelinguistic exchanges with caretakers can draw them into a web of subtle parentifying processes. As they mature, their early concern and intersubjectivity are mediated by increasingly sophisticated behavioral and cognitive systems, including interpersonal schema of themselves as caretakers (cf. Hoffman, 1976; Zahn-Waxler & Robinson, 1995). Yet, also at variance with Karpel's observations, there is evidence to suggest that even these processes may begin to develop early in the life of the child.

Consider the following observations of a 15-month-old and his friend, indicating that some nascent forms of social perspective taking and attendant helping behavior may occur before two years of age, especially in the context of familiar relationships.

> The boy, Michael, was struggling with his friend, Paul, over a toy. Paul started to cry. Michael appeared concerned and let go of the toy so that Paul would have it, but Paul kept crying. Michael paused, then gave his teddy bear to Paul, but the crying continued. Michael paused

again, then ran to the next room, returned with Paul's security blanket, and offered it to Paul, who then stopped crying. (Hoffman, 1976, pp. 129–130)

Schneider, Pollock, and Helfer (1972) cite an example, from their clinical work with abused children, of a 20-month-old who, whenever her mother was upset, comforted her.

Data supporting these anecdotal findings indicate that as early as one year of age, children physically comfort others in distress (e.g., hugging, patting) and within their second year engage in other prosocial and reparative actions (e.g., helping, sympathizing) (Zahn-Waxler & Radke-Yarrow, 1982; Zahn-Waxler, Radke-Yarrow, Wagner, & Chapman, 1992). By the age of two or three, children have developed rudimentary sociocognitive skills to support their emotional responsiveness to parental figures and their possible functioning in a parentified role.[5]

Attachment

Also contributing to early caretaking on the part of children is attachment behavior. Although acquired through experience, attachment is conceptualized as a basic behavioral system, along with other systems underlying such behaviors as reproduction, feeding, and exploration, all of which are biologically based and thus species-characteristic (Ainsworth, 1989; Bowlby, 1979). Consistent with Stern's thesis that the relationships of infants are predicated on their initial differentiation of self and other, research by Sroufe and his colleagues (Sroufe & Rutter, 1984) indicates that attachment becomes a prominent developmental concern between 6 and 12 months of age (cf. Cicchetti, 1989). Functioning to maintain proximity between the young and preferred adults, whether primates in savannah gorilla troupes or human infants in familial settings, the attachment behavior system is assumed to have survival value. Its biological roots help to explain why children can

---

[5]See also Bridgeman (1983), Cohn & Tronick (1983), Rheingold (1982), Rheingold, Hay, & West (1976), Zahn-Waxler & Kochanska (1988); Zahn-Waxler, Radke-Yarrow, & King (1979), and Zahn-Waxler & Robinson (1995).

develop and maintain affectional bonds, albeit of poor quality, to attachment figures who are abusive (Bowlby, 1979; Cicchetti, 1989).

Infants of abusive, traumatized, alcoholic, or affectively disordered parents have been shown to exhibit a disorganized/disoriented attachment pattern (Carlson, Cicchetti, Barnett, & Braunwald, 1989; Main & Hesse, 1990; Main & Solomon, 1986, 1990; O'Connor, Sigman, & Brill, 1987; Radke-Yarrow, Cummings, Kuczynski, & Chapman, 1985). Unpredictable emotional displays and other disruptive behaviors by these parents may confuse the infants, who become disorganized and disoriented in their presence. They also learn that their attachment behaviors, which are erratically reinforced or even punished, are not always welcomed by parental figures. Under such conditions, infants are at risk of assuming an increasingly caretaking role, especially to the extent that parentified behavior functions to maintain affectional ties that otherwise would not be available to them (see Main & Hesse, 1990; Main & Cassidy, 1988; Zeanah & Klitzke, 1991).

PROXIMAL SETTINGS

Developmental processes unfold within different microsystems, the most immediate of which in our culture, and to a large extent in many other cultures, include the children's family, peer group, and school. Of these, the family plays the central role in both the genesis and the perpetuation of parentification. The others function primarily to reinforce and maintain the child's caretaking style.

Family

Stressors

Various stressors that affect the structure, role patterns, and legacies of the family increase the likelihood of destructive parentification of the children. These stressors include the number, spacing, and birth order of the children; major illnesses and disabling conditions in the parents and siblings, including substance dependence and severe psychopathology (e.g., schizophrenia, bipolar and unipolar mood disorders, obsessive-compulsive disorder); parent absence, marital conflict, separation, divorce, and custody disputes; and other stressors (e.g., parental imprisonment) that overextend the economic and human resources of the family system. Some of these are considered in greater detail in the following paragraphs:

Substance Dependence. We discovered that adult children of alcoholics reported a greater degree of destructive parentification during their childhood than a comparison group of individuals of nonalcoholic parents (Goglia, Jurkovic, & Burge-Callaway, 1992). This finding, however, was restricted to the female participants, raising questions at a macrosystemic level, which are addressed later, about the moderating function of gender-role socialization patterns in the parentification process.

Birth Order and Family Size. Oldest children, particularly girls in large families, tend to be assigned and to accept significant responsibility, increasing the likelihood of their parentification (Bossard & Boll, 1956; Toman, 1961). The level at which different siblings enact characteristic patterns of behavior, however, may depend on their degree of differentiation (Kerr & Bowen, 1988). An elder but immature child may attempt to care for needy family members in a controlling and intrusive fashion. In this instance, reflecting the complementarity of functioning positions in the family, a younger sibling often assumes a more functional, first-born role.

Single Parenting. Children of single parents are also at risk for parentification. In addition to sharing responsibility with their parents and siblings for various instrumental tasks, they frequently perform expressive functions, such as serving as their parents' confidants, companions, and even supervisors (Dawson, 1980; Fry & Trifiletti, 1983; Wallerstein, 1985; Weiss, 1979). A single parent of a preadolescent boy in Weiss's study reported:

> I called my house and Mark said, "When are you coming home?" And I said, "Pretty soon." And he said, "Ma, it's a quarter of eight. Now you had better get home here quick." And I said "Okay, Mark. I'm just having drinks with a few friends." And he said, "Well, don't drink too much and be home soon." (p. 104)

Of course, not all children who live in single-parent homes or who are experiencing other stressors are harmfully parentified, particularly if their relationships with parental figures are moderated by various protective processes, as discussed throughout this chapter. As Weiss observes, the horizontal structuring of parent-child relationships in such homes, in which the children assume a "junior-partner" role, is both common and adaptive. The apparent maturity of many of these youngsters, however, can belie underlying stress and adjustment problems (Dawson, 1980; Weiss, 1979; Wallerstein, 1985).

Marital Dysfunction. Another potential stressor is the parents' marital relationship, which when healthy is a primary source of parental support (Belsky, 1980; Belsky & Vondra, 1989). Before parentifying their children, parents with emotionally impoverished developmental histories often seek parenting from their mates. An all-consuming involvement with a dominant partner, however, can be threatened by the birth of a child. Women who attempt to give equally to their infants without jeopardizing their marital relationships parent inconsistently, placing their newborns at risk for parentification (Zeanah & Klitzke, 1991).

Clinical observation reveals that extreme dissatisfaction, underorganization, stress, and abandonment during pregnancy in this subsystem in the family, even if not potentiated by deprivation in one or both of the partners' families of origin, is often a primary determinant in the destructive parentification of children (cf. Karpel, 1976; Minuchin, Montalvo, Guerney, Rosman, & Schumer, 1967). Children of violent marriages are especially at risk of being pathologically parentified. In addition to comforting their parents, they assume responsibility for preventing violence between them. A seven-year-old boy treated by Elbow (1982) said:

> I help Mom. She tells me to call Grandmother to come
> and help. When I go to the phone, Daddy stops. (p. 468)

It has been empirically documented that even two-year-olds actively intervene in parental conflict by attempting to stop it, by encouraging their parents to make up, or by consoling one of them. Interestingly, when seen several years later, these children exhibited a similar pattern, except that their marital interventions were more effective. They, moreover, appeared less angry and upset, perhaps reflecting the adaptiveness of their role as mediators or peacemakers (Cummings, Zahn-Waxler, & Radke-Yarrow, 1981, 1984).

Role Induction

The process by which parentification assumes pathological proportions can follow either a direct or an indirect path. For example, children often serve in loco parentis as a direct consequence of their parents' overpermissiveness, physical abandonment of the family, abdication of parental responsibility, co-parenting difficulties, incompetence, or preoccupation with unmet needs and fears (Karpel, 1976; Minuchin, Montalvo, Guerney, Rosman, & Schumer, 1967; Zeanah & Klitzke, 1991).

In addition to parental underfunctioning, parents' prematurely demanding independence of young children figures directly into the parentification process. Such demands do not teach children independence but, rather, *nondependence* on their parents (McClelland, 1961). When children's requests for help (e.g., in getting dressed) or need for guidance (e.g., in doing homework) are rejected by parents, they are likely to turn to their older siblings for assistance.

Obvious displays of parental neediness, helplessness, and dependency also directly elicit caretaking responses from children. These can range from suicidal gestures in their children's presence to chronic somatic complaints (see e.g., Kreider & Motto, 1974). One of my clients presented me with a graphic example of this process. When she was diagnosed with a degenerative disease at the age of 12, her mother said to her after the doctor left the office, "You're going to have to help me through this one."

Other direct forms of parentification include threats (Bowlby, 1979), persuasion, and moral exhortations to behave in an overresponsible fashion. One of my parentified clients, Johnny, was repeatedly informed by his mother that it was his role to take care of his younger sister—"that's what big brothers are supposed to do." Whenever his sister complained or resisted her brother's parenting efforts, however, Johnny was severely reproached. His job description also included maintaining his mother's equanimity.

More often, children are induced to assume a parentified role in an indirect and insidiously captivating fashion. Karpel (1976) suggests that they are subjected to two types of directives: (1) *instructions,* prescribing what the youngster should be and do, and (2) *injunctions,* proscribing what he or she should not be or do. Such mandates not only interfere with clear communication but impose parental definitions onto the child's intentions, emotions, needs, and actions. In effect, the parent "misdefines the child to himself" (Stierlin, 1974, p. 42).[6]

For example, parents may subtly instruct their children to behave in a pseudomature fashion by reinforcing such behavior and depicting them as precociously grown-up and sensitive (Karpel, 1976). One nine-year-old I saw several years ago described himself as a "pre-adult," an appellation fully endorsed by his parents. Yet, they were uncomfortable with his desire to become increasingly independent of them. Another parent of an extremely parentified 16-year-old supported her daughter's desire to drive, particularly because she could then take her shopping, but found her age-appropriate requests for a later curfew outrageous (Jurkovic, Jessee, & Goglia, 1991).

As discussed earlier, destructive parentification may be disguised further by overprotective, devoted, or solicitous parental behavior. Although apparently a response to the child's anxiety, this caretaking style is in reality a projection of the parent's anxiety. Children's guilt-induced efforts to repay their self-sacrificing parents are often rejected, leaving them forever in their parents' debt (Boszormenyi-Nagy & Spark, 1973; Bowlby, 1973, 1980; Zeanah & Klitzke, 1991).

Overinvolved parents may also alternate between parentifying and infantilizing behaviors, which ultimately results in the parentification of their children. In fact, this pattern, which often typifies enmeshed parent-child relationships, may be part of the disorganized/disoriented attachment process referred to earlier. The behavior of these parents involves an iterative pattern of (1) engulfment, followed by (2) sudden and often angry disengagement,

---

[6]One of the stages in projective identification, as described by Ogden (1982), also involves induction. The ability of children to recognize and to cope with inductive processes, possibly feeding back parental projections in an altered form, is limited. Thus, they are unable to complete the last stage of the projective identification process.

when it becomes apparent that the child cannot gratify the parent's needs and has pressing needs of his or her own, and, repeating the cycle, (3) a guilt-laden reengagement of the child. The unpredictability of this interactive sequence is disorganizing and disorienting for the developing child, who increasingly attempts to become a satisfying object for the parent (cf. Main & Hesse, 1990; Minuchin, Montalvo, Guerney, Rosman, & Schumer, 1967).

Boundaries

The various means by which children become involved in a pathogenic parentified role reflect marked boundary distortions in the family. In some cases overrigid boundaries around the spousal subsystem can result in neglect of the children, who then turn to one another for support and protection (cf. Gunderson, Kerr, & Englund, 1980; Zeanah & Klitzke, 1991). Many parentified children are enmeshed with one parent and disengaged from the other ("cross-generational coalition") or involved in shifting coalitions ("triangulation") in which the parents actively compete for the child's support and allegiance (Minuchin, 1974; Minuchin, Montalvo, Guerney, Rosman, & Schumer, 1967). These shifting coalitions entrap youngsters in a "predicament of split loyalty" (Boszormenyi-Nagy & Krasner, 1986). They are told by one parent of the failings of the other and are often drawn into the role of refereeing and attempting to reconcile the parents' differences or induced to cut off from one of their parents.

A particularly pernicious form of this process came to my attention recently. A young adolescent, who had long functioned as an intermediary between his parents, learned of his drunken father's intent to shoot his mother. The parents had recently separated. Rather than directly oppose his father at the risk of being disloyal, he accompanied him to his mother's residence "to help them work it out." Despite his father's threatening gestures with a gun, this youngster intrepidly prevented the conflict from escalating further.

In the case of parents who relinquish executive and/or nurturing responsibilities, parentified children also become overinvolved with their siblings. The role of parentified children in the sibling subsystem under these conditions, however, is stressful. Like managers in the business world, they are caught in the middle. They are the targets, not only of their younger charges' anger against neglectful parental figures, but also of their parents' criticism and blame, when they themselves or their charges fail to live up to parental expectations (Jurkovic, Jessee, & Goglia, 1991; Minuchin, Montalvo, Guerney, Rosman, & Schumer, 1967).

Just as physical or sexual abuse continues, in part, because of the passive participation of the nonabusing parent, so does pathological parentification. Children are abandoned in various ways, such as through their nonparentifying parent's failure to interdict the parentification process. As a result, boundary distortions in the family persist. Talking about her own severe parentification by her mother, Miller (1979/1981) wrote:

> I had been subjected to this terror for years because no one close to me, not even my kind and wise father, was capable of noticing or challenging this form of child abuse. Had just one person understood what was happening and come to my defense, it might have changed my entire life. That person could have helped me to recognize my mother's cruelty for what it was instead of accepting it for decades, to my great detriment, as something normal and necessary. (viii–ix)

In addition to functional co-parenting, signs of healthy family boundaries from a transactional perspective include developmental appropriateness, clear definition, and supervision of assigned tasks. Responsibilities, moreover, are distributed throughout the family, including the sibling subsystem (Minuchin, Montalvo, Guerney, Rosman, & Schumer, 1967; Minuchin, 1974). Children who are given considerable instrumental work in the home also feel less exploited if they (1) perceive that the work is necessary and shared with parents and (2) are granted autonomy in the discharge of their duties (see Goodnow, 1988).

Peers and School

Writing about young children of alcoholics, Walsh (1992) noted that with teachers and peers, these children tend to assume the role (e.g., hero, scapegoat, clown) they characteristically play at home. Through a process referred to as "family transference" in the clinical literature (Boszormenyi-Nagy & Framo, 1962; Brown & Beletsis, 1986), a concept that anticipated subsequent theorizing about internal working models (Bowlby, 1979), children appear to re-create family relationships with extrafamilial figures. Although not empirically documented, we have observed the same phenomenon with parentified children.

For example, parentified children tend to overfunction with their friends just as they do with family members, thinking excessively about them, assuming most or all of the responsibility for initiating and maintaining contact, and going to great lengths to avoid hurting them at their own expense. Not surprisingly, parentified youngsters are frequently sought out by their peers for advice and support. On the other hand, because of their excessive orientation to adults and lack of age-related social skills, many of these children are socially isolated.

These relational patterns outside the home contribute to children's identification with and enactment of a parentified role. For example, social isolation increases the availability of parentified children to adults, whose parentifying behaviors are reinforced, which in turn contributes to greater social isolation. Further complicating matters are effects of an even higher order. As socially isolated children become increasingly enmeshed with parentifying caretakers, the parents' spousal relationships, which may have contributed to the parentification process in the first place, further deteriorate. The result is still greater pressure on children to satisfy parental needs and to maintain the family's equilibrium. The complexities of cause and effect in this area have yet to be captured empirically.

The pseudomaturity of parentified children also endears them to their teachers, although some respond with concern. Consistent with their interactions with parental figures, these children are often exceptionally helpful, functioning like a teacher's aide. Alternatively, they may parentify their teachers, projecting parental qualities onto them. One parentified third-grader recurrently dreamed that her teacher, whom she visited at her home on occasion, was a maternal figure who disciplined her. Discipline symbolized caring to this youngster whose mother was too preoccupied with her own needs to recognize those of her daughter. Interestingly, in high school, this girl sought "mentoring" from teachers to meet her parenting needs.

Thus, school represents a source of relief for some parentified children. This is more likely if the school's climate is a supportive one. Growing evidence, however, indicates that large consolidated middle and secondary school systems (often in excess of 2,000 students) are problematic, significantly impairing students' scholastic performance, extracurricular involvement, and sense of belonging, especially for those who are academically marginal (Barker & Gump, 1964; Garbarino, 1980; Fowler & Walberg, 1991).

Moreover, the increasing industrialization and product-orientation (as exemplified by grades and standardized test scores) of school systems in this country are pressuring children to accommodate to schedules of achievement and productivity that violate fundamental principles of child development and learning (Elkind, 1981). The school, therefore, may be just one more setting, hurrying parentified children into adulthood and ignoring their basic needs for recognition and empathy.

INTERRELATION OF SETTINGS

How do the different settings in which the parentified child is an active participant interrelate? To my knowledge, this question has received little, if any, attention. Yet the nature of the family-peer-school system has important implications for the developmental course of parentification.

Home–School

Parentified children experience demands to perform both at home and in school. Stresses at home can detract from performance at school, creating a feedback loop that may result in aversive consequences for the child in both settings (Garbarino & Abramowitz, 1992; Foster, 1984; Lusterman, 1985). As in the case of Nicholas, referred to in the Introduction, poor grades resulting from burdensome duties at home may occasion punishment by parents. Unless parents and school personnel communicate about the child's needs, this pattern is likely to continue and to intensify. Parents protect their children by actively managing not only intrafamilial boundaries but also boundaries between the family and other social institutions such as the school.

Parents who are struggling to survive psychologically and financially, however, often lack the time and energy to form cooperative partnerships with teachers and others involved in the lives of their children. Negative information from school, for example, only adds to their stress, intensifying the demands they place on their children to behave in ways that do not require parenting. Moreover, some parents are not ready or able to respond to the advice of teachers. For instance, Mrs. Stein, one of the mothers studied by Karpel (1976), observed:

> Eva's sixth grade teacher told me once that we were making her, like we were asking her to grow up too fast. He said, "She's still a child. Let her act like one." ... At that time I couldn't see it as much as I could now. (p. 85)

It is noteworthy that this teacher was both sensitive to parentification and able to process his observations with Eva's mother. *Although school personnel have become increasingly aware of child abuse and neglect and play a key role in their detection, their understanding of pathological parentification and its sequelae is limited.* Moreover, large class sizes and the growing role demands of teachers impede their ability to foster the necessary parent-teacher alliances to help interdict destructive parentification processes.

Parent–Peer

Another systemic dynamic that affects parentification is the link between parents and their children's peer groups. Do parents encourage their children to form healthy peer relationships? Are they actively aware of their children's social world? By definition, destructive parentification is captivating and thus inimical to positive bonds external to the family. Peer relating is threatening to parental figures who rely on their offspring for support and self-definition. Thus, they may interfere either directly or indirectly in their children's peer interests. To the extent that their children do become involved in relationships outside the home, parents often do not closely monitor them because of their own self-absorption. In these cases, the children are at risk of forming problematic affiliations.

DISTAL SETTINGS

Many parents are attempting to raise their children not only in the absence of adult partners but also without supportive ties to relatives, neighbors, social networks, work settings, community agencies, and other social institutions. Although children are not directly involved in all of these contexts, they are affected by them. For example, if their parents are isolated from formal and informal sources of support, they are at great risk of being abused and neglected (see Belsky, 1980; Garbarino & Kostenly, 1994). During times of stress, their parents have no one to turn to for help and feedback. Along with increasing the possibilities of abuse and neglect, this state of affairs places children at risk for parentification, becoming compensatory support systems for socially isolated parents.

Neighborhood

The role of community support for parents has become paramount with the decline of stable, extended family structures in many segments of our society. One of the most robust sources of such support is the immediate environment of the family, namely, the neighborhood. Garbarino and his colleagues (Garbarino, 1981; Garbarino & Crouter, 1978; Garbarino & Kostenly, 1994; Garbarino & Sherman, 1980) found, in part, that compared to neighborhoods with high rates of child maltreatment, those with low rates had more neighborly exchange, greater residential stability, more interaction among children, superior housing, better relations with institutions, such as schools, and less overall stress. These findings influenced the U.S. Advisory Board on Child Abuse and Neglect (1993) to recommend, as the top priority of a national strategy to combat child maltreatment, the creation of "protection zones"—safe neighborhoods for children that facilitate neighborly interactions and socioeconomic growth (Melton & Barry, 1994).

The harsh realities and pressing needs of parents residing in high-risk neighborhoods impede their ability to receive and to give help to others. Many of these parents have also failed to develop the skills and the motivation necessary to establish and sustain friendships as well as to seek assistance (Belsky, 1980; Garbarino, 1981).

In our work with inner-city, multiproblem families, one goal has been to build parents' "ecological competence," a term we coined to refer to a set of social skills involved in seeking help and dealing assertively with social institutions to meet personal and familial needs. Ecologically competent parents fight being victimized by "red tape," incompetence, unresponsiveness, and discrimination.

Employment

Employment can also serve to empower parents and enhance family relationships. Joblessness, a correlate of child abuse and neglect (Belsky, 1980; Pelton, 1994), is often in the family backgrounds of parentified children whom we and others (e.g., Minuchin, Montalvo, Guerney, Rosman, & Schumer, 1967) have seen. In addition to the direct effect of unemployment on family functioning, this variable is associated with other factors (e.g., depression, stress) that increase the likelihood of child maltreatment, including pathological forms of parentification.

Other conditions of parental employment (e.g., frequent relocation, demanding work loads, negative attitudes toward maternal and paternal leave policies, lengthy commuting, travel, inflexible working hours) that promote geographic mobility, separation from family members, fragmentation of the extended family, long workdays, and stress also contribute directly to the destructive parentification of children (cf. Stipek & McCroskey, 1989).

The "working poor," whose jobs often require odd hours and yield limited income, may rely heavily on their children to help manage the household. For example, a child might be required to assume full responsibility for her younger siblings while her single mother works the 4:00 to 10:00 P.M. shift at a convenience store. Interestingly, cross-cultural data also indicate that sibling caretaking is common in many other societies when (1) mothers have much work to complete, (2) their work takes them away from home, (3) their jobs cannot be interrupted, or (4) they have caretakers (e.g., older children) available to them (Weisner & Gallimore, 1977).

Even children in more advantaged families and stable neighborhoods, particularly those with parents who both work outside the home, are frequently called upon to perform various parental tasks. Children of parents whose career obligations and choices compete with the needs of their families are at increased risk of parentification as well. The spouses of such parents may turn to the children to fill the void in their marriages. Mitchell and Cronson (1987) describe such a dynamic in the "celebrity" families that they have treated. By assuming full responsibility for child rearing and home management, often with the help of one of the children, the spouses of celebrities enable their mates to devote themselves to their careers.

Social Services

Another factor influencing parentification is the availability and responsiveness of various social service systems to families, particularly to those with limited resources. Mental health facilities, juvenile courts, and protective service agencies continue to be understaffed with qualified personnel and overly focused on identifying, investigating, and treating problems after the fact. As the U.S. Advisory Board in Child Abuse and Neglect (1993) recommends, the delivery of human services should be neighborhood based and reoriented to help families before they experience crises.

Moreover, professionals who are working with children and families, both in the public and the private sectors, are not sufficiently conscious of the problem of pathological parentification. For these practitioners, as for schoolteachers, changes in professional training and mandatory reporting laws have focused attention on physical abuse and neglect. Further changes are needed, however, to broaden the awareness of the various professional groups to include destructive forms of parentification as well.

CULTURAL CONSISTENCIES

In an address a number of years ago to the American Orthopsychiatric Association, Brim (1975)—whose work helped shape Bronfenbrenner's ideas—was one of the first investigators to challenge his colleagues to integrate macrosystemic determinants into their formulations of child development. Various social forces at this level of analysis, including technology, cultural values, politics, law, mass media, economics, and historical changes, significantly influence the other processes and settings discussed earlier. Several of these forces are considered in this section.

Societal Attitudes

Insufficient federal funding of children's programs, a concern raised by Brim that continues to be a problem today (Adler, DeAngelis, & Moses-Zirkes, 1993), reverberates throughout the ecologies of vast numbers of children and families. As Brim observed, when budget cuts and limitations are needed, "children are the first to go." The actions of many policymakers reflect an ideology, born of individualistic culture, that overemphasizes family autonomy and privacy. Thus, programs empowering the community as a support system for children and families are seen as expendable. The undervaluation of social interdependence in our society represents a significant part of the macrosystem of child maltreatment, including destructive parentification (Garbarino, 1980a; Garbarino, Gaboury, Long, Grandjean, & Asp, 1982).

Social Legitimacy

The larger sociocultural context in which children are enacting various parental tasks is also a critical consideration in this area. Cross-cultural research, for example, indicates that sibling caretaking is widespread; indeed, siblings play a central socializing role in many societies around the world (Weisner & Gallimore, 1977). Gallimore, Boggs, and Jordan (1974) recall one of their interviews with a native Hawaiian mother who helped them appreciate that the parent-child dyad is not always the culturally appropriate focus in socialization research.

> Q. Did you have any trouble with her [toilet training]?
> A. Oh, I didn't [have anything to do with it]. Sister teach 'em that. (p. 124)

In many societies, especially in simple agricultural communities (Murdock & Provost, 1973), even infants are cared for by their older siblings to allow mothers to complete household economic tasks. For example, Super and Harkness (Harkness & Super, 1983; Super & Harkness, 1981, 1982) discovered that in a community of farm families in Kenya, an older sibling, a *cheblakwet,* is assigned responsibility for the immediate care of infants over 4 months of age. The sibling's task, which usually falls to a sister during her eighth year, is to entertain and to protect the baby. However, if the baby becomes inconsolably upset, the *cheblakwet* returns him or her to the mother. After being nursed and comforted, the infant often sleeps. Parental supervision, definition, and legitimization of children's caretaking tasks—important protective factors—are normative in this community.

Clinical and empirical observations of families of various national origins in this country also reveal that sibling caretaking has roots in wider social processes. Culturally related variations in family roles, kinship patterns, values, and even alcohol consumption are causal factors in this area, although whether they result in destructive parentification depends on the nature and context of the assigned tasks.

For example, a recent study of socialization goals and adaptive strategies of African American, Native American, Asian-Pacific American, and Hispanic families discovered that older siblings in each of these groups are routinely required to assume responsibility for their younger brothers and sisters (Harrison, Wilson, Pine, Chan, & Buriel, 1990). Sibling caretaking, along with alternative family structures (e.g., shared living quarters with extended family members) and job responsibilities outside the home for both parents, reflect (1) adaptations by ethnic minority families to their situation within the larger society (e.g., inadequate community support systems, economic and social discrimination) and (2) worldviews derived from earlier generations that emphasize group loyalty, cooperation, and kinship ties (cf. Boyd-Franklin, 1987).

Yet, just as the kinship group has eroded in majority American culture, so it has in minority cultures. For example, economic and social pressures have contributed to increasing geographic mobility and other socioemotional problems among African Americans, significantly attenuating their extended family relationships (see, e.g., King, 1993). Growing numbers of upwardly mobile members of their culture are further depleting the ranks of their natural support systems. Many of those climbing the socioeconomic ladder, moreover, are finding that an unexpected cost of their success is the loss of connections with kin, community, and heritage (McAdoo,

1988; Lightfoot, 1992). A child's enactment of adultlike roles in an interdependent, extended family network qualitatively differs from that in a fractionated and discordant one. The potential for exploitation and destructive parentification is much greater in the latter case.

Other culturally defined family patterns can also contribute to parentification. For example, in patriarchal familial systems, such as traditional Greek, Iranian, and Asian families, sons are encouraged to exercise executive authority as preparation for future leadership roles in their family groups (Jalali, 1982; Shon & Ja, 1982; Welts, 1982). Brothers in Iranian families traditionally assume the role of supporting and protecting their sisters. Because of the role rigidity in many patriarchal systems, however, the children's mothers often use them as go-betweens to express differences with their husbands (Jalali, 1982), a process that can set the stage for an unhealthy form of parentification.[7]

Recent immigrants of various cultural groups are especially dependent on relatives who immigrated earlier. In the event that they are among the first to relocate in this country, perhaps in an ethnically divergent or diffuse neighborhood, the emotional and instrumental aid of their children becomes essential. Our observations indicate that the offspring of these parents often act as necessary links to American culture (cf. Landau, 1982). Indeed, the youngsters' help in translating the language, practices, and mores of mainstream Americana to their parents has immediate survival value. Although the growing acculturation of these children enhances their role as "cultural go-betweens," it can also can be a source of conflict and stress. For example, as the 13-year-old son of East Indian parents became increasingly involved with girls who called him at home, which was absolutely forbidden in his household, he was subjected to draconian measures by his parents to preserve their traditional Indian values.

---

[7]It is important to remember that, in considering the role of culture in parentification, numerous variables affect the way families in the U.S. uniquely integrate their cultural backgrounds. Examples of these variables include migration processes, place of residence, degree of assimilation of mainstream values and practices, and socioeconomic mobility (McGoldrick, 1982).

Gender Roles

The collective orientation of many ethnic groups in our country is at variance with Western ideals of independence, self-reliance, individualism, and competition. This contrast is drawn even more sharply for female children. Indeed, the sex-role socialization practices that have traditionally characterized dominant American culture, and many other cultures worldwide, pattern girls to organize their behavior, goals, and personalities around responsibilities to others, caring, and interdependence (Gilligan, 1982). In light of the fact that these themes are also central to the parentification process, it is understandable that gender differences in parentified behaviors have repeatedly surfaced in both cross-cultural research (see Weisner & Gallimore, 1977; Whiting & Edwards, 1973) and data collected in this country.

In our studies, for example, on a measure of overt parentification that we developed, females typically report greater caretaking responsibilities in their families of origin than males (Goglia, Jurkovic, Burt, & Burge-Callaway, 1992; Sessions & Jurkovic, 1986; Wolkin, 1984). They disproportionately endorse such questionnaire items as "In my family, there were certain family members I could handle better than anyone else"; "At times, I felt like the only one my mother/father could turn to."

This is not to suggest that males are necessarily less caring on a genotypic level. Their phenotypic expression of such caring, however, may be muted by or embedded within more traditional male attitudes and activities, such as distracting misbehavior, reflecting their status as a loyal object rather than an overt parentification process. For example, we found that although adult female children of alcoholics scored higher than their male cohorts on the parentification measure, they did not differ on an indirect projective measure of generational boundary distortions. Men were as likely as women to create stories about pictures in the Thematic Apperception Test that portrayed children in a parental or spousal role (Goglia, Jurkovic, Burt, & Burge-Callaway, 1992).

Differences between boys and girls in parentification may gradually dissipate as gender roles and socialization practices continue to change. There are suggestions in the empirical literature, however, that increasing egalitarianism is not significantly relieving females of traditional "feminine" activities as much as adding more "masculine" ones to their repertoires (Goodnow, 1988). Confusing transitions in this area, spawned by our rapidly changing postmodern society, are contributing to the contemporary pressures on parents to cope with competing demands, divorce, separation, role conflicts, job dissatisfaction, and other stressors. The result is that many parents are overwhelmingly stressed and turn to their children for support, companionship, and self-definition (Elkind, 1981, 1994).

Consideration of various sociocultural patterns in which the parentified behavior of children appears to be an adaptive and legitimate response helps check tendencies to pathologize the parentification process. Nevertheless, as noted in Chapter 1, an ecological–ethical perspective raises questions about culturally related practices that possibly limit the developmental potential of children. That which is adaptive at one level of analysis (e.g., familial or societal) may not be at another (e.g., individual).

Friedman (1982), moreover, posits that different cultural customs, rituals, beliefs, and practices do not determine family dynamics but rather *"supply the medium through which family process works its art"* (p. 501). One important implication of his thesis is that cultural forces can be exploited by families to support dysfunctional relational patterns. For example, culturally sanctioned sibling caretaking may be used by a particular family to justify abrogation of parental responsibility. Cultural legitimacy and adaptation, therefore, are not sufficient grounds for establishing justice in family relationships.

ETHICAL CONTEXT

Balance of Fairness

In this discussion of determinants in the destructive parentification process, a number of questions have been implicitly, if not explicitly, asked. For example, as a result of parental deprivation, marital dysfunction, life circumstances, and/or sibling pressures, are children's natural loyalty, concern, and attachment needs being wittingly or unwittingly exploited by family members? Is sibling caretaking embedded in a cultural context that not only endorses such behavior but also prescribes appropriate parental supervision, support, and crediting? Do parents who enlist their children's help, in the absence of cultural guidelines, recognize and credit their offspring for their caring attitudes and contributions to the family's welfare? Is sociocultural legitimacy used by parents to justify dysfunctional and ethically illegitimate child-rearing practices? Do corporate leaders counterbalance the often heavy demands made on employees with benefits to relieve family stress? Are the priorities of school officials, curriculum designers, and other educational personnel informed by the developmental needs, characteristics, and rights of students? Do state and federal funding patterns discriminate against children and families? Is the solidarity of transgenerational relationships valued in this country?

The answers to many of these and related ethical queries moderate the effects of the primary causal agents discussed in this chapter, determining whether parentification follows a destructive or nondestructive course. How the various and often competing claims of individuals, families, future generations, social institutions, corporations, governmental bodies, and cultural traditions should be balanced ethically to protect and nurture children and the different settings in which they develop is difficult to determine. This question defies answers based on simple absolutistic rules, especially to the extent that interpersonal justice is an inherently collective or dialogic process, involving an ongoing balancing of relational claims and obligations. As such, it cannot be reduced to a particular set of values, norms, ideologies, motives, or reasoned judgments (Boszormenyi-Nagy & Krasner, 1986).

There are, however, numerous ethical principles to justify relational actions and outcomes (see Reis, 1986). For example, it can be argued that in light of children's dependence on parental figures, a justice based on developmental need, rather than other principles (e.g., reciprocity), should be the matrix of justice in parent–child relations (Sampson, 1986). However, if the balancing of give-and-take is viewed from a transgenerational perspective, then at any given point in time a singular ethical principle does not apply (Boszormenyi-Nagy & Krasner, 1986). That is, at the same time that parents are giving to their children (need), they are repaying, in part, their own parents for their investment in them (reciprocity). To think of justice in these terms requires an expansion of one's conception of time and space. The claims of former and future generations for due consideration, caring, and action must always figure into the just balancing of parent-child relationships in the present.

Entitlement

As noted in Chapter 1, children who are deprived of their inherent right or entitlement to appropriate parenting often later seek compensation from others, including their partners and children. Unsettled accounts, therefore, are often forwarded to members of the next generation, who are unjustly expected to assume responsibility for a debt incurred by their grandparents. This process of "destructive entitlement" represents a key intervening mechanism in Boszormenyi-Nagy's explanation of the transgenerational transmission of parenting problems.[8]

From an ethical perspective, it is imperative that the developing youngster's entitlement to due care from his or her parents guide the philosophy, organization, and functioning of the various settings that directly and indirectly affect children and families. *Our priorities and practices as individuals, parents, educators, therapists, citizens, community leaders, and policymakers must be evaluated, not only scientifically in terms of their reverberations throughout the ecosystem, but also ethically in terms of their intergenerational fairness.*

A critical consideration along these lines is that entitlement is not transferable from one relationship to another (Boszormenyi-Nagy & Krasner, 1986). Children's right to responsible caretaking from their own parents cannot be met from an ethical perspective through alternative care-giving arrangements (e.g., therapeutic foster care, school-based entitlement programs), however psychologically and physically helpful these arrangements might be. Thus, to the greatest extent possible, support should be given to parents at various levels of the ecosystem to empower them to parent their children and to maintain strong ties with them, even if their children

---

[8]Supportive evidence for Boszormenyi-Nagy's hypothesis can be found in Bavolek's (1984) normative data on the Adult–Adolescent Parenting Inventory. Abused adolescents obtained less mature scores on the Role Reversal scale than both the adults and the nonabused adolescents.

are placed in foster care or other settings away from home (cf. Melton & Barry, 1994). An elemental measure of a society's success in supporting the solidarity of intergenerational relationships is the well-being of children. Unfortunately, various indices of this variable in our country (e.g., the increasing number of youngsters living in poverty, appearing on the rolls of juvenile courts and protective service agencies, joining gangs, and/or dropping out of school) are not favorable (Garbarino & Garbarino, 1992).

CONCLUSIONS

Viewing parentification from both an ecological-developmental and existential-ethical perspective reveals a wide array of causal variables at various levels of analysis. As discussed in Part II of this book, the integrative framework proposed here can significantly inform applied work with parentified children and their families. It also promises to spur further investigative activity into such important theoretical and empirical questions as how the different variables considered in this chapter moderate and mediate one another in the development and maintenance of destructive parentification.

CHAPTER 3

Multilateral Consequences
of Parentification

A s discussed in Chapter 2, the consequences of children's parenting form the matrix of their parenting of the next generation. Therefore, to consider the effects of parentification is to elaborate further the context of this process. From a multilateral perspective, everyone in the parentified child's immediate and future relational systems is potentially affected. This chapter focuses, in particular, on the impact of parentification on the children themselves as well as on their siblings, parents, and families of procreation.

Simple cause–effect relationships cannot be assumed. For example, as discussed in Chapter 2, the immediate consequences (e.g., social isolation) of destructive parentification often recursively increase children's participation in the process. Furthermore, changes within and outside the family (e.g., improved ties between parents and their families of origin, new relationship opportunities for the children) may disrupt the pathogenesis of destructive parentification, occasioning more balanced interactions within the family. Thus, signs of inappropriate role behavior early in a child's life are not inevitably linked to a negative outcome (Karpel, 1976). Prognostic difficulties notwithstanding, our clinical and empirical observations, along with those of others, point to many of the probable risks and benefits of parentification.

PARENTIFIED CHILDREN

Whether parentification has deleterious or beneficial effects on children depends on a number of factors. As noted previously, these include not only the overtness, type, extent, and object of parentified behaviors expected of a child but also the developmental, psychological, sociofamilial, and ethical context in which such behaviors are embedded.

In the event that children's parental responsibilities are appropriate and fair, then parentification can facilitate their development in a number of ways. For example, they can earn trustworthiness and gratify their need to care for and to reciprocate the caring given them by significant others in their lives. In the process, they often learn important social skills related to responsibility, independence, empathy, nurturance, and fair give-and-take in relationships. Such skills enrich children's developing sense of identity and self-worth and serve them well in future roles, including those of parent and mate (Boszormenyi-Nagy & Spark, 1973; Boszormenyi-Nagy & Krasner, 1986; Karpel, 1976; Minuchin, Montalvo, Guerney, Rosman, & Schumer, 1967; Minuchin & Fishman, 1981; Tharp, 1965; Weisner & Gallimore, 1977).

It is possible that youngsters whose parentification is exploitative also derive some of the same benefits. The age and gender of the child, however, appear to be moderating factors. Because many adolescents have personal and social resources to cope with households, such as single-parent homes, that are physically and emotionally demanding of them, their sense of competence and self-worth often grows. In contrast, their younger and less mature cohorts may not fare as well. For example, consistent with Weiss (1979), we have observed that they have difficulty expressing dependency needs directly even when their parents are accessible, which results in quarrelsome and frustrating interactions between child and parent. Neither the child nor the parent is able to identify the child's underlying desire for contact and support, which then continues to be met indirectly through his or her parentified role.

Girls may suffer more ill effects from destructive parentification than boys. It is plausible that parentification, particularly if it involves child care and emotional caretaking, fosters a more extreme, traditionally feminine gender role in girls, but encourages an androgynous orientation in boys (see, e.g., Ember, 1973). Because relationships are more salient in the socialization of girls than of boys, the involvement of boys in their parents' difficulties also tends to be less emotionally upsetting (Gore, Aseltine, & Colten, 1993). On the other hand, as one of my students (Wolkin, 1984) discovered, the congruence of parentified girls' responsibilities with sex-role expectations can bolster self-esteem.

In addition to gender of the child, gender of the parent with whom the child reverses roles may be another variable that differentially affects outcome (see Jacobvitz, Fullinwider, & Loera, 1991; Johnston, Gonzalez, & Campbell, 1987). For example, in comparison to same-gender parentification, cross-gender parentification most likely induces more matelike than parentlike functioning and may have a greater impact on the child's future romantic relationships.

Regardless of sex or age, pathologically parentified children are at risk of experiencing a variety of emotional, cognitive, and sociofamilial difficulties: loss of childhood, parents, and trust; anger and resentment; stress; guilt and shame; physical and sexual abuse; peer problems; school difficulties; disruption in identity development; conflicts about leaving home; occupational concerns; and personality dysfunction.

Loss of Childhood, Parents, and Trust

Perhaps the greatest loss experienced by destructively parentified children is loss of childhood, although the bitterness, disappointment, depression, and other effects of this deprivation may not be realized until later in their lives (Boszormenyi-Nagy & Krasner, 1986; Karpel, 1976). As one young adult gradually awakened to this loss in therapy, she became fixated on a brief time in her childhood when she felt "carefree." Placed in the custody of relatives by her father who wanted "space" to pursue a business interest, she began to blossom, especially socially. Within six months, her father's business failed, and, despite her protests, she was immediately returned home in the middle of the school year. Her father "needed" her.

In her analytic treatment of adults who were severely parentified as children, Miller (1979/1981) found that they often had dreams in childhood of being partly dead, symbolizing the moribund state of their "true selves"—their spontaneity and aliveness. One of her analysands, who as a child parented her younger siblings, recalled the following recurrent dream:

> My younger siblings are standing on a bridge and throw a box into the river. I know that I am lying in it, dead, and yet I hear my heart beating; at this moment I always wake. (p. 13)

Destructive parentification also entails an insidious loss of parental figures. The earliest memory of an adult client I saw a few years ago, whose history included extreme parentification, was as follows: "I am in my crib, crying, and no one is there." As this individual confronted the unavailability of his parents, the "low-grade" depression that he had experienced all of his life dissipated.

A parentified adolescent confided in me recently that she feels "homeless" psychologically. Talking about a story she read, in which the central character is an orphan, she said:

> I'm like that orphan, but I don't have the up-side of being an orphan; I'm still responsible to my family.

Like Jenny (who was presented in the Introduction), many parentified children and adolescents become suicidal as they realize that their helping efforts in the family are ineffectual and unappreciated, or even criticized, and that no one notices their increasing psychic pain. Reflecting on her recurring depression and suicidal feelings since childhood, a parentified late adolescent explained:

You suffer from profound feelings of alienation and loneliness, because you know that when it comes down to it,
your feelings don't matter. Nobody really knows your
feelings at all. You feel worthless. I feel like I don't really
exist. I know that I exist but I don't know why and if it
matters to anyone at all.

Concomitant with parentified children's loss of childhood and
parents is a loss of trust, in parental figures specifically, and in
others generally. The implicit contract or dialogue between parents and children is broken when parents consistently fail to care
(Boszormenyi-Nagy & Krasner, 1986; Elkind, 1981). "When I
needed something," a formerly parentified individual said, "I was
alone." For much of his adult life, this client has struggled to trust
others.

Pervasive mistrust also compromises parentified individuals' capacity to trust themselves, that is, to believe their perceptions and
to experience their own inner life. This capacity is fostered by caretakers who accept and appropriately respond to their offsprings'
spontaneous thoughts, emotions, and needs (Miller, 1979/1981).

The feelings of abandonment and loneliness that many parentified
children experience, but are unable to access or to express for fear
of alienating parental figures, are often unconsciously acted out,
for example, through their subsequent substance abuse, overeat-
ing, or promiscuity. They may also attempt to elicit caring from
others through these and other symptoms, for example, suicidal
gestures or hypochondria (Bowlby, 1979). When I suggested to a
parentified adolescent that he seemed to use drugs whenever he felt
neglected by and angry with his mother, he immediately said:

Well, yeah. If I told her my real feelings, she'd fall apart.
There wouldn't be much left of her. Then what would I
have?

Anger and Resentment

Along with feelings of loss, deprivation, depression, and nonbeing,
anger and resentment are common in the lives of parentified chil-

dren. These feelings typically remain dormant, however. A parentified adolescent explained to me that to express anger would only make matters worse. She said:

> It's like when my mother is late picking me up from school. I go, "Oh, where is she? I'm the last kid being picked up again; I can't believe this!" When she gets there and says something about being late, I say, "It's OK, Mom, I understand." If I told her I was angry, she'd cry and tell me how overwhelmed she is.

The implication is that displaying anger, frustration, and disappointment would not only further burden and hurt parental figures but also encumber parentified children with additional responsibility. Moreover, anger or differences of any kind might threaten the parent-child bond that exists, however tenuously. Disagreement, characteristically regarded in such families as attacking and disloyal, reflects problems in differentiation, as discussed later.

Stress

Stemming from the bind of having excessive responsibility without the maturity, knowledge, or power to handle it adequately, another effect of destructive parentification is overwhelming stress, with associated insecure feelings, anxiety, and low energy, and psychosomatic disturbances (Elkind, 1981; Karpel, 1976; Kerr & Bowen, 1988; Minuchin & Fishman, 1981; Wallerstein, 1985). A 10-year-old parentified girl told me that she liked being treated by her mother as an adult, but having so much responsibility for her younger brother "scared" her. In addition to having chronic headaches, she worried incessantly about her brother's welfare.

In many cases, parentified children meet diagnostic criteria for generalized anxiety disorder (American Psychiatric Association, 1994). However, rather than anxiety about academic, athletic, and social performance, which is characteristic of children and adolescents with this disorder, they worry about adult-oriented matters (such as finances or possible misfortune to someone in the family). A parentified 13-year-old was reluctant to continue therapy with me. Although he found the sessions beneficial, he worried that his mother could not afford them.

Attuned to their parents' problems, many parentified youngsters regard their parents as people with the same vulnerabilities as their own. Although this insight is a marker of maturity, it can contribute to even greater insecurity. How can such children rely on parental figures who, because of their own insecurities, rely on them? The result is precocious self-reliance or counterdependence (cf. Weiss, 1979).

Guilt and Shame

The sequelae of destructive parentification also include overweening guilt and shame. The anxiety and depression of pathologically parentified individuals often partially relate to their guilt about the troubles of family members. They find it difficult to be happy and to enjoy their life successes, knowing that family members whom they care for or have cared for are not doing well emotionally, physically, financially, or in other ways. As suggested in the following quotation from an adult, their affective dilemma is akin to survivor's guilt:

> If you're benefiting yourself but everybody else is not doing well, then you feel guilty that you haven't done enough.

The ongoing problems of parents and other family members are persistent reminders to parentified children of their inability to fulfill their roles. Thus, they often perceive themselves to be a disappointment to their families. Although Zeanah and Klitzke (1991) suggest that the affect underlying this perception is guilt, shame is likely as well. Indeed, being a disappointment implies shame and associated feelings of worthlessness.

Many parentified children are also disappointed in their parents, although they seldom voice these feelings to them. After describing her family situation, noting especially that they had little food to eat, Jenny said, "It's embarrassing." Another parentified adolescent recalled:

I was in the hospital and my parents didn't visit, and the nurses and doctors felt sorry for me. I'm saying, "It's OK," but it's embarrassing. Everybody else knows you need something, and you say, "OK. God, this is embarrassing. Why can't I have a regular mom or dad who will take care of me when I'm sick?"

These children's struggles with guilt and shame, in addition to the problems discussed earlier, leave them extremely vulnerable to the illness or loss of parents. Such life events often intensify their anxiety and self-recrimination; in the event of parental death, these feelings contribute to a pathological grief reaction (Bowlby, 1979). The children assume that they should have done more to help their parents. Many also experience anticipatory anxiety and despair about life-threatening events. One parentified child frequently cried at night when she imagined her parents' dying.

Physical and Sexual Abuse

That parentified children cannot possibly gratify all their parents' needs may result in their being physically maltreated. They are also at risk of being sexually abused by parents or drawn into covertly incestuous relationships with them. The subtext of destructive parentification in cases of incest is well documented in the clinical literature, although not always identified as such (see, e.g., Borgman, 1984; Butler, 1978; Hays, 1987; Hyde, 1986; Russell, 1986). In instances of father-daughter incest, for example, the mother is often found to have played a parentified role in her family of origin. Although drawn to a dependent man, she eventually tires of caring for him. Her daughter then fills in, assuming responsibility for the expressive needs of the family, including those in the sexual domain (Hays, 1987).

Peer Problems

Children and adolescents suffering from extreme forms of parentification typically have peer problems. Because of their exaggerated sense of responsibility for and excessive loyalty to family members, many of them have difficulty forming extrafamiliar relationships and thus are isolated from their peers (Buchholz & Haynes, 1983; Karpel, 1976).

Oriented to adults, such youngsters are also impatient with and, in some cases, even intolerant of their age-mates. Describing her son to the family therapist, one of the mothers in Karpel's sample noted:

> He's fine with adults. He can hold a conversation with you, really. But when it comes to being with children.... (p. 86)

These children often complain that they do not "fit in." Upon seeing the toys in my office, Jenny, age seven, said, "That's baby's stuff."

It became apparent that Jenny, like a lot of parentified youngsters, not only viewed age-related interests and activities as immature but also simply did not know how to engage her peers in a meaningful way. The social skill deficits of these children perhaps relate to decreased opportunities for peer contact and, in many cases, underinvolvement or conflictual interactions with siblings (cf. Stoneman, Brody, Davis, & Crapps, 1988). Indeed, the parentification process often disrupts the healthy socializing influence of the siblings subsystem (Minuchin & Fishman, 1981). Moreover, parentified children's interest in peer activities may be threatening to parents who rely on them for support and self-definition. Thus, they often interfere, either directly or indirectly, in their children's social world.

Also contributing to the social isolation of parentified children is the perception by their peers that they are too serious and grown-up (cf. Weiss, 1979). To the extent that peers interact with them, it is often in a dependent and exploitative manner. For example, peers may use them for advice or companionship when lonely but fail to reciprocate. Many parentified youngsters, however, tend to tolerate such asymmetrical and unfair relationships because of the social contact and narcissistic gratification they provide. They may also cognitively construe peer interaction in nonreciprocal terms. In effect, they replicate their attachment with parental figures (cf. Dean, Malik, Richards, & Stringer, 1986).

Through their overfunctioning, moreover, these youngsters emotionally bind their friends to them, or "take hostages" (as this process is labeled in the addiction field), which alienates them from their peer group in the long run. It also compounds their tendencies to overextend themselves socially and to enter into, as well as to have difficulty ending, unhealthy and emotionally draining relationships with boyfriends and girlfriends (see Jacobvitz, Fullinwider, & Loera, 1991).

A 17-year-old I treated functioned as his friends' therapist. Although we often joked about his "practicing without a license" with both peers and family members, the consequences of his overhelpful behavior were serious. He suffered from many of the same problems as "burned-out" clinicians, worrying excessively about his friends, assuming full responsibility for them, overidentifying with their problems, and trying to manage situations well beyond his control.[1]

Other parentified children turn to a peer group to escape the pressures of their role at home. They may become involved in delinquent group activities, abuse alcohol and drugs with peers, or join a gang. Destructively parentified girls are also at risk for early pregnancy (Minuchin, Montalvo, Guerney, Rosman, & Schumer, 1967). Although these behaviors often represent rebellion against their exploitation in the family, they add to the problems of pathological parentification.

On occasion, the dyssocial actions of parentified children signal their distress at home, resulting in a beneficial response from parents, school personnel, and other helping agents in the community. Many parentifying parents, however, do not closely monitor their children's peer activities, which further increases the risk of their forming problematic affiliations.

---

[1] A developmental precursor of parentified adolescents' overinvolvement with troubled and needy peers is suggested by research of children of depressed parents. Zahn-Waxler and her colleagues (see Zahn-Waxler & Kochanska, 1988) found that two-year-olds whose mothers suffered from unipolar depression became more preoccupied and upset in the face of distress in others, including peers, than children of well mothers.

School Difficulties

Parentified children often excel in academic and extracurricular activities. Such success, however, may be the result of excessive work in response to the achievement needs of their parents as well as those of the school. In other cases, school performance and attendance suffer as a result of parentified children's home responsibilities. They may be inattentive, preoccupied with family concerns, or simply exhausted, both mentally and physically.

One parentified ninth grader, who had long attended to his mother's needs after her divorce when he was three, uncharacteristically began skipping school and, in his words, "blowing off homework." It quickly became apparent that he felt entitled to take a break from school because of his years of hard emotional and physical labor at home. Indeed, he had earned merit, a fact that figured centrally in his therapy.

Disruption in Identity Development

It was suggested earlier that parentification confers a sense of identity and self-esteem to children, especially girls. This identity, however, revolves around the needs of family members and thus is other-directed, reactive, or undifferentiated. Indirectly commenting on this process, one of the adult children referred to by Ackerman (1989) recalled that she functioned well in a parentified role in her family until the age of 16, at which point her family seemed to be "out of control" and no longer responsive to her input. She said:

> So I ran off and got married. I found someone who was very needy and married him. I was in control, 16 years old, and I had complete control. (p. 22)

The control that this individual sought doubtless reinforced her identity as a caretaker. Indeed, through their caretaking activities, parentified individuals create order in their psychic worlds. They define themselves. For many, rescuing others also meets an even more profound ontic need, confirming their very existence.

A highly anxious college student with obsessive-compulsive symptoms and a long history of emotional caretaking in her family sought my help. Her presenting complaint was an overwhelming fear of losing her mind. When asked what she feared most about such a prospect, she said: "I'd lose my connection to my family, my *definition*." As she increasingly differentiated from family members, providing herself a platform from which to explore her own identity and life goals (e.g., major in college), her symptomatology remitted.

The importance of parentified children's identities as caretakers for their own psychological survival and that of family members significantly interferes with their experimenting with alternative roles and questioning previous identifications (Erikson, 1980; Fullinwider-Bush, & Jacobvitz, 1993; Karpel, 1976). Asking the question "Who am I?" is not only anxiety provoking but also a source of guilt. At an intrapsychic level, such a reaction reflects "counter-autonomous superego" processes (Boszormenyi-Nagy, 1965). At an ethical level, it reveals the workings of a relational system that requires unwavering loyalty at the expense of individual family members' development. Consequently, parentified individuals are not able to wrestle with the self-definitional issues that contribute to the formation of an autonomous ego identity.[2]

Conflicts About Leaving Home

Related to destructively parentified adolescents' failure to form an independent sense of self and their extreme filial loyalty is their difficulty in leaving home. Parentification is frequently a factor in the crisis reactions, depression, and suicidal behaviors of college students (Held & Bellows, 1983; Lopez, 1986). Earlier evidence of separation anxiety (e.g., refusal to attend school or to spend the night with friends) is also often present in the histories of these individuals.

---

[2]More specifically, for females, recent evidence suggests that weak father-daughter boundaries, marked, in part, by role reversal, are associated with the daughters' disinterest in even establishing an identity. On the other hand, similar boundary disturbances between daughters and their mothers related to a premature commitment to their family's values and beliefs (Fullinwider-Bush & Jacobvitz, 1993).

A parentified youth announced during one session that she found the task of applying to colleges too arduous to complete. Her paralysis was directly traced to increasing guilt about leaving her parents, who had long found it easier and more gratifying to interact with her than with each other. In a subsequent session, she explained to her parents:

> I feel like I'm a security to both of you. And, leaving is ... there's a whole lot of guilt there. I feel like in leaving, I'll take a big part of the family with me.... Somewhere along the line, I've developed more responsibility for the family than I should have.... I feel responsible not just to each of you but to the unit.

Another adolescent client assumed that her mother, whom she had emotionally cared for, could not survive her leaving home. She recurrently dreamed that her mother was nagging her to fill the empty cupboards with food (Jurkovic, Jessee, & Goglia, 1991). Parentified adolescents are often referred to therapy for amorphous reasons. In one such instance a 17-year-old, Susan, was making plans to attend college. Her family, however, feared that she might "go crazy." I learned from her that she was the third child in her family to have inherited parental responsibilities. Her two older siblings were able to leave home, in part because they had a younger brother or sister who was prepared to assume the role they were vacating. However, being the youngest, Susan could not do the same. The family faced a dilemma. It appeared that concerns about Susan's mental health were a projection of the parents' own anxieties, particularly her mother's. As these dynamics emerged in therapy, Susan's mother sought to reconcile deeply rooted conflicts with her estranged husband. Susan, in turn, was able to resume making preparations for college.

With therapeutic help, the adolescents referred to in this section were finally able to leave home with only a modicum of guilt. Others are not so fortunate. They conspire with their parents to sabotage their own separation. Or, if they do manage to leave physically, they experience excruciating guilt, shame, and a sense of disloyalty. They may continue to take care of family members, especially emotionally, even if living hundreds of miles away.

Occupational Concerns

Parentified children in adulthood are at risk of experiencing job dissatisfaction, as they discover that their work, however rewarding in material and other ways, cannot fulfill unmet needs for dependency and nurturance (Weiss, 1979). As we and others have speculated, their occupational choices are often extensions of their role in their families of origin (Jurkovic, Jessee, & Goglia, 1991; Lackie, 1983; Maeder, 1989a; Miller, 1979/1981; Racusin, Abramowitz, & Winter, 1981; Sussman, 1992; Titelman, 1987; Welt & Herron, 1990). An emergency room nurse realized in therapy that he had chosen his career to ensure that people would "need" him, just as his mother had throughout his childhood years. When not working, he had disturbing feelings about his identity. "It feels like I no longer exist," he commented in one session.

Destructively parentified children as adults may be overrepresented in the helping professions, including the psychotherapeutic field. Sessions (1986) asked groups of clinical psychology graduate students and advanced undergraduates in engineering to report their degree of parentification while growing up. As expected, the former were significantly more parentified. The various ethical, professional, and personal problems of therapists whose backgrounds include destructive parentification range from boundary distortions in the therapist-client relationship to occupational burnout. These problems are discussed in depth in Chapter 8.

Personality Dysfunction

Implicit in the discussion of parentification and its relation to self-development is the effect of this process on personality structure. Suggestions in Chapter 2 that parentification is often rooted in infancy imply that core personality processes (e.g., attachment, narcissism, separation-individuation) are affected. Many parentified children, therefore, are at risk of forming unhealthy traits and personality disorders. For example, they may not fully develop object constancy, self-soothing skills, and the capacity to be alone—features of a borderline personality organization (Gunderson, Kerr, & Englund, 1980; Karpel, 1976; Malerstein & Ahern, 1979).

Following the loss of her husband, one of my parentified clients rediscovered her terror of being alone. She had been plagued with this fear as a child. Separation from her seven-year-old daughter was especially problematic for her. Sensing her mother's panic, the child frequently feigned illness during the school year to remain home with her.

According to Miller (1979/1981), various manifestations of narcissistic disturbance (grandiosity, depression) in adults may also be products of destructive parentification from an early age. The grandiose individual successfully fulfills the expectations of the parental introject, whereas the depressive individual experiences him- or herself as a failure in this regard. Both, however, are driven by a need to maintain a persona, defined initially by parental figures and supported later by introjects. Thus, narcissistically driven depression and grandiosity reflect similar dynamics: loss of self, fragility of self-esteem, perfectionism related to a high ego ideal, need to be special, intense fear of loss of love, strong tendency to conform, and denial of true feelings.

Many of these personality attributes are embodied in descriptions of co-dependency. Indeed, co-dependency is a probable outcome of the parentification process (Olson & Gariti, 1993). In an effort to delimit the definition of this broadly used term, Cermak (1986, 1990) differentiated co-dependent traits from co-dependent personality disorder. He suggested the following five diagnostic criteria for the latter:

1. Self-esteem related to ongoing efforts to control oneself and others despite adverse consequences.
2. Taking responsibility for others' needs at the expense of one's own.
3. Boundary problems and anxiety associated with intimacy and separation.
4. Enmeshment with substance-dependent, impulse-disordered, and personality-disordered persons.
5. Evidence of at least three of the following: excessive use of denial, emotional constriction, depression, hypervigilance, compulsions, anxiety, substance abuse, recurrent victimization by physical or sexual abuse, stress-related medical ill-

nesses, and involvement with an alcoholic or other drug addict for at least two years without seeking help.[3]

A diagnosis under consideration at one time for inclusion in the *Diagnostic and Statistical Manual of Mental Disorders* (American Psychiatric Association, 1987), "self-defeating personality disorder," also contains elements of narcissistic disturbance and co-dependency.

> The essential feature of this disorder is a pervasive pattern of self-defeating behavior, beginning by early adulthood and present in a variety of contexts. The person may often avoid or undermine pleasurable experiences, be drawn to situations or relationships in which he or she will suffer, and prevent others from helping him or her. (p. 371)

Although not identified as such, parentification is a likely predisposing factor (cf. West & Keller, 1991). Along these lines, Jones and Wells (1996) recently discovered that childhood parentification, as measured by Sessions and Jurkovic's (1986) scale, was significantly related to self-defeating and narcissistic characteristics in a college student sample.

The co-dependent, self-defeating qualities of parentified individuals greatly interfere with their giving and receiving of care. Having originally been trained to meet parental needs, the parentified child does not later in life associate giving with spontaneous pleasure. Rather, giving represents a duty that is compulsively discharged to avoid loss of love. The inauthenticity of such caring is further evidenced by its being directed by what the care giver thinks the other needs rather than by what the other thinks he or she needs. Giving under these circumstances, then, is not related to intimacy per se, but to security. As a result, it is often invasive and controlling. The recipients of compulsive care giving are frequently showered with help at untoward times and blocked in their efforts to reciprocate,

---

[3]Whitfield (1991) suggests that "alcoholic or other drug addict" should be replaced with *"actively mistreating or abusing person"* (p. 51).

thus leaving them indebted to the care giver (see Boszormenyi-Nagy & Krasner, 1986; Bowlby, 1979; Miller, 1979/1981; West & Keller, 1991; Zeanah & Klitzke, 1991).

Indeed, asking for and receiving help are also problematic for pathologically parentified individuals. Although desirous of attention, nurturance, and succor, they have learned in their families of origin to deny their needs—to remain strong for others. Accepting help is a sign of weakness and is incongruous with their definition of themselves as helpers (see Valleau, Bergner, & Horton, 1995).

At a deeper level, parentified individuals also often feel unworthy of care. Children who are deprived assume that the fault lies with them. The extent of their shame and self-loathing can be startling. An adult with a long history of parentification and related difficulties in accepting help from others, including therapists, asked rhetorically:

> Why do they really care about me? What is their investment? Once they find out that my family doesn't care about me, they'll know there's something inherently wrong with me. So I've learned not to expect nurturance from others. When they try to give it to me, it throws me off.

FAMILY OF ORIGIN

Siblings

Not only are parentified children affected by the parentification process, but so are other members of their families of origin and procreation. For example, the effects—both positive and negative—reverberate throughout the sibling subsystem. Cross-cultural studies suggest that when mothers share child care responsibilities with one of their children, it lessens the other youngsters' separation anxiety and attachment to a single primary caretaker and enhances their affiliation motivation (Weisner & Gallimore, 1977). They may also have greater freedom to develop normally if they are not the primary object of pathological parentification (Miller, 1979/1981). For instance, because Jenny absorbed the greater part of her mother's anxiety, her younger brother showed no signs of clinical disturbance.

Yet the siblings' access to nurturing and socializing interactions with parental figures are often significantly limited because of parental overinvolvement with the parentified child. Relatedly, their peer contacts may be restricted to those of their older sibling caretaker, depriving them of enriching relationships with age-mates (cf. Mead, 1961).

Preadolescent and young adolescent caretakers also tend to show little empathy or tolerance for the emotional behavior of their siblings and still need parental help to temper intensely ambivalent feelings toward them (Essman & Deutsch, 1979; Rosenbaum, 1963). Ethnographic accounts further suggest that being cared for primarily by slightly older siblings who lack well-defined personalities impedes the younger siblings' self-differentiation, although this result may be less deleterious, or may even be functional, in societies that do not support or value personal achievement and independence (Mead, 1968; Park & Gallimore, 1975; Weisner & Gallimore, 1977).

Extensive sibling caretaking may also lead to intense sibling conflict, which is often attributed by the parentified child to the troublesome behaviors of his or her charges. One of these "troublemakers" complained in a family session that he already had parents and failed to see the need for another. In this case, as in many others, jealousy of the special relationship that his sibling caretaker enjoyed with their mother contributed to their rivalry. Yet, reflective of the circularity of family systems processes, I have been impressed clinically with the extent to which parentified youngsters covertly incite sibling conflict and embellish the negative images of their siblings to perpetuate their own role.

Sibling incest may be another deleterious consequence of the parentification process. We once treated an impoverished single-parent family in which the oldest son, a 16-year-old who had long played a parentified role, sexually abused his 5-year-old sister. It became clear that his behavior reflected, in part, increasing sexual tensions in his relationship with his mother. In other cases, parentified children may sexually use their younger brothers and sisters, for whom they have excessive responsibility, to gratify longstanding needs for emotional contact and, perhaps, to attempt to balance the ledger of fairness in the family, albeit destructively.

Parents

Parents who assign caretaking responsibilities to their children are affected in various ways as well. Although often at the youngster's expense, the parentification process reduces parental stress and increases role flexibility (Boszormenyi-Nagy & Spark, 1973; Weisner & Gallimore, 1977; Weiss, 1979). As a result, the parents' parentifying behaviors are reinforced. This was the case for Jenny's mother. Her daughter's parentification freed her of child care responsibilities and facilitated her college studies. In many families, sibling caretaking also allows parents to interact more with their children (Weisner & Gallimore, 1977).

On the other hand, as discussed earlier, a parent who relies on one of the children may become increasingly distant from the others, especially as the siblings increasingly orient to their parentified brother or sister. Such sibling interaction may also increase the youngsters' opposition to parental control and the parentified child's competition for a leadership role in the family (Minuchin, Montalvo, Guerney, Rosman, & Schumer, 1967; Weiss, 1979).

Despite parents' overinvolvement with their parentified children, many eventually discover that they have co-opted their offspring's childhood, a discovery that is painful and guilt inducing. They realize a profound loss. A poignant example of this dynamic is presented in Chapter 5.

Parents who exploitatively use their children also miss the opportunity to offer due care and, in the process, to validate their own worth and to earn merit. Such merit entitles them to fair consideration from others, including their children over time. Paradoxically, when parents are not accountable in relationships and thus fail to earn entitlement, they also severely compromise their ability to become responsibly independent (see Boszormenyi-Nagy & Krasner, 1986).

In families characterized by destructive parentification, the parents' marital relationship is often strained. As pointed out earlier, not only are children parentified in part to compensate for marital dysfunction, but the effects of parentification further stress the marriage. For example, we have observed that in divorced families in which parentification is evident, one of the children may have assumed a parentified role well before their parents separated. Indeed, the triangulation of this child into the parents' marital conflict, although initially stabilizing, blocks effective communication between the parents and may ultimately contribute to the dissolution of their relationship. Unless a careful history is taken, these dynamics are frequently missed. Rather, the child's parentification is assumed to be part of the postdivorce process.

For example, in one family, the father's overinvolvement in his new business, which eventually produced tremendous profits and catapulted the family into a higher income bracket, left his wife feeling resentfully alone. Their son soon became father's proxy at home, long before his parents entered divorce proceedings. With his mother's tacit support, he regularly undermined his father's attempts to exert any influence in the family. The father's repeated requests that his wife support him in setting limits with their son fell on deaf ears. On the advice of their lawyers, the parents entered therapy to attempt reconciliation. The depth of his wife's and son's pain over his abandonment rapidly became apparent to the father. It took him some time, however, to appreciate fully the injustice and distrust they felt intensely as a result of his efforts to compensate them with "money and things" for his "not being there."

Although the parentification process is often an adaptive feature of single-parent families, particularly when children are credited for their contributions and perceive their duties as fair, it may become a liability when parents remarry. The role confusion and hierarchical imbalances that characterize the formative stage of blended family systems are exacerbated when a parentified child is involved. Stepparents, for example, may find their authority severely challenged by parentified children who are unwilling to relinquish their power or their special relationship with their biological parents. The biological parents, in turn, may become caught in the middle, unable to relate satisfactorily to either their new spouse or the parentified child (Jurkovic, Jessee, & Goglia, 1991).

FAMILY OF PROCREATION

In addition to the immediate effects of parentification on children and members of their families of origin, it is important that the long-term consequences of this process for parentified children's families of procreation be considered as well. In particular, what are the implications of having been parentified as a child for an individual's future couple and parent-child relationships? As discussed in Chapter 2, clinical observation and research reveal several possible relational outcomes.

Perhaps most common is that many simply reenact their parentified role in future relationships. For example, they tend to overfunction as parents, intrusively caring for their infants and infantilizing their children (see Jacobvitz, Morgan, Kretchmar, & Morgan, 1992). However, the uncertainty and anxiety they experienced as children while taking care of siblings and other family members without adequate support often pervade their caretaking efforts as adults. They may also continue to serve in a caretaking capacity in their families of origin, which divides their loyalties. The increasing and conflicting demands of family life and a career, possibly involving service to others, can lead to emotional and physical exhaustion. Should such a person fail in his or her parentified role as an adult, other family members (one of the children or the spouse) may then fill the void. For example, in Jenny's family, the father's childhood history of parentification was reenacted with her mother. He rescued her. When he was no longer available to meet her needs, Jenny assumed the role.

Another common pattern that I and others (Crandall, 1976, 1981) have seen in the couple relationships of parentified individuals is a collusive giving and taking of destructive care. Although only one partner may indulge the other, both are often acting in a parentified and parentifying role at once. These dynamics are discussed at length in Chapter 7.

CONCLUSIONS

This chapter has considered a variety of potentially negative, as well as positive, consequences of parentification for children and other members of their present and future families. Further systematic investigation of the short- and long-term effects of parentification is necessary to verify clinical observations in this area and to help explain the mechanisms responsible for different types of outcome. It is critical that work along these lines consider the multilateral impact of destructive parentification. An appreciation of the widespread effects of this process has critical implications, as discussed in the rest of this book, for treatment and prevention.

Part II

TREATMENT AND PREVENTION

CHAPTER 4

Evaluating Childhood Parentification: The I-D-C Model

Daughter:	What does "objective" mean?
Father:	Well. It means that you look very hard at those things which you choose to look at.
Daughter:	That sounds right. But how do the objective people choose which things they will be objective about?
Father:	Well. They choose those things about which it is easy to be objective. (Bateson, 1972, p. 47)

It is not easy to objectify parentification. The temptation is to focus only on its overt role properties (e.g., the type and extent of caretaking responsibilities assumed by the child), thus missing the less demonstrable aspects of the context within which this role exists. As Bateson said to his daughter later in their exchange about objectivity, a potential pitfall of operationally defining phenomena for purposes of scientific study and classification is that it "slices everything to bits," splitting the part from the whole (Bateson, 1972, p. 49). To avoid this problem in the area of parentification, it is critical that parentified role behaviors be evaluated relative to the developmental-psychological, sociofamilial, and existential-ethical processes discussed earlier.

This chapter draws from theoretical and empirical material considered in Part I of this book to suggest a holistic approach to assessing pathological forms of parentification in children and adolescents. Specifically, a three-stage evaluative model is proposed: Identify, Describe, and Contextualize (I-D-C). The first stage involves identifying children and adolescents who are at risk or possible victims of destructive parentification. In the second stage, the overt properties of the parentified child's role are described. Developing an understanding of the developmental-psychological, ecological, and ethical context of these properties, including their multilateral effects, constitutes the third stage. A case example is presented to illustrate the utility of this approach. Consideration is also given to research instruments that we and others have developed that promise to help operationalize various applications of the I-D-C model to parentification.

STAGE 1: IDENTIFY

Children and adolescents suffering from various forms of destructive parentification, as well as those at risk of being pathologically parentified, are frequently not identified by therapists, teachers, probation officers, physicians, and other helping agents. In many cases, because of their overcompliant behavior, they are simply not seen as having significant problems. Rather, their symptomatic siblings are the focus of concern. The noncompliant behaviors of others (e.g., truancy, poor grades, delinquency) often elicit diagnostic, treatment, educational, medical, and legal responses that ignore destructive parentification as an etiologic factor.

Behavioral signs of parentification in children and adolescents include excessive compliance, adultlike demeanor or pseudomaturity, overachievement, perfectionism, social isolation, overinvolvement in peers' problems, sadness, psychosomatic complaints, fatigue, nervousness, preoccupation, and chronic worrying, particularly about family members and peers. Destructively parentified youngsters who are underachieving, abusing substances, and engaging in other problematic activities may also evince many of these behaviors.

More direct evidence of burdensome and unfair parentification of young children typically requires clinical observation and interviews of parents and other family members. For example, drawing from the early work of Schneider, Pollock, and Helfer (1972, p. 62), questions that can be asked of parents include the following:

1. When should parents start toilet training a child? At what age should the child be fully trained?
2. How well do your children understand your feelings?
3. How have your children been of help to you?
4. Can they tell when you're upset, and do they help then?
5. Do any of your children seem to have a problem in being warm and loving enough?
6. Do all your children live up to your expectations?
7. When you're upset, do your children comfort you?

The interviewer should be sensitive to parents' spontaneous comments regarding their expectations and conceptualizations of their children and of themselves as parents. Evidence of "egoistic" thinking (Newberger, 1977; Newberger & Cook, 1983; Newberger & White, 1989), in which the parents' own needs and projections predominate, supports a finding of parentifying behaviors. In evaluating the conceptions and expectations of parents, one must consider their optimal level of functioning. Various psychosocial stressors may contribute to an unevenness in their understanding. On the other hand, the clinician should not equate cognitive sophistication with emotional empathy, sensitivity to the child's affective cues, or responsible parental behavior.

Siblings of parentified youngsters can also provide important diagnostic information. Questions to ask them include the following:

1. Does your brother (or sister) ever take care of you? How often and when?

2. Do your parents check on the way he (or she) cares for you? Do you tell them? How do they respond?
3. Does your brother (or sister) help you, for example, with your homework or with problems that you may have?
4. Do you often go to your brother (or sister) for help rather than to your parents? Is he (or she) more helpful to you than your parents? If so, in what ways?
5. Are there things about the way your brother or sister takes care of you that you don't like?

In addition to observations and parent and sibling interviews, older children can be asked directly about their caretaking activities. For example, questions that we frequently pose include these:

1. How well do you know your parents' feelings?
2. Can you tell when your parents are upset? What, if anything, do you do to help?
3. In what other ways do you try to help your parents?
4. Do your parents talk to you about their problems?
5. Do you ever feel caught in the middle between your parents?
6. In what ways do you help your brothers and sisters or other family members?

Again, one should be alert for evidence of parentification in the spontaneous remarks and behaviors of children and adolescents. For example, when I returned the telephone call of a mother who was seeking therapy for her daughter, an adolescent boy answered. After identifying himself and learning who I was, he informed me that his sister was depressed and needed help. He further recommended that I see the whole family. Not only did he prove to be parentified but he also suffered from a serious addictive disorder.

It is important that therapists and other helping professionals not underestimate very young children's tendency to contribute actively and in self-limiting ways to the welfare of their families. They must keep in mind that children's attunement to the needs of their parents appears to manifest early in their development and that many begin to caretake overtly at one or two years of age (see Chapter 2).

A couple recently saw me in therapy. At their third session, because of child care problems, they brought their 34-month-old daughter, Sara. Before I became aware of subtle tensions between the parents, Sara crawled into her father's lap and made distracting humming noises. Her father said: "It's OK, darling; Mommy and Daddy aren't going to fight." Her mother contradicted him, however, and stated: "She knows I'm upset with you." I learned that for the past several months Sara often intruded into her parents' conflicts at home, physically moving between them with her hands up—like a referee at a boxing match—and saying, "Y'all stop fussin'; it be all right."

This session reminded me of the importance of considering the needs of all family members, not just of those who present for treatment. The children of parents who enter couple therapy because of long-standing conflicts in their relationship are at risk for destructive parentification. As discussed in Chapter 2, other families with increased risk in this area include single-parent and blended families, families with many children, substance-abusing and workaholic families, immigrant families, physically and sexually abusive families, two-career families, families in which parents lack meaningful links to family of origin, neighbors, church, and social services, families composed of emotionally dysfunctional and undifferentiated parental figures or disabled members, and families with parents who experienced abuse, deprivation, or other boundary problems as children, including pathological parentification.

Unpredictable events (e.g., parental death, divorce, or unemployment) often require children to assume increased instrumental and expressive responsibilities. Although these events may occasion parentification, consideration should also be given to the possibility that they serve only to exacerbate an already existing parentified pattern.

Another potential risk factor to consider in evaluating parentification is children's temperament. Those who are extremely sensitive interpersonally and inhibited or shy are likely to be inordinately attuned to the needs of family members. Similarly, the needs of children who are temperamentally easy may be ignored, especially by parentifying parents whose own concerns and issues are prominent.

Evidence of an anxious, insecure, or disorganized attachment between parents and their infants should be noted. Attachment disturbances may not only place young children at risk for destructive parentification but also represent an early marker of role reversal, stemming from the young child's attempts to maintain affectional bonds with his or her parents.

STAGE 2: DESCRIBE

The next step after identifying a potentially pathological form of parentification is to describe its behavioral properties. These include the overtness, type, extent, and object of the youngster's caretaking.

Overtness

Are the child's caretaking behaviors directly or indirectly expressed? If there is no evidence of overt helping, we then think in terms of a loyal-object rather than parentification process. In our experience, indirect caretaking is often accompanied by direct expressions of protection, mediation, and helpfulness. Unless formally evaluated, however, the latter may not be identified. For example, had I not asked the parents of the toddler described earlier whether she overtly attempted to help them at home, more direct evidence of her parentification may not have been obtained.

Type

Does the child engage in instrumental and/or expressive caretaking? Exactly what responsibilities does he or she appear to have, such as caring for siblings, mediating marital conflict, nursing a chronically ill family member, providing companionship to a parental figure, acting as a surrogate mate, contributing to the family's income, or maintaining the house? The interview questions listed for Stage 1 often yield useful information in this regard. Of course, the therapist should not rely solely on parent or child self-reports. Direct observation of the type of caretaking behaviors expected of and enacted by children is helpful.

Extent

How extensive are the child's caretaking responsibilities? Are they situational or long-standing? In calculating the extent of various caretaking behaviors, consideration should be given to the fact that some tasks are probably more burdensome than others and thus merit a differential weighting. Caring for a younger sibling for six hours may be more demanding and certainly involves greater responsibility than cleaning house for an equivalent period of time.

Object

Who is the primary object of the child's caretaking efforts: mother, father, or sibling(s)? The possibility that he or she has responsibility for more than one family member, as well as for the parents' relationship and the family as a whole, should be considered. The diagnostician should also look for evidence of a same- or cross-gender parentification pattern (e.g., mother-daughter, mother-son). Often, reflecting the splitting of loyalties that destructively parentified children experience, they are overtly solicitous toward one parent while equally but subtly concerned about the welfare of the other parent. They may not reveal their multilateral worries unless asked directly and by themselves, however.

STAGE 3: CONTEXTUALIZE

At the end of Stage 2, the diagnostician should have formed a clear behavioral picture of the child's parentified role. The final stage, placing this role in context, is necessary to understand its significance at different levels: developmental-psychological, sociofamilial, ethical, and consequential.

Developmental-Psychological

Many of the developmental-psychological variables that place youngsters at risk for destructive parentification (e.g., temperament, attachment needs, concern) and contribute to the parentifying tendencies of parents (e.g., conceptions of parent-child relationships, emotional adjustment, level of differentiation, family background) were noted in Stage 1 of the evaluation process. In addition to assessing these via a genogram, a developmental history, and other methods, the therapist should ask questions about the developmental timing and age-appropriateness of caretaking assignments.

Does the child have the requisite skills? Because of their counter-dependency and pseudomaturity, many destructively parentified youngsters present themselves as being more self-assured and competent than they actually are. Parents are misled by these qualities; it is critical that therapists and other professionals are not.

It is also important to evaluate the degree to which the child has internalized the parentified role. Is the child enacting a parentified role for concrete, functional reasons or as part of a long-term, internalized, and captivating commitment? To determine the latter, one must obtain information about the following: Does the youngster's self-esteem, happiness, and identity depend on his or her caretaking of family members? Does he or she assume blame for their continued troubles? Does he or she worry about them at school? Are the child's peer relationships limited because of his or her extreme loyalty and devotion to needy family members? Do parents rely on the youngster for self-definition and self-worth? Is his or her excessive caretaking evident not only at home but also in other contexts (school, peer group)? Is the child perceived by parents, teachers, and others as exceptionally mature, precociously self-reliant, and highly responsible? Does he or she have difficulty moving into new developmental stages requiring greater autonomy and separation from family, for example, attending school, going to an overnight camp, or leaving home later in life?

Another important question to ask is whether parental role assignments are diffused throughout the sibling subsystem. If so, then the parentification process is probably not as psychologically captivating (cf. Boszormenyi-Nagy & Spark, 1973; Minuchin, Montalvo, Guerny, Rosman, & Schumer, 1967). This is more likely, however, when children are entreated to meet instrumental rather than emotionally based demands. Instrumental tasks are more easily exchanged and shared with siblings, because they typically do not have the same fundamental (ontic) significance to parents and children as expressive tasks. The diagnostician should, however, consider the possibility that children's socioemotional development may organize around instrumental caretaking tasks as well and thus be equally binding.

Sociofamilial

Parentification entails a parentified-parentifying dialectic. The role activities and commitments of parentified children are embedded within sociofamilial settings that are parentifying. The nature of these settings figures importantly in the pathogenicity of the parentification process and thus merits careful attention.

Role Induction Processes and Family Boundaries

At the family transactional level, chronic boundary distortions are part of the definition of destructive parentification. The way children are induced to help in the family provides important information about this variable. Are they asked overtly? Are their responsibilities, even if extensive, clearly delineated and supervised by parental figures, as well as shared with other family members? We have found that in comparison to instrumental activities, expressive role behaviors are not as likely to be monitored, because they are (1) less explicit and, more important, (2) often supportive of undifferentiated parental figures whose appreciation of family boundaries is limited.

There are a number of other questions to ask concerning role induction processes: Are the children simply directed by their parents to discharge various age-inappropriate responsibilities? Are their overresponsible behaviors subtly cued and shaped by various prescriptive and proscriptive attributions as well as by expressions of neediness and helplessness on the part of parents? For example, do parents define their children as being more grown-up than they actually are? Do they proscribe behaviors (e.g., autonomy) that are incongruous with a captivating parentified role? Are they jealous of their children's friendships? Do they burden their children with their own problems? Do they, in their children's presence, act in such a manner (e.g., despondent, suicidal) to elicit a caretaking response?

One must also attend to the hidden messages in parents' communications that are parentifying (see Love & Robinson, 1990). Jenny's mother, for example, often said to her: "I don't know what I'd do without you." The metamessage here is, "I'm dependent on you. Give all of your loyalty to me. Disregard your own needs to meet mine." A father going through a divorce said to his oldest daughter, "You're the only one in the world who loves me." She interpreted his comment to mean that she was now responsible for his welfare.

The nonparentifying parent is another aspect of the parent-child subsystem that requires attention by evaluators. Although both parents may be actively violating the child's boundaries, often one is more involved than the other. If so, is the nonparentifying parent aware of the parentification process? Has he or she taken steps to intervene? If not, why?

Evaluation of generational boundaries often reveals a poorly defined and dysfunctional spousal system. Does one of the children help stabilize his or her parents' marriage? It is important to remember that undifferentiated partners whose relationship either fails to meet their needs or is all consuming are at risk of parentifying their children.

One should also consider the presence of other boundary violations in the parent–child subsystem that are often part of the problem of destructive parentification, namely, neglect and physical and sexual abuse. Conversely, as noted earlier, families who present with these other abusive patterns should be evaluated for pathological parentification processes.

In addition to evaluating how parental figures are contributing to boundary violations in the family's caregiving system, the diagnostician should consider the role of the siblings. Are they turning to their parentified brother or sister for nurturance and structure instead of to parental figures? Do they oppose the authority of their parents?

Family–Community Relationships

Another level of the transactional structure of parentification pertains to the interrelation of the various settings in which children are involved. Relationships between the family, school, and peer group are seldom systemically evaluated by clinicians, even though they significantly influence one another and, consequently, affect the behavior of children.

At this level of analysis the following questions should be asked: Are the youngster's caretaking behaviors at home affecting school performance? Is he or she triangulated between the conflicting and increasing demands of school and home? If so, to what extent are teachers and parents aware of such problems, and are they communicating with one another about them? Do parents have the skills, time, and energy (ecological competence) to collaborate with school personnel? Are they also sensitive to the potential effects of childhood parentification on peer involvement? Do they know their children's friends and support healthy peer relationships?

Gathering information about the interrelation of different systems of which the child is a part typically raises questions about the nature of the parents' support system and involvement outside the home. Are they gainfully employed? Is their work highly stressful? Does it demand that the children assume increased responsibilities at home? Do parents have friends and social skills? How stable is the family's neighborhood? Are affordable and competent social and heath-related services available to the family? In the absence of meaningful social ties and self-empowering activities, parents often call on their children to fill the void.

Larger Societal–Cultural Factors

The role of macrosystemic variables in the parentification process should also be noted. These include, in part, cultural values and traditions, political processes, mass media, technological changes, the legal system, and economic factors. For example, is the child's parentified role socially legitimate? Are the parents' involvement in different social-legal institutions, such as the welfare system, disempowering them and fragmenting family relationships? What role do racism, ethnic prejudice, and institutional discrimination play in the child's parentification? How well connected is the family's ethnoracial group to the economic mainstream? Have traditional gender role socialization practices played a part in the child's parentification?

Ethical

The evaluative focus to this point has been on the personal histories, qualities, and expectations of parental role assignors, the developmental characteristics and commitments of the parentified role assignees, assignor-assignee transactions, the interface of family, school, and peer variables, and the sociocultural legitimacy and context of the parentification process. The existential–ethical significance of and relationship between these elements are also part of the fabric of parentification. The ethical context should be evaluated at both intrafamilial and extrafamilial levels.

Intrafamilial Ethics

Important considerations at the intrafamilial level include the balance of justice, unsettled accounts, legacies, loyalty, and trust (see Boszormenyi-Nagy & Krasner, 1986; Karpel & Strauss, 1983).

Balance of Justice. Are mutual obligations and entitlements fairly balanced in the family? Do parents act responsibly toward their children? Are they accountable for their parenting behaviors? Do they recognize their children's inherent entitlement to caring, despite the children's inability to reciprocate equally? As part of this process, are family members acknowledged or given credit for their contributions (entitlements) when due? And are their claims or requests of one another actively considered?

In cases of destructive parentification, parents (1) exploit their children to meet their own needs, (2) do not acknowledge and may criticize their efforts to help the family, and (3) fail or refuse to consider their claims (e.g., of unfair treatment). Accordingly, the parent-child relationship becomes increasingly imbalanced, a fact that must be considered at the ethical level of analysis whether or not internally experienced by either the parent or child.

Children often do not voice grievances about their parents because of loyalty processes within the family, although evidence of inequities and lack of reciprocity often surfaces in their answers to such questions as, Are your parents aware of how you feel when you're upset? If so, how do they help? What happens in your family when you need help? Do your parents notice your feelings? Can you talk to your parents about your problems? Does it seem as though your parents expect you to be grown-up? Do you think that you are asked to do too much in the family?

Justice issues can also be framed in contractual terms (Elkind, 1979). Does a "reasonable balance" obtain between children and parents in the following areas: (1) achievements expected and supports provided, (2) responsibilities expected and freedoms provided, and (3) loyalties expected and commitments provided? Contractual violations may be the result of either an imbalance (e.g., parents' expecting more than they provide) or expectations that exceed the child's developmental capacities.

The balance of justice in the family is an ongoing dynamic process that spans multiple generations, including those of the future. Justice is subject to reevaluation and rebalancing at any time. In the assessment of justice, one must attend closely to life events (e.g., birth of a child, death of a parent), because they often occasion changes not only in the structure of the family but also, from an ethical perspective, in the distribution of relational burdens and benefits (Boszormenyi-Nagy & Krasner, 1986).

Unsettled Accounts. The ethical implications of individual psychological and historical factors, as discussed earlier, must be considered, particularly abuse, deprivation, and exploitation in the parent's family of origin. Is the parent destructively entitled? Parents with unsettled accounts in other relationships may turn unfairly to one another or to their children to achieve equity.

Legacies. Relational justice is further influenced by legacies, which refer to universal and specific expectations or obligations that are rooted in one's origins (e.g., parental accountability, filial loyalty, maintenance of family traditions, compensation for a parent's unrealized aspirations). It is important to determine whether these legacies have empowered family members or entrapped them (Karpel & Strauss, 1983).

Loyalty. Loyalty is a universal aspect of human relationships that reflects not only differential attachment patterns but also ethical indebtedness (Boszormenyi-Nagy & Krasner, 1986; Karpel & Strauss, 1983). People may be indebted to others for helping them in various ways (e.g., providing support during a time of need) or for existential reasons. Children, for example, owe their existence to their parents, regardless of the merit or deservedness of the latter. This fact is reflected in the Vietnamese adage "Children live to repay the debt of their birth."

Filial loyalty is a potential resource that enters into the ethical balancing of parent-child accounts. Evaluators should consider, however, whether it is misused and divided by parental figures, as well as whether it is overdeveloped in the youngster. Children's loyalty helps explain why they tolerate and even actively participate in their own exploitation and suffer greatly when they are caught in the middle of their parents' conflicts and bids for attention.

Trust. It has been noted that one of the most serious consequences of ethically imbalanced relationships is the loss of trust. Family members' increasing readiness to depend on one another is the direct result of interactions that are reliable, responsible, and duly considerate. In other words, trust accrues within the context of a relationship that is just and caring. As such, its ambit extends beyond psychology and transaction to include relational ethics. Mistrust by family members is prima facie evidence of ethical imbalances in their interactions with one another and possibly with extrafamilial figures and institutions (Boszormenyi-Nagy & Krasner, 1986; Karpel & Strauss, 1983).

An important part of the process of assessing the ethical dimension entails encouraging family members conjointly to evaluate the equity of their relationships with one another. They should be helped to focus not only on debits but also on credits and resources (e.g., parental caring and empathy, filial loyalty), including those that inhere in the parent-child relationship (e.g., children's indebtedness to their parents for giving them life) (Boszormenyi-Nagy & Krasner, 1986; Karpel, 1986a; Karpel & Strauss, 1983).

Children, disempowered members of families, as well as future generations, however, cannot be expected to enter fully, if at all, into family discussions about ethical issues. It is therefore incumbent upon clinicians to represent their claims and points of view. It is also important to determine the parentifying parent's capacity to acknowledge the availability and beneficence of the child. Resistance to being accountable and to giving credit when due may be a sign of narcissism, transactional-communication difficulties, or destructive entitlement (Boszormenyi-Nagy & Krasner, 1986). These problems notwithstanding, diagnostic efforts to confront ethical imbalances lay the groundwork, as discussed in Chapter 5, for helping family members to reallocate relational costs and benefits and to earn constructive entitlement.

Extrafamilial Ethics

In evaluating the ethicality of relationships, it is also critical from an ecological-ethical perspective to consider the balance of fairness not only in the family but also in other systems that affect children. Chapter 2 presents a number of questions to ask about ethical processes in these various systems. Further such questions include, for example, Is the child exploited by peers? Do school personnel duly acknowledge and consider students' and their parents' claims of mistreatment? Does the school system expect its charges to negotiate problems, curricula, and circumstances (e.g., those inherent in large consolidated middle schools and high schools, sex education and family planning programs, experimental and untested classroom structures and pedagogic approaches) too soon and without sufficient support? Are parental figures treated fairly in their places of work? Are there sociocultural structures to support responsible and caring parenting? Have traditional gender socialization practices played a role in unjust parent-child and marital interaction patterns? Do the widespread injustices in the histories of ethnoracial groups (e.g., African Americans, Jews) leave the present generation with legacies and entitlements that are either destructive or empowering? Finally, what are the ethical implications of past and current family and sociocultural practices for posterity?

Unethical practices and policies at the extrafamilial level directly or indirectly affect the balance of fairness in the family. Parents who experience discrimination and exploitation in contexts outside the home, for example, are at risk of recreating the same experience within their homes, perpetuating the cycle of injustice not only transgenerationally but socially as well. By considering the wider ethical context in which family justice is embedded, we can better understand the problems presented us by children and families and avoid unfairly blaming them.

That is not to say that an ecologically based, ethical stance fails to hold people accountable. Indeed, it does. The balance of responsibility, however, should be fairly evaluated and apportioned. This often involves noting destructive entitlement. At its extreme, an ecological-ethical orientation also recognizes that we all affect and are affected by one another and thus collectively share in the responsibility of determining the ethicality and saneness of the various contexts in which we live.

Consequential

The consequences of parentification constitute the final contextual dimension in the I-D-C evaluative model. As discussed in previous chapters, because the effects of this process influence the development of parentified youngsters, other family members, and the family as a whole, consideration of such effects is an important component in a comprehensive contextual evaluation.

The identifying behavioral signs of destructive parentification (referred to earlier) reflect many of the sequelae that should be assessed. One should also ask, What is the parentified youngster's level of destructive entitlement? Has the parentification process resulted in the child's social isolation, further reinforcing his or her overresponsible role at home? Is there evidence of other emotional, learning, and health problems that may or may not be specific to parentification? Often, these problems (e.g., visual acuity disorders, learning disabilities, hypoglycemia) have gone undetected or untreated because of parental neglect.

Also to be considered is the impact or potential impact on other members of the parentified child's current and future families. For example, in the case of sibling caretakers, have they met the basic physical needs of their brothers and sisters? Have they disciplined them harshly or abusively? Have they limited their peer contacts? Has sibling incest occurred?

Concerning the parents, has the process served to maintain their undifferentiated and dysfunctional status? Has it exacerbated problems in their marital relationship? Has it blocked their interactions with the other children? If families are attempting to blend, has a parentified child complicated the process?

Finally, the clinician should not ignore the positive effects of the parentification process. For example, as we have seen, although negatively affecting the child in many ways, it may provide him or her with status and much needed self-esteem. Parentified children may provide relief for overwhelmed or upwardly mobile parental figures. Siblings are frequently beneficiaries of their brother's or sister's parentification as well (e.g., allowing them to have healthier interactions with their parents). Moreover, knowledge of positive consequences helps to illuminate factors that are maintaining a destructive parentification process.

CLINICAL EXAMPLE

To illustrate the usefulness of the I-D-C model in evaluating parentification, we return to a case that was briefly mentioned in Chapter 3. In a project that served inner-city, court-involved families, we saw Zach, a handsome and gregarious 16-year-old. An African American, he lived with his mother, who was unemployed, and a 5-year-old sister in a housing project near the juvenile court facilities. A few months before Zach's birth, his father left his mother and had no further involvement with them. His parents were not married. Zach's sister was also born out of wedlock to another man, whose contacts with the family were sporadic.

Since the age of 14, Zach had been referred to the court several times for possession of marijuana and truancy. His mother also discovered that he had been fondling his sister. After she reported her observations to Zach's probation officer, he was referred to us for court-ordered treatment.

Exploration of Zach's court history uncovered his long-standing and pathological parentification within his family. His truancy, for example, related to his working late nights at a warehouse, a well-paying job that he took to help support his family. Constantly fatigued, he frequently missed school to sleep. Recently, Zach had begun selling marijuana to supplement his income. Smoking it also helped him to relax.

Zach was, as he said, his mother's "main man." In addition to supporting her financially, he was helpful to her in other ways, acting as her co-parent and spouse. She could always count on Zach to help her feel better, which included holding her whenever she needed physical contact. It was apparent that the incestuous overtones in their relationship, reflecting extreme boundary problems, were being acted out by Zach in his interactions with his sister.

At the same time, there were signs that Zach was attempting to distance himself from his mother. He often exploded when she commented about his attire or behavior, leading her to withdraw from him. Zach confided to the evaluator that he wanted a "divorce" from his mother and often considered running away from home. He worried, however, that his mother and sister could not make it without him, reflecting the degree to which he was captivated by his parentified role and the reality of his family's situation.

Although he was popular at school and talented athletically, the demands of his home situation impeded Zach's ability to pursue friendships and extracurricular interests. His increasing marijuana use, often in the company of his co-workers after work, was not only a relaxant but a much needed social-recreational activity for him as well. Another source of gratification for Zach at work was his immediate supervisor's paternal interest in him.

Zach's mother was uninvolved in her son's peer, school, and court activities. She simply warned Zach that he had better complete school lest he end up like all the other men in her life: "losers." Yet she did not object to his working late at night.

Zach was his mother's sole support system. Other sources of

support (e.g., friendships, stable neighborhood, work) were either unavailable to her or beyond her capacity to cultivate. When she was 14, her mother died of a gunshot wound; like her son, she had never had any contact with her father. Although her three half-siblings lived in the same city, she had little involvement with them. They had been placed in separate foster and group homes after her mother's death. Thus, Zach's mother was as isolated from her family of origin as she was from others in her social system.

Additional information gained from her genogram revealed that she was a survivor of sexual abuse. She recalled having been abused by several of her mother's boyfriends. Although aware of the abuse, her mother did not protect her. Zach's mother was plagued with suicidal feelings as an adolescent, feeling unprotected and unworthy as well as destructively entitled. When she became pregnant a few years after her mother's death, she felt hopeful that her child-to-be would give her reason to live. Indeed, he did. Forming an undifferentiated relationship with Zach, she depended on him not only for emotional support but for self-definition. Accordingly, her parenting attitudes and behaviors reflected an underlying egoistic orientation.

Noteworthy about Zach's early development was the fact that he served as a primary attachment figure for his mother. At a young age, he was oversolicitous toward her. He suffered extreme separation problems, which affected his school attendance during his early school years. It is likely that his separation anxiety was reactive, functioning to keep him in his mother's emotional and physical orbit.

An evaluation of Zach's sister by the Department of Children and Family Services revealed that she had not been traumatized by her brother's sexual misconduct, which appeared to be minimal. Rather, she seemed most upset about Zach's distancing from her after the problem between the two of them was discovered. That her mother intervened is interesting; it appeared that her reliance on Zach over the years allowed her to have a more appropriate parental relationship with her daughter.

Macrosystemic factors that were implicated in Zach's parentification included socioeconomic status and race. Discrimination and related economic hardships suffered by African Americans in our culture have contributed to father absence, poverty, transgenerational fragmentation, and overinvolvement of social agencies in their families. The role of the latter in separating Zach's mother from her siblings was unfortunate. As alluded to earlier, family and children's service agencies often benevolently intervene in families and, in the process, disempower parents and strain familial relationships. These agencies, however, because of a lack of funding, personnel, and public support, are as stressed as the families they serve.

The balance of obligations and entitlements in Zach's relationship with his parents was clearly unfair, reflecting the injustice of earlier generations of parent-child relationships in his extended family and, at another level, years of prejudicial treatment in society. Clearly, future generations in Zach's family are at risk of being treated in exploitative and uncaring ways as well. Moreover, to the extent that the familial and sociocultural conditions that gave rise to the ethical imbalances within his family system persist, society at large and its progeny, from an ecological-ethical perspective, are also at risk.

Despite the unfairness of Zach's situation, helpful resources are identifiable. For example, although Zach's relationship with his supervisor at work could not directly undo the ethical imbalances in his family system, it helped him to delineate a clearer sense of himself and of his self-worth. One result of this change was that he began to rebel against his mother's controlling dependence on him, claiming his independence.

Zach's existential indebtedness to his parents could motivate him to seek to rebalance his relationship with them. Part of this process often involves exoneration and/or forgiveness of errant parents through a greater appreciation of their past. However, it was recognized that Zach's willingness to take these steps would most likely occur later in his life and perhaps then only if his mother initiates some type of corrective action.

The mother's siblings also represented a potential resource. Helping her to reconnect with them could be a powerful way of reducing her dependence on Zach for her identity and existence. Along the same lines, encouraging her to exercise the job skills she possessed would further empower her.

Finally, both she and Zach would benefit if she were helped to appreciate and to credit her son's contributions to the family. This would be both validating for Zach and self-affirming for his mother. The ability to acknowledge children's helpful activities is a potent resource that many parents possess but greatly under use.

INSTRUMENTATION

In the identification and exploration of Zach's parentification, we used a variety of standard clinical procedures: individual and family interviews with attention to both content and process; a genogram, including detailed developmental histories; a review of records; and reports of teachers and other agency personnel (e.g., probation officer). No objective measures of parentification were administered; most have not been sufficiently developed for clinical use. A number of such instruments, however, have been constructed in recent years for research purposes.

One of the first, the Parentification Questionnaire (PQ), grew out of our efforts to study the long-term effects of parentification in late adolescents and young adults (see Appendix B). Drawing from theory, clinical experience, and a previous measure developed by one of my students (Goglia, 1982), we designed a 42-item, true-false questionnaire, which asks respondents to report the degree of instrumental and expressive parentification and relational injustice that they experienced in their families during their childhood and adolescent years (Sessions, 1986; Sessions & Jurkovic, 1986). The instrument has acceptable internal and test-retest reliability, as well as content, discriminative, and criterion validity (see Goglia, Jurkovic, Burt, & Burge-Callaway, 1992; Sessions, 1986).

Mika, Bergner, and Baum (1987) have also independently developed a measure of parentification in a college student population. Respondents to their Parentification Scale report parentification both before 14 years of age and between ages 14 and 16. The scale, which has acceptable psychometric properties, is composed of four subsets of items: spousal role vis-à-vis parents, parental role vis-à-vis parents, parental role vis-à-vis siblings, and nonspecific adult role-taking. A major shortcoming of this measure is that it does not include items pertaining to the sociofamilial and ethical contexts of the various role patterns assessed.

In her studies of generational boundary disturbances in undergraduate students, Jacobvitz (see, e.g., Fullinwider–Bush & Jacobvitz, 1993) has used two subscales from her Family Relations Questionnaire (Father-Daughter Boundary Dissolution and Mother-Daughter Boundary Dissolution) to measure parental dependence on daughters for emotional support. The scales have adequate internal and test-retest reliabilities. They are useful as an index of same- and cross-gender parentification.

Another relevant self-report instrument in this area is the Relational Ethics Scale. Designed by Hargrave, Jennings, and Anderson (1991), this scale is not a measure of parentification per se. Rather, it isolates the ethical dimension of individuals' relationships with (1) their families of origin (vertical relationships) and (2) persons of equal status (horizontal relationships). See Hargrave, Jennings, and Anderson (1991) and Hargrave and Bomba (1993) for discussion of its development and psychometric characteristics.

A projective measure of parentification processes has also been created (Walsh, 1979). Developed to identify generational boundary problems in research of severely disturbed adults, Walsh coded stories to selected pictures (taken mostly from the Thematic Apperception Test) according to the presence of themes reflecting the child character in (1) a caretaking or sacrificial role (child-as-parent) or (2) a perverse triangle or sexualized relationship with parental figures (child-as-mate). Illustrative of the former is a story from a subject in one of our studies (Goglia, Jurkovic, Burt, & Burge-Callaway, 1992):

> The older woman is the mother, and the man is the son. The woman intensely looks out the window, hoping that her husband would return. The husband has been dead for several years, and the son knows and realizes that his father isn't coming back home. The son witnessed the death of his father, but he can't bring himself to con vince his mother that he is dead, because it will hurt her so much. (p. 297)

We have speculated that Walsh's measure may identify parentification in individuals who, because of cultural reasons, defensiveness, or social desirability, fail to report parentified role behaviors on objective instruments. It is not clear, however, whether self-constructed stories with child-as-parent or child-as-mate themes necessarily reflect actual parentified role behaviors. Instead, they may symbolize generational boundary distortions generally, as Walsh originally interpreted such thematic material, or a loyal–object process.

Burt (1992) also suggests that Walsh's scoring scheme is over-conservative. For generational boundary distortions to be coded positively, the story characters must be cast as having fully enacted a child-as-parent or child-as-mate role. Burt recommends that stories in which the characters merely consider enacting such a role may also be indicative of boundary problems. Whether she is correct raises an interesting empirical question, the answer to which may help further refine Walsh's method.

Internal dynamics related to the parentification of others can also be reliably and validly measured on the Thematic Appercep-tion Test using the Pathogenesis Scale (see Meyer & Karon, 1967; Mitchell, 1968; VandenBos & Karon, 1971). This scale evaluates the conscious or unconscious tendency of individuals to ignore the needs of others in a dependent position or to exploit dependent others to gratify personal needs.

All of the instruments discussed thus far were developed with late adolescent and adult samples. Fosson and Lask (1988) designed the Pictorial Assessment Instrument, which can be used with children and adults. It depicts various stylized family patterns, consisting of normal and detouring families, two- and three-generational enmeshment, parental child, undermined mother, and chaotic family. Family members, either alone or in combination, are asked to select depictions that are most like their own family systems.

Although Fosson and Lask reported statistically significant concordance between the selections of a group of clinic families and those of their therapists, the correlations were small. The ability of their instrument to differentiate family structure has also yet to be established. Seventy-five percent of their sample was rated by the therapists as enmeshed; none characterized as parental child. Nonetheless, because of the efficiency of graphically based evaluation methods, the Pictorial Assessment Instrument warrants further attention.

The Sibling Inventory of Differential Experience (SIDE) authored by Daniels and Plomin (1985) contains a scale, Differential Sibling Caretaking, that also may be useful in identifying an important aspect of the parentification process. Developed for individuals ranging in age from preadolescence to young adulthood, the SIDE measures siblings' perceptions of their relative experiences within their families. The SIDE is psychometrically sound and appears to tap experiences within families that are environmentally rather than genetically based.

Other researchers have attempted to identify parentifying actions of parents. For example, as part of their research of child disturbance and postdivorce conflict, Johnston, Gonzalez, and Campbell (1987) developed clinical rating scales to assess the degree to which parents involve their children in their conflicts (Role of Child in Dispute Scale) and the extent of role reversal in the parent-child relationship (Role Reversal Scale). The scales have adequate interrater reliability and were useful in Johnston and associates' study in predicting various behavior problems in children.

Clinical ratings of parentification were also used by Burkett (1991) to research parenting behaviors of women who were sexually abused as children. Parental interviews, based on all questions of an adapted version of the Child Rearing Practices Scales (Sears, Maccoby, & Levin, 1957) rather than from a specific item or group of items, were rated along two related dimensions: (1) use of the child as a primary companion and (2) use of the child for emotional caretaking.

For example, pertinent information from one of the mothers in Burkett's study was elicited by a question about what she did for fun with her 10-year-old:

> One of the things we'll do together is sleep together and we'll stay up late, like twelve-thirty, one o'clock in the morning, and talk, just talk. We'll talk, mostly, about all sorts of stuff. We'll talk about her friends, and we'll talk about my friends. I love it, I just love it. I love to do it. I wish I had ten times the time to do it. (p. 428)

When asked to describe her relationship with her 9-year-old daughter, another mother said:

> It's her and I, and sometimes I get support from her, and I'm not sure if she's old enough to give it. I forget that she's a child, especially when I'm confiding in her, I'm talking to her at an adult level, and I forget that she's not an adult. I've decided I can't confide in her like she's

another adult because she just can't keep it to herself. (p. 429)

Ratings of parent–child interaction can also be used to assess parentification. For example, Sroufe, Jacobvitz, Mangelsdorf, DeAngelo, and Ward (1985) constructed a 7-point rating scale measuring "boundary dissolution" (i.e., the extent to which the parent remains in a supportive parental role vs. a peer or child role) to assess parental behavior in interactive laboratory situations requiring parents to guide and teach their children. A group of mothers were observed to flirt with and look to their 42-month old sons for support and affection on such tasks. Evidence of boundary dissolution in these mother-son pairs helped predict attention deficit/hyperactivity disorder later in the boys' development (Jacobvitz & Sroufe, 1987).

Another innovative approach to capturing caretaking on the part of young children can be found in the longitudinal studies of Zahn-Waxler and her colleagues (Zahn-Waxler & Radke-Yarrow, 1982; Zahn-Waxler, Radke-Yarrow, Wagner, & Chapman, 1992). They trained mothers to observe their one- and two-year-olds' reactions to naturally occurring or simulated distresses and reliably coded instances of prosocial and reparative behaviors on the part of the children in the mothers' observational records.

The Adult-Adolescent Parenting Inventory (AAPI), a 32-item, self-report measure developed by Bavolek (1984) to identify abusive and neglectful parenting behaviors and attitudes, is composed of scales that are also related to parentification: developmental expectations, empathy, and role reversal. The measure includes a scale pertaining to corporal punishment as well. Standardized on large samples of adults and adolescents, including abusive adults and abused adolescents, the AAPI has good psychometric properties.

Newberger's (1977, 1980) semistructured interview schedule also assays parental conceptions that mediate parentification. It is composed of both direct questions and hypothetical dilemmas, relating to the parents' concept of the child's development and personality, parents' and children's rights and responsibilities, and the meaning and management of various issues (e.g., maintaining trust and communication). Interview data are classified in terms of one or more hierarchically organized levels of parental awareness: (1) egoistic, (2) conventional, (3) subjective-individualistic, and (4) systems.

The value of Newberger's scheme is that rather than measuring surface attitudes and beliefs, the underlying logical structure of parents' thinking about their children and the parent-child relationship is evaluated. Parents, for example, may endorse attitudes that suggest they are concerned about their children's needs; the conceptual basis for their endorsement, however, may be egoistic in nature. Also noteworthy about Newberger's stage descriptions is that they include an ethical component, reflecting an internal psychological counterpart of relational ethics.

CONCLUSIONS

Although common, destructive parentification is frequently overlooked by clinicians or diagnosed late in the therapeutic process. Moreover, to the extent that parentified behaviors are identified, especially in adults, they are often simply attributed to co-dependent or self-defeating personality traits or structures. Such processes may very well be involved, but from an ecological-ethical viewpoint their role should not eclipse data at other levels of analysis in the evaluation process. The utility of the I-D-C framework presented here is that it systematically guides clinicians to describe and to contextualize parentification on a broader spectrum.

Clearly, the measurement of parentification and related processes is in an early stage. Continued work in the design of standardized and clinically relevant indices of both parentifying and parentified behaviors in parent-child relationships promises to contribute to our ability to identify and to evaluate parentification in its various forms.

CHAPTER 5

Treating Destructively Parentified Children and Their Families: Systemic and Ethical Perspectives

I n our treatment of parentified children and their families, a number of issues have recurrently emerged. Informed by clinical experience as well as by theoretical and empirically based considerations detailed in Part I of this book, guidelines are presented in this chapter for (1) joining with family members, (2) addressing the parentification process, (3) negotiating emergent problems, (4) restoring parental accountability, (5) empowering parentified children, (6) helping family members grieve their losses, (7) fostering new relational possibilities, and (8) facilitating the children's socioemotional growth. The first three tasks are associated with the beginning phase of treatment, the next three with the middle phase, and the last two with the ending phase, although it is recognized that the various tasks may be negotiated and renegotiated throughout the therapy process.

Prior to a discussion of the specific therapeutic tasks, our treatment of Jenny is summarized, along with general orienting perspectives that undergird ecosystemic-ethical intervention strategies. Jenny's therapy represented our early efforts to implement an integrated therapeutic approach. Despite our misapplication at times, Jenny and her family steadily improved. In the process, they taught us invaluable lessons about the complexities and demands of working simultaneously at different contextual levels.

JENNY REVISITED

Recall that during the intake interview, we learned of several pressing issues: (1) the mother's threats to abandon the family, (2) her abusive relationship with her boyfriend, (3) Jenny's hopelessness about being able to help anymore and attendant suicidal feelings, and (4) the scarcity of food in the house.

Upon hearing our concern about these issues near the end of the first session, Jenny's mother, Barbara, immediately reassured her daughter that she would never leave. Her threats, she explained, reflected mounting tensions with her boyfriend and fears of financial ruin. Barbara added that she, too, had felt suicidal until distracted by Jenny's depressive behavior.

Visibly relieved, Jenny began to cry but quickly regained her composure and advised her mother to leave her boyfriend. We said that we could help her mother with that issue but, respectful of Jenny's vital role in the family, also acknowledged that Jenny might feel threatened as a result. She urged us to intervene, although she pointed out that our task would not be an easy one.

During the next several months, we met with Jenny and her mother individually and, occasionally, together. Jenny's brother was also included in some of the joint meetings. Efforts were made as well to involve Jenny's father in the therapy. Our initial concerns about Barbara's rapidly deteriorating condition and her ability to meet her children's physical and emotional needs abated rapidly. We helped her obtain food stamps, apply for jobs, and, at her request, terminate her relationship with her boyfriend. Barbara's response to these interventions was dramatic. Her concern about "falling" into another self-destructive relationship helped shift the focus in her individual sessions to family-of-origin issues, particularly her sense of abandonment by her own father and exploitation by family members.

Jenny's individual work was largely child centered. Initially declining my invitation to play with the toys in the consulting room, she talked about school and her family. Jenny had difficulty accepting my acknowledgment of her helpfulness to her mother. She focused instead on her perceived shortcomings, such as her errors on homework and her inability to sustain her mother emotionally. Jenny needed validation for her contributions to the family directly from her mother. Although therapists can recognize imbalances in the family ledger and offer due credit, as I did by commenting on Jenny's helpful behavior, family members must be encouraged to negotiate these issues themselves (Boszormenyi-Nagy & Krasner, 1986).

Nevertheless, Jenny seemed intrigued by therapeutic inputs, which presented her with a view of herself different from the unfavorable one she had held previously. For example, during one session she slumped in her chair, devastated by the fact that she had made several mistakes on a math assignment. To challenge her perfectionistic tendencies, I graphically portrayed her self-concept (see Harter, 1977). After drawing two circles to represent Jenny, I labeled one "stupid" and the other "smart," descriptors she had alternately applied to herself during that session. We discussed her tendency to vacillate between feeling "all stupid" and "all smart," depending on her school performance. Less than perfection, as Jenny informed me, was unacceptable.

To introduce the notion that she might conserve positive feelings about herself in the face of imperfection, I constructed another circle with a line drawn through the middle. One half symbolized her sense of "stupidity" in reference to math, and the other her "smartness" in different areas, such as spelling. In the following session, Jenny continued to work with the "circle," spontaneously identifying other parts of herself about which she felt positive. Later that session, she also wondered if we might play a game, which, of course, we did. Her ability to play freely increased remarkably in subsequent sessions. She also began to entertain the idea that perhaps she did not have to be "perfect."

The change in Jenny's behavior during the therapy hours doubtless related to the undivided and unconditional attention she was receiving. It was also apparent that her mother had begun to assume more responsibility at home, gradually relieving Jenny of her caretaking tasks. In the joint sessions, which we scheduled on a more regular basis beginning in the third month of therapy, we continued to help Jenny and her mother develop more appropriate boundaries. For example, when Jenny criticized her mother's purchase of a used car, we directed Barbara to set a limit with her daughter.

During this period, our ongoing attempts to include Jenny's father in the therapy were finally rewarded. He explained that because of heavy travel commitments he did not return our telephone calls initially and then delayed scheduling an appointment with us. We met with him alone at first to explore his willingness to be involved in Jenny's life. Immediately expressing concern about his daughter and a desire to reconnect with her, he attributed his absence to depression, partially related to the court's denial of his request for liberal visitation, as well as to his new wife's extreme reactivity to his former family. However, he declined our offer to involve his wife in the therapy as well.

Although her father was responsive to our concerns about his availability to Jenny, we were unsure about the genuineness of his feelings and his ability to negotiate his parental responsibilities with his wife. Therefore, we focused on the added pain that his daughter would experience if he reconnected with her only to vanish again when stressed. It was critical ethically, in our view, that he be accountable for the consequences of his behavior, regardless of the mitigating circumstances. Obviously consumed with guilt about his abandonment of Jenny, he reassured us that he would take remedial steps immediately.

And he did. Within a week, he had contacted Barbara to arrange regular visitation with Jenny again. The elevation in Jenny's mood was striking, although she was fearful that her father's reinvolvement in her life would be short-lived. In a subsequent session with the two of them, Jenny's deep-seated distrust was discussed. To her father's credit, he was able—with little prompting—to acknowledge the painful consequences of his actions and to reassure his daughter that he would make every effort to be trustworthy.

For the next several months of therapy, we helped Jenny and her family to work through the many changes they were experiencing. In one session, for example, Barbara suddenly announced that they had "gone back to *Go.*" In a despondent voice, she explained that Jenny and her brother had begun fighting—a new behavior for them. She interpreted the change as a sign of her inadequacy as a mother. "To the contrary," we asserted. We suggested that her children's rivalrous behavior was normal, indicative of the family's growth and increasing differentiation of parent-child roles. It was a sign of Jenny's engagement in the sibling subsystem as a sister rather than as a parent.

Although significant shifts were occurring in the family, we underestimated the stressful impact of these changes at an individual psychological level. This serendipitously came to our attention near the end of the fifth month of treatment. As part of a project in the clinic where we were seeing Jenny, she was administered the Rorschach and the Thematic Apperception Test (TAT). Despite evidence of significant improvement in Jenny's behavior at home and school, the results suggested that she was still emotionally troubled, related, in part, to possible iatrogenic effects of the treatment.

One of her TAT (3GF) stories, for example, was about a "girl who felt very angry with her mother, because her mother would not let her cook for her." It seemed that the change in her familial role had threatened the only secure way of relating to her mother that she had known. In subsequent sessions, we addressed Jenny's anger and her fears that her mother would abandon her emotionally and physically if she were not allowed to caretake as she had in the past. We realized at this point the importance of helping Barbara to counterbalance generational boundary marking with acknowledgment and legitimization of her daughter's caring feelings and actions.

We also recognized that Jenny needed direct assistance with peer relationships. She was becoming more tolerant of her age-mates but still struggled with tendencies to be "bossy," as one of her teachers described Jenny. Thus, we enlisted her mother's help in teaching her social skills. For example, Jenny was encouraged to invite friends to her home and to practice playing cooperatively. We coached Barbara to signal Jenny unobtrusively whenever she was "bossy."

Therapy ended successfully after nine months. A one-year follow-up found Jenny to have grown not only physically but also emotionally. She had many friends, continued to perform exceptionally well academically, and related comfortably with her mother. Along with working part-time, Barbara was completing requirements for a teaching certificate. She had not become involved in another relationship.

Jenny's father had fulfilled his promise of adhering to a regular visitation schedule. Interestingly, he later sought marital therapy. It appeared that Jenny's half-brother was also doing well. Influenced by changes in Jenny's paternal relationship, Barbara reported that she had persuaded the boy's father to take a more active interest in him. Thus, not only was Jenny affected by the therapy but so were others in her ecosystem. The groundwork, moreover, had been laid for the next generation to experience a different legacy of familial give-and-take.

GENERAL ORIENTING PERSPECTIVES

As demonstrated in our work with Jenny, a variety of therapeutic techniques were employed at different contextual levels. For example, self-concept issues were addressed at the individual psychological level, generational boundaries and the home-school relationship at the sociofamilial level, and parental accountability, trustworthiness, and acknowledgment at the ethical level. Our interventions were increasingly guided by two interrelated perspectives: one rooted in ecosystemic-developmental thinking and the other in existential-ethical analysis.

Multilevel Systemic Orientation

A basic derivative of ecosystemic theories is that therapists, regardless of their approach, cannot avoid practicing at multiple levels of analysis. Interventions aimed at one level perturb interrelated processes within and at other levels. Just as planners of new developments, such as highways, dams, airports, and waste storage sites, are constrained by environmental impact studies, so should therapists concern themselves with the broader implications of their treatment. At the same time, they can systematically design interventions that take into consideration the spread of effects (Jurkovic & Berger, 1984; Jurkovic, Jessee, & Goglia, 1991).

For example, Jenny's therapy involved many interventions that strategically traversed several levels of analysis (or issues within levels) simultaneously. For example, her father was helped to re-connect with her, while also encouraged in the process to address ethical imbalances between them. We facilitated the mother's link-ing with her daughter's school, which further reinforced her parental role. Similarly, suggesting that Barbara inconspicuously cue Jenny when she behaved inappropriately with friends affected both family and peer processes.

Relatedly, a multilevel orientation also helps therapists lay the groundwork for interventions at one level by addressing associ-ated issues at other levels. For example, techniques to facilitate Barbara's relying less heavily on her daughter were effective, in part, because of interventions early in the therapy process designed to provide her with alternative sources of support and esteem (e.g., employment, individual therapy sessions focused on her needs). Assisting Barbara at both an individual and an ethical level with unresolved grief and resentment, as well as relational imbalances in her family of origin, also freed her to interact differently with Jenny.

Multilateral Ethical Orientation

Integral to thinking and practicing at multiple contextual levels is the therapist's appreciation of an "inclusive, fair multilaterality." Coined by Boszormenyi-Nagy and Krasner (1986), this term points to the necessity, from an ethical perspective, of considering the con-sequences of justice between family members for all affected or potentially affected. For example, changes in fairness between marital partners affect the balance of fairness with their children. A multilateral ethical perspective is achieved by therapists through a basic or essential therapeutic quality (referred to as "multidirected partiality" by Boszormenyi-Nagy) involving sensitivity to the hu-manity of and accountability to everyone potentially affected by the treatment process.

In the practice of multidirected partiality, therapists abandon therapeutic neutrality to enter into the often competing psychosocial and ethical frames of reference and experiences of family members and other concerned parties. The goal of such a process is to help all involved to confront their differences, to be accountable to one another, and to learn to process and rectify imbalances of fairness between them.

Therefore, although cognizance of the different analytic levels and multiple persons potentially influenced by the therapeutic process aids the therapist in designing elegant and powerful interventions from a systemic perspective, the strategy pursued must always be constrained by ethical considerations. That is, does the intervention treat clients and others (relatives, teachers, peers) as objects to be manipulated, controlled, or changed to achieve a "therapeutic" end (e.g., symptom relief, personal autonomy, boundaries, conformity)? Or does it accept them, including children, as persons with their own subjective-experiential sources of being, uniqueness, entitlements, and potential to enter into an authentic and fair relationship with others?

For example, in the process of helping Jenny's family to restructure, we unfortunately failed first to address long-standing ethical imbalances in their system. Her parents should have been prompted to acknowledge and to process their daughter's previous contributions to them, her brother, and the family as a whole, however inappropriate structurally. The result was that in the course of drawing boundaries, Jenny's ethical worth and hard-earned entitlement were disregarded and, from a multilevel perspective, her attachment to her mother was threatened. When our mistake finally became apparent to us later in therapy, we took corrective action, which greatly facilitated Jenny's participation in her family's reorganization. The boundary-making process seemed less arbitrary and oppressive to her and, at another level, proceeded more justly.[1]

---

[1]Recent trends (e.g., Anderson & Goolishian, 1988; de Shazer, 1991; Hoffman, 1990; White & Epston, 1990) to fashion therapy as a co-constructive process, in which therapists and clients share equally in the recontextualizing of problems, may help prevent therapeutic practices that have untoward and possibly harmful effects at levels typically disregarded by treatment providers. Of concern, however, is that even the constructivists may not pay sufficient attention to the psychosocial and ethical plight of family members, particularly current and future generations of children, and others in the community who are unable to articulate their perspective and to make their rightful claims for fair and sensitive treatment.

THERAPEUTIC TASKS

Beginning Phase

Joining

Establishing a therapeutic relationship with parentified children and their families can be challenging. Indeed, their system is often a juggernaut, defying easy entry by outsiders, however benevolent their intent. Because of parentified children's excessive loyalty to family members and underlying distrust of adults, they view the therapist as a potential intruder and someone with whom they should not develop a relationship. Therefore, it is incumbent on therapists to recognize and process these dynamics with parentified children and their families.

Recall that Jenny struggled with loyalty issues in her first session. Invested in protecting her mother from criticism, guilty about her inability to help her, and ashamed of her family situation, yet also keenly aware of her family's need for assistance, she was in a bind. My commenting on her dilemma and reassuring her that she did not have to violate any confidences helped her to feel understood. Jenny did confide in me about pressing problems in her family. By doing so, however, she risked dividing her loyalties between me and her family.

Many parentified children also resist joining with therapists because they are reluctant to relinquish their caretaking role. Can family members whom they have long nurtured be entrusted to a stranger, regardless of his or her credentials and helpful demeanor? Will their relationship with parental figures, which has depended on their caretaking efforts, be attenuated? Although parentified children are also often concerned about loss of influence in the family, especially as therapy proceeds, their initial resistance has much less to do with power than with psychological and existential-ethical issues related to attachment, caring, commitment, loyalty, and responsibility.

Therapists who are sensitive to these issues are, therefore, disinclined to handle their young clients' resistance with conventional strategic or structural techniques, contrived to establish boundaries prematurely. It is often helpful to process the various fears that parentified children experience as a result of therapeutic involvement in their families, particularly feelings of being displaced. We have also had success in giving parentified children tasks early in treatment to help us with other family members, for instance, monitoring a parent's mood. One adolescent who was assigned this task reported in the next session, "Maybe with your help, we can get my mother out of her depression" (Jurkovic, Jessee, & Goglia, 1991, p. 307).

A multilateral ethical orientation also requires therapists to develop a trustworthy relationship with the other members of the parentifying family system. For example, while the therapist is joining with the parentified child, the adults may feel slighted or criticized. It is thus important to recognize their victimization and related destructive entitlement stemming from stressful issues and exploitative experiences in the present and past. Pointing to signs of appropriate parenting on their part is also essential, lest they feel uniformly and unfairly discredited by the process of therapy, which will unavoidably uncover their inadequacies as parents (Boszormenyi-Nagy & Krasner, 1986).

Finally, successful joining with parental figures helps assuage the sense of disloyalty that parentified children experience in therapy. If the therapist attends as much to their parents as to them, then they are freer to enter into the therapeutic enterprise (Boszormenyi-Nagy & Krasner, 1986). For instance, although unsure of our ability to help, Jenny was relieved by our concern about her mother's welfare and less worried about violating confidences about the family.

Addressing the Parentification Process

In an earlier publication (Jurkovic, Jessee, & Goglia, 1991) we suggested that addressing destructive parentification in the opening phase of treatment is probably not helpful and may reflect the therapist's efforts to rescue the child from a process in which he or she is playing an active part. As our appreciation of the existential-ethical dimension of family dynamics and its determining role in processes at other levels has grown, we have come to agree with Boszormenyi-Nagy and Krasner (1986) that early acknowledgment of relational imbalances in the family is foundational. If sensitively handled in light of the perspectives of everyone involved, a healing context develops within which to work at the other levels of analysis.

Excerpts from the second session of our therapy of a single-parent family, involving two children, Ansley, age 12, and Brett, age 15, illustrate the utility of processing parentification in the beginning phase of treatment. After years of suffering from debilitating depression and physical problems, for which she finally received help, the children's mother, Anne, decided to pursue therapy to restore "harmony and organization" in her family. She complained that the children were disrespectful, often hurling expletives at her and generally disregarding her attempts to exercise any authority. She felt particularly victimized and unappreciated by them in light of the fact that their father left the family when they were toddlers and maintained only sporadic contact with them. Near the end of the initial interview with the family we learned that both Ansley and her brother had been parentified.

Rather than proceed in the second session to rebuild the hierarchical structure of the family, we engaged them in an ethical discussion about their relationships with one another. The transcript begins after the first 10 minutes of the session. During the previous week, Ansley had been going to the library after school to study in an effort to improve her grades. Problems arose, however, in regard to her mother's picking her up on a timely basis, resulting in what Anne regarded as a disrespectful and thoughtless reaction by her daughter.[2]

Mother:	Well, from my standpoint, I thought it was helpful for her to go to the library, except that she was super ugly about dropping her off and picking her up, like I'm supposed to materialize instantly. I'm not allowed to see a client or have a phone call. So she ran screaming up the stairs and slamming her door but not before saying, "You bitch," you know.
Daughter:	I didn't say that!

---

[2]Therapists 1 and 2 in this case were Lori Jurkovic, M.A., and the author, respectively.

Mother:	Yes, you did say that.
Daughter:	No, I did not say that!
Mother:	Friday night, that's what you said.
Daughter:	I didn't say that!
Mother:	I was supposed to pick her up at 6:00, and I picked her up at 6:01.
Daughter:	You did not pick me up at 6:01 … the library had closed, the wind was blowing, and it was raining outside, and I was standing outside, waiting for Mom to come get me, and it was cold.… It made me angry because I was done a half-hour before that. I tried to call her but she wasn't where she said she'd be.
Mother:	I told you I was going to be with a client.
Daughter:	I didn't hear that.
Mother:	This is a real problem with her, with communication. It's always, "I didn't hear it; you didn't tell me."
Therapist 1:	*(looking at Ansley)* So what arrangements did you understand?
Daughter:	Well, she told me she'd pick me up around 6:00.… I was mad at you *(now speaking to mother)* because you got all sassy and got that face. And I was mad already, then she gave me that look, and that made me mad.
Mother:	And she let me have it all the way home in the car. From the minute she got in the car, she would never lay it down.
Daughter:	I was going to try to be quiet, but I got angrier and angrier.

It was at this point that we might have buttressed mother's authority. Instead, as will be seen, we shifted the focus to underlying grievances and relational imbalances from an individual psychological and existential-ethical perspective.

Therapist 2: I wonder if there is something else going on. Did you feel let down by your mother?

Daughter: She's always forgetting about me. I always feel left out.

Son: (*speaking to mother*) You do forget about her, you've got to remember that.

Mother: I did forget about her once this week. Was it yesterday? Saturday?

Daughter: I don't know. You're forgetting about me all the time.

Therapist 1: When you do forget Ansley, how do you work it out with her? Do you apologize?

Daughter: She just blames it on me.

Mother: This is another thing. This word "blame." There was no blame. I admit that I forgot.

Daughter: You turn things around and make it my fault!

Therapist 2: (*speaking to mother*) When Ansley is angry with you, it's obviously hard for you to hear.

Mother: Yes.

Therapist 2: I could see that; you were putting your hands over your ears when Ansley was talking. Why is that so difficult?

Mother: Because she is so unrelenting and screaming and slamming doors, using foul language, and she won't stop and listen.

Therapist 1: Do you ever acknowledge her feelings?

Daughter: No!

Mother: I acknowledge that I'm wrong. And I always say that I'm wrong when I'm wrong.

Therapist 1: As we learned in the first session, part of the problem in the family right now is that, Anne, you've been depressed, and a major part of the kids' history with you has involved your depression. Ansley has been doing a lot to help you; she's always been there to help you.

Mother: She's been a good one.

Therapist 1: She's always stayed connected with you; she focuses on you. It's like she's been a parent to you. And she's still emotionally in that position.

Mother: That's why she's always telling me what to do.

Therapist 1: Like a parent. The hope of kids who have been there for their parents is that eventually their parents will meet their needs. And now you're not depressed. You're doing better. I suspect that Ansley is feeling entitled. "Mom's well enough now to take care of me." So when she feels forgotten by you now, she lets you know. She gets angry. It would be helpful to simply acknowledge her angry feelings and to say you're sorry, if appropriate. What else would help?

Daughter: When she does say it, to mean it.

Mother: She won't accept my apologies.

Therapist 2: Ansley, could you model for your mother how you'd like her to say it? Show her.

Therapist 1: Pretend like your Mom was left outside in the rain and cold, and you drove up and picked her up.

Mother: It was cold out there, all right!

Daughter: *(putting her hand on her mother's shoulder)* I'm sorry. Are you all right? Why are you sitting outside in the cold? "Because the library closed 16 minutes ago!" I'm sorry, are you OK?

Mother: I'm never gentle like that.

Therapist 1: So you'd like nurturing, touch, concern about how you felt.

Mother: Well, if I'd put my hand on your shoulder, you would have knocked it off.

Daughter: Only if you gave me that look.

Therapist 2: Show your mother what she's doing.

Daughter: (imitates mother)

Therapist 1: What does the look say?

Daughter: It says she's all happy, and I'm mad. It's like you don't even care about my feelings.

Mother: But I did care about how you felt.

In this segment, we supported Ansley's request for more sensitive and responsible parental treatment and facilitated her mother's consideration of her claims. At the same time, mother and daughter were encouraged to communicate with each other more effectively (e.g., having Ansley model what she wanted) at a transactional level. The dialogue, however, began to lapse into another power struggle, prompting the therapists in the next sequence to return to the problem of unfair and hurtful family dynamics.

Therapist 2: I think Lori's earlier comments may be important. There's a long history of Ansley's feeling forgotten. So there's this incident, the library incident ...

Mother: So it gets blown up.

Therapist 2: That's right. It's magnified by a history of feeling forgotten and left out.

Mother: And I can accept that. I can understand that because I've been in the long, dark night of the soul. But my selfish feeling right now is: Are these two kids going to make me a trained dog, jumping through hoops of fire?

Therapist 2: I think the first step is for you, Anne, to simply acknowledge the fact that you weren't available to them for the reasons we've talked about. And that you appreciate that they helped take care of you and the family.

Mother: And you know I tried all along during those bad years to talk to them and say, "You know, I'm really sorry;

I know this is not the way it's supposed to be." I hope that you both remember ... I was aware that I was being a real shit.

Therapist 2: *(to the children)* Do you remember your mother talking about these things?

Daughter: *(shaking her head no)*

Therapist 2: You may not; you were small.

Therapist 2: Do you remember, Brett?

Son: Yes, I remember.

Therapist 2: What do you remember?

Son: Just what she said, but I was running out the door.

Therapist 1: *(speaking to mother)* When we talk about this, I want you to understand that we appreciate the pressure you were under, having two children, a husband who abandoned you, physical problems ...

Mother: Well, it hurts, but we want it all up and out because I want to go on with life.

Therapist 1: It's obvious that your kids have an attachment to you; they're beautiful kids who care about you, and you care about them. There's a lot of strength in this family. But there's also fallout from your years of depression.

In keeping with a multidirected stance, note the support and credit that the mother was given here to help her confront long-standing inequities in her relationship with her children and to recognize that she too was victimized.

Mother: It's too important that they really don't get hung up on the past; it's hard enough these days.

Therapist 2: That's why we're focusing on the past; past resentments are playing a role.

Mother: Yes.

Therapist 2: Ansley, you said that you don't remember your mom's talking to you about her inability to do as much as she would have liked as a mother.

Daughter: (again shaking her head no with tears in her eyes)

Therapist 2: (speaking to mother) Maybe you could talk to her about that now.

Mother: Remember that you were my greatest comfort. I remember when I grieved after the death and funeral [of my mother] ... and I'm the kind of person who grieves very openly and loudly. We had gone into a fabric store at Christmastime, and I just fell apart. So Ansley came to me and sat outside with me and took care of me. Another time when I was running a tub of water for the children, it hit me again. And I remember little six-year-old Ansley put her arms around me and had just the right things to say.... I've always appreciated her strength.

Therapist 2: What are you thinking, Ansley?

Daughter: I didn't know she felt that way about me.

Therapist 1: As I listen to you talk about this, Anne, I'm keenly aware that both of your children helped you. Ansley was obviously nurturing. How did Brett help you?

Mother: Ansley was old and wise and there.

Therapist 1: And Brett?

Mother: He was my big man. I've probably always asked him for too much. (to Brett) It was a natural thing for you to fix the toilet, fix the seat, a natural thing for you to pick up the cords and the ends I got for the cords. You could do that when you were just a little boy.

Son: She was afraid she was going to get shocked.

Mother: He didn't have a daddy there.... I think it kind of got screwed up in a way because probably to him it's like I was looking to him like the head of the household to do those little things that husbands would do. I wanted it to be just a natural thing. Yet, it was a lot

of things. It wasn't just fixing the cords. I wanted it
to be natural. He had to learn how to do them some-
how, sometime, from someone.

We learned that the children were, indeed, parentified: Ansley
expressively and Brett instrumentally, in large measure. Although
it is not obvious in the transcript, Ansley was touched by her
mother's acknowledgment of her devotion and caring. Upon hearing further confirmation of his parentified role, Brett seized the
opportunity to express his own grievances and wishes.

Son:	I've heard this! You always want me to be learning stuff. I've already learned a lot and can do it by my-self, like camping. She will not let me go camping!
Therapist 2:	So you're in a bind. On the one hand, you're her big man …
Therapist 1:	But you don't get the benefits that go along with it.
Son:	I wasn't a little kid long enough. I had to grow up too fast, and now she doesn't want to let go of me. In two and a half years, I'll be gone, taking care of myself [at college].
Therapist 1:	Are you preparing your mom for leaving home?
Mother:	It sounds like it.
Son:	I keep on telling her.
Therapist 1:	So you hope she'll be ready.
Son:	I don't want to have to send her to a mental ward.
Therapist 2:	You're afraid your mother will fall apart when you leave.
Son:	Yeah! She can't program a VCR. All this stuff lying around the house that needs to be fixed. She can't fix it.
Therapist 1:	What would convince you that your mom is ready?
Son:	Let me go camping.

Therapist 2: You feel like you've earned the right. You've paid your dues.

Mother: He's still a boy.

Therapist 2: But he's been the man of your house. Do you see the dilemma here?

Mother: Yes. But what if a catastrophe happens?

Therapist 2: I think it would be helpful to let Brett know whether your concern about camping has to do with you and your fears of being apart from him or whether your concern is for him and his safety.

Son: It's more for you, and I've tried to tell you that.

Mother: No, my concern is for him. And the mothers of the other two boys have said no.

Therapist 1: That's a normal motherly response. But like Ansley, Brett is not used to the idea of your responding like other mothers.

Mother: He doesn't know how much I worry about him when I do let him go places. I'm always on the phone with Sally [the mother of one of Brett's friends].

Therapist 2: Do you think your mother has a right to set limits?

Son: Yes.

Mother: You do?

Son: Some of the things you let me get away with are ridiculous.

Therapist 1: So you want limits.

Son: Yes!

Therapist 1: But when your mother does set limits, you give her a bunch of crap. Does she fall apart and sometimes give in?

Son: Eventually. If she would hold out longer.... I realize that after it's over, she's right.

Therapist 1: You want a normal interaction, where you give your mom a bunch of crap, and she sticks to her limit.

Son: Yeah, I hold out longer than she does.

Therapist 2: It's your way of making things normal. If your mother holds out, it shows you that she really does care.

Son: If I can convince her to do something, imagine what someone else can do after I leave.

Therapist 2: So in your own way, you're also still taking care of your mother.

The issue of filial respect and limits that prompted this mother to seek family therapy can now be seen in a new light. On the one hand, the mother has needed her son to grow up quickly to be the "man of the house"; on the other, she is reluctant to accord him the perquisites that attend such a position, particularly at this point when she is beginning to realize that she has missed his childhood. Her reluctance, of course, is understandable but unfair if based largely on her needs rather than Brett's. Simply to have supported the mother's limits without considering the larger ethical context would have been a mistake.

We also discovered that Brett's pushing limits with his mother represented (1) an attempt to elicit a normal parental response; (2) consistent with his parentified role, concern that if she were unable to protect herself from his manipulations, then she would be vulnerable to the manipulations of others; and, relatedly, (3) preparation for his leaving home.

Therapist 1: Is this news to you, Anne?

Mother: Yes, it is news to me that he's worried about what will happen to me after he leaves. That he thinks I can't get along by myself in the world. You know, that's kind of really hurtful.

Therapist 2: How so?

Mother: To think that either one of them thinks that. I've felt for a long time that both of them thought of me as a nothing, that I'm worthless. To think that I can't get along ...

Therapist 2: Not at all. Because of your worth, they have invested so much of themselves in taking care of you.

Therapist 1: You're very meaningful to them.

Son: Yeah, I'd hate to see my childhood go to waste.

Therapist 2: *(speaking to Brett)* You've invested a lot.

Mother: *(speaking to Ansley)* Do you think your childhood has been a waste? You've invested a lot too.

Therapist 1: *(speaking to Ansley)* You don't want to hurt her.

Therapist 2: Are you afraid you've hurt your mother?

Daughter: *(shrugs her shoulders)*

Therapist 2: It's different for you to be talking to each other this way. You argue about camping and about being picked up at the library, while underneath are all of these other issues that are not being addressed.

Mother: Together, we haven't been a functional unit. I want us to be a nice unit.

Therapist 2: You have been a unit. That's what I'm hearing loud and clear. When you weren't able to mother the way you wanted, the kids filled in. Things are changing now.... the kids would not be able to say what they've said today and to share their feelings with you, if they didn't have some sense that you're ready to hear them.

Therapist 1: The fact that they're able to do this with you means that they know there's something in you that can handle it.

Mother: Well, I think I'm made of pretty tough stuff.

We again commented on the mother's redeeming qualities at a point in the session when questions were raised about her parenting, for example, the "news" of her children's concerns about her ability to take care of herself. Note, also, that rather than interpret the projective significance of the mother's assertion that Brett and Ansley regard her as a "nothing," we were simply supportive. The children too needed our support. For example, we addressed their feelings of disloyalty and fears of having hurt their mother in the session.

Processing relational imbalances in this family early in therapy prepared them, not only for deeper consideration of inequities in their system, including the mother's relationship with her own parents, but also for facilitation of clearer boundaries and communication. A few sessions later, for example, the children spontaneously expressed concern about their disrespectful behavior toward their mother. At the same time, Anne began to take on more appropriate parental responsibilities.

Negotiating Emergent Issues

In the course of joining, evaluating, and addressing relational imbalances in the families of parentified children, pressing issues related to destructive parentification may surface, demanding immediate attention. These often include parent-child and sibling incest, neglect, physical abuse within the spousal, parental, or sibling subsystems, addictive disorders, and other problems (e.g., physical disability, financial crisis).

It was necessary, for example, to help Jenny's mother feed her children and protect herself from her boyfriend's violent behavior. These "primitive family" interventions, as Clark and his colleagues (1982) refer to them, take priority. It is unrealistic to expect family members to dialogue about relational imbalances when they are hungry or consumed with fear for their physical safety.

Yet it is often possible, from a multilevel systemic perspective, to handle emergent issues in such a way as to promote growth in other areas. Rather than merely provide Jenny's mother with food stamps, for instance, we taught her how to obtain such assistance, thus facilitating her ecological competence. Helping alcoholic parents to join AA and obtain a sponsor not only addresses their addictive disorder at an individual level but also expands their social support network.

Middle Phase

Restoring Parental Accountability

Central to the middle phase of therapy are interventions to help parents assume more appropriate responsibilities. Effective parenting is a multifaceted undertaking, involving such emotional, cognitive, transactional, and existential-ethical processes as self-differentiation, perspective-taking, understanding, communication, authenticity, caring, commitment, fairness, and trustworthiness.

It is little wonder that boundary-marking operations at a familial level are ineffective in many cases. With parentifying parents, we find that their appreciation of generational boundaries and, more fundamentally, of their children's personages is frequently limited by profound neediness, depression, isolation, stress, narcissism, destructive entitlement, and general socioemotional, cognitive, and moral immaturity.

For example, in the fourth session with Anne and her children, Brett tentatively informed his mother that he was uncomfortable in being treated by her as an "equal." In particular, he did not like her talking to him about "30-year-old stuff." She retorted: "And I don't like hearing hours of your 15-year-old stuff.... Who am I supposed to talk to? There are no other adults at home."

Lecturing parents about the asymmetrical nature of parent-child relationships typically contributes little to what they already know, at least on the surface. However, the therapist must not assume that such knowledge is within everyone's repertoire. One parent of a parentified youngster finally said to us in frustration, "Just tell me what I'm supposed to do, because I don't know" (Jurkovic, Jessee, & Goglia, 1991, p. 308). Her ability to act more responsibly, however, depended on more than our direct guidance. Like Anne, she required help in developing a more empathic and cognitively sophisticated view of her child as a developing person in need of parenting (cf. Newberger, 1980).

One way of fostering such a perspective is to sensitize parents to what their children experience as a result of their parentified role (Boszormenyi-Nagy & Krasner, 1986). Parents are typically unaware of their children's suffering. Once they understand, their motivation to change often increases. Anne, for example, was distressed upon learning of Brett's inner experience when she confided in him about adult matters. At those times, he thought about running away, saddened that she treated him like a "husband" rather than a "son."

As illustrated earlier in our work with Brett and Ansley, it is also essential to help parents acknowledge their children's contributions to the family. Acknowledgment not only helps balance the ledger of relational burdens and benefits from an ethical perspective but also psychologically affirms their existence. As such, it represents a healthy parental response, supporting the youngster's true rather than false self (see Bacal, 1989).

Awareness of the impact of parentification on children and of the importance of acknowledgment, however, is usually not sufficient to maintain more responsible parental behavior on a consistent basis, unless parents find other sources of support. In many cases, the therapist assumes the role previously held by the parentified child, particularly early in the treatment process. As therapy proceeds, parents can be encouraged to access or develop natural support systems through a variety of interventions designed to help them reconnect with their family of origin, to acquire social skills, to establish friendships, to resolve marital or relationship problems, to find gainful employment, or to join self-help groups and other organizations (e.g., church).

We noted in an earlier chapter that through their lack of awareness or interdiction of the parentification process, nonparentifying parents also play a pivotal role in the maintenance of destructive parentification. Thus, they must also be held accountable and encouraged to take on appropriate parental responsibilities. Reasons for their underinvolvement can often be found in unresolved family-of-origin processes as well as in marital dysfunction.

As parents attempt to resolve their marital differences, which often results in an increase in conflict, the parentified youngster may continue to be triangulated into their relationship. Even though parental figures learn in the course of therapy to resist handling their conflicts in this way, parentified children have difficulty relinquishing their mediating role. Parents should be taught ethically to acknowledge their children's ongoing efforts to help, but also at a transactional level to draw a boundary.

Addressing family-of-origin issues is particularly critical to help parentifying parents work through possible destructive entitlement. We have found that if such issues are not addressed, the effects of most, if not all, of the interventions suggested here will not last. Until relational imbalances in Barbara's and Anne's families of origin were considered, neither was able fully to release their children from their destructively parentified roles.

As parents' support systems grow and as their sense of destructive entitlement diminishes, they can also be encouraged to become involved, if they are not already, in their children's schooling (e.g., by attending parent-teacher conferences, participating in other school functions, and taking an interest in their youngsters' homework). Helping them to monitor their children's friends and peer activities is another intervention that contributes importantly to responsible and trustworthy parenting. Although children, particularly adolescents, often resist such parental behavior, the fact of their parents' concern is not lost on them. Recall that Brett was chagrined by his mother's inability to set limits.

Empowering Parentified Children

It is essential, in the process of helping the grown-ups in the parentifying family system, that the children are not ignored. *Disregarding them in the treatment setting subtly re-creates destructive aspects of parentification.* Certainly, crediting their contributions and challenging implicit or explicit efforts by parents to hold them responsible for their families' problems are useful, particularly early in therapy. Many parentified children also benefit from being educated about their parents' difficulties. For example, information about the nature of their mother's long-standing depression helped Ansley and Brett to appreciate that her parenting failures were neither their fault nor purposive on her part.

In the middle phase, when loyalty and trust issues are less toxic, the children can also be taught about the parentification process and prompted to express feelings and needs (e.g., anger, sadness, dependency) and to assert their claims for fairer treatment (e.g., Brett's desire to be regarded as a "son" rather than a "husband"). However, after years of being encouraged to suppress or mislabel their thoughts and feelings, many parentified youngsters have difficulty identifying and expressing their inner experience and thus may need therapeutic assistance to do so. They frequently discover that they are emotionally depleted by their family's dependence on them. Thus, they may also need stress management training, an important part of which involves their resisting overextention of themselves and being assertive when they are asked to do too much or are triangulated into their parents' conflicts.

Of course, empowering parentified children in these ways without educating and involving their parents in the process sets them up for failure. Parental figures must be helped to listen to and to consider their children's concerns or, at a minimum, to give them permission to have feelings and thoughts, however unpleasant, upsetting, or different from their own. The latter further modulates the parentified child's loyalty conflicts. The ability to tolerate, not to mention actively consider, the inner lives and claims of one's children assumes a level of differentiation that many parents have not achieved.

Anne, for example, tended to confuse Ansley's and Brett's complaints about her parenting with the verbally abusive remarks that members of her family of origin showered on her as a child. Helping the children to state their feelings in a nonblaming fashion facilitated their mother's ability to respond to them nondefensively. For example, Ansley was taught to say, "It makes me angry when you don't get up in the morning to help me make breakfast." In response to these interventions, Brett and Ansley felt better understood and thus less victimized, even though Anne was unable to alter her behavior in many areas for months.

Helping Family Members Grieve Their Losses

As changes occur in therapy, family members become aware of the pain that the destructive parentification process helped them avoid. Parentifying parents, for example, are often faced, perhaps for the first time, with losses and privations that they experienced in their childhoods and, possibly, marriages. Many, moreover, realize that as a result of their parentifying behaviors, they did not really know their children as children. Anne's sense of loss along these lines contributed to her difficulties in allowing Ansley and Brett to exercise more independence as adolescents.

Parentified children also painfully confront lost aspects of their own childhoods, especially as they grow older. Brett speaks to this dynamic in the following excerpt:

Brett: I had to grow up too quickly. I always wanted to play sports ... but I couldn't because there was no one there who could take me to the practices or games.

Therapist 2: There's sadness in your voice.

Brett: *(beginning to cry)* Yeah.

Mother: He never had a chance to be expert at the things he wanted to do. When he got to high school, they chose their teams by who's the best. Brett had not really learned yet.

Therapist 2: Do you hear Brett's sadness? What I hear him saying at a deeper level is that he missed his childhood, and ...

Mother: *(interrupting)* And I want my little boy.

Brett: It's too late for that. I've come too far. There are only two years left [*before attending college out of state*].

Mother: I'd like to think that there's something we could do.

Brett: I'll be moving out of the house, a thousand miles away, taking care of myself ...

Mother: *(interrupting)* You'll still be my boy.

Therapist 2: Brett, I hear a part of you who wants to be her little boy and to have that experience. But another part is saying, "Look, Brett, you must get on with it; you've only two more years." I agree with you that you cannot go back and be two years old again. But there are things your mother can do now to help you feel more like her son, such as not talking to you about grown-up things that make you feel uncomfortable or simply putting her foot down and saying no to you at times. You may also need your mother to understand that you did miss important childhood experiences. That makes you sad.

Brett: She didn't plan it that way.

Therapist 2: No, she didn't. But it's OK to be sad about what happened. You experienced a lot of loss.

Mother: We've talked about it. He rented the movie *The Sandlot* over the weekend. It's about kids playing baseball. Brett was sad and cried while he watched it. He watched it three times.... I tried to give him activities as a child.

Therapist 2: I think you did the best you could, Anne. What you could do now as Brett's mother is to hear your son's sadness and be there for him. I don't know if he'd accept a hug to let him know that you're with him, that you understand.

Brett: *(nodding affirmatively)*

Mother: I've probably kissed him thousands of times over the years ...

Brett: Not kisses.

Therapist 2: How about a hug?

Brett: I'd take that.

Like Brett, youngsters tend to discuss the losses they experienced as a result of their parentified role in terms of concrete activities and events, such as being unable to participate in sports. Although the fact of loss in the parentifying family system cannot be undone, family members can be encouraged, as we attempted to do with Brett and his mother, to acknowledge and process their losses and disappointments at multiple levels: (1) to provide a corrective emotional experience, (2) to support developing generational boundaries, and (3) to redress relational inequities.

Ending Phase

Fostering New Relational Possibilities

Indications that family members are genuinely striving to relate to one another in differentiated, caring, and just ways presage the ending of therapy. The path to termination, however, is fraught with obstacles. Perhaps most formidable is parentified children's fear of losing their attachment to parental figures, however distorted.

Jenny's TAT story reflected her concerns along these lines. It was helpful for Barbara to recognize her daughter's continuing need to take care of her in order to feel connected and valued, despite changes in their relationship. As Barbara increasingly met her own needs and those of her children and thus became more trustworthy as a parent, Jenny's compulsive need to caretake diminished. The basis of their attachment shifted. To facilitate this shift, we encouraged Barbara not only to assume appropriate responsibilities but also to engage in child-centered activities and play—both at home and in therapy sessions. Many parentified children and their parents lack recreational skills, and, to the extent that they do play or recreate together, it is typically on the parent's terms.

Even if issues pertaining to parental responsibility, relational imbalances, and attachment have been addressed, some children, especially those with a long history of parentification, continue to reject generational boundaries. Conventional boundary-marking interventions are needed at this point. For example, disgruntled about his mother's appropriate refusal to buy him an automobile, Brett said to her, "You know how I wanted you to say no; I didn't mean it about getting a car!" His unrelenting badgering of her about this issue, which in the past often persuaded her to give in, failed. We supported his mother in maintaining her limits and at the same time helped Brett to adopt more age-appropriate means of dealing with his wishes (e.g., delaying gratification, negotiating a compromise with his mother).

The siblings of parentified children, too, need extra help in adjusting to therapeutic changes in the family's caregiving system. Like their parentified brother or sister, whom they may have become attached to and dependent on, they may not know how to relate to their parents, who are emerging as responsible caregivers. It is thus unrealistic to expect them to look primarily to parental figures for parenting until later in the therapy process. Their parents, however, can be helped to accept this fact and to support the parentified member of the sibling subsystem as changes gradually take place (see Jurkovic, Jessee, & Goglia, 1991).

In many cases, because of circumstances that overwhelm the parental subsystem, the responsibilities of the parentified child are not readily transferable to parental figures. At a minimum, however, they can be redistributed throughout the sibling subsystem (Minuchin, 1974). Special attention must also be given to the younger members of the sibling subsystem. They may inherit caretaking responsibilities when their older parentified brothers and sisters leave home. The result is that they frequently are unable to separate. Their older siblings, therefore, may need to be recruited by the therapist to share the burden or to assist a younger brother or sister to de-role.

We recently invited one of the older sisters of a parentified young adult to a therapy session. She was fully aware of having precipitously stepped out of her parentified role upon leaving home, a source of consuming guilt for her, but had underestimated the burden with which she had saddled her youngest sibling. Her ongoing participation in therapy was essential in helping him to understand and change his role in the family and in other relationships. In the process, she also reworked the way she left home, rebalancing her relationship with her brother and dealing with her chronically depressed and alcoholic mother differently. Her guilt, in turn, abated.

Facilitating the Parentified Child's Socioemotional Growth

As relational patterns and ethics change in their families, parentified children are typically confronted with a void in both their personal and social development. As discussed in Chapters 2 and 3, their identities and interpersonal relationships have centered on their role as the family's caretaker. Thus, they may need therapeutic help to focus on their own needs and interests and to develop healthy peer relationships. These are challenging developmental tasks, however. The parentified child may avoid negotiating them by reverting to his or her overresponsible position in the family. As illustrated in our work with Jenny, parents can play a central role in facilitating their children's personal and social development. In many cases, individual and group therapy are useful. Teachers may also be enlisted to help, especially to foster healthier peer relations.

CONCLUSIONS

Having a working knowledge of the various levels of analysis that encompass ecosystemic and existential-ethical spheres of understanding allows the therapist to intervene into parentifying family systems in a refreshingly creative, effective, and just fashion. Of course, many aspects of the larger system of the parentified youngster (e.g., state and federal policies regarding children and families, racial discrimination) are not amenable to therapeutic input. As discussed in Chapter 9, however, efforts to effect molar changes through sociopolitical and community intervention strategies are equally important in reducing and preventing the destructive parentification of children. Further clinical evidence of the power of a combined ecological and ethical approach to extremely serious forms of this problem is presented next.

CHAPTER 6

Breaking the Deadlock:
The Case of Jamie

J amie and her family presented one of the most ruinous and vex-
ing cases of parentification that we have encountered. A few
months prior to her 16th birthday, she was referred to the juvenile
court for soliciting sex. She also used heroin and other drugs and
had a long history of acting in a parentified role within her family.
The nurse at the hospital where she had received an abortion earlier in the year likened Jamie's physical condition to that of a "50-
year-old in poor health."

Not only was her mother actively supporting her parentified
role and other self-destructive behaviors, but so were her boyfriend,
her juvenile probation officer, and an older consort, her "sugar
daddy," as Jamie occasionally referred to him. As often happens in
work with difficult families, however, these dynamics did not surface until our initial efforts to facilitate change failed.

Time was of the essence. Along with the immediate dangers of
her substance abuse and other problematic behaviors, Jamie was

within seven months of turning 17 and, thus, of falling outside the jurisdiction of the juvenile court. Her boyfriend was also scheduled to be released from prison within a week. Continued complicit behavior and ineffective action on the part of Jamie's family and associates, as well as those charged with helping her, had lethal implications. This chapter illustrates how key members of a destructively parentified youngster's ecosystem can be mobilized quickly to become a force for responsible action.

BACKGROUND

Jamie's father died when she was 18 months old, leaving her alone with her mother, Carol. Although her marriage had been riven by alcoholism, unemployment, and perpetual bickering, Carol was devastated by her husband's death. Having escaped her abusive family by marrying him, she had never been on her own. Carol plummeted into an incapacitating depression for the next several years, presenting Jamie with yet another loss.

Carol recalled her daughter's valiant efforts to comfort her: bringing her food, cuddling with her, and generally attempting to cheer her up. Although they constituted a reversal of roles, Jamie's caretaking activities served to maintain ties with her mother. Indeed, Carol's emotional survival depended on their contact just as much as Jamie's. They became extremely enmeshed, sharing the same bed initially and, over time, all of their thoughts and feelings. "We became best friends," Carol observed.

Jamie's world, however, dramatically changed again when she started attending school full time at the age of six. Both mother and daughter had difficulty managing the anxiety of being apart. Not coincidentally, Carol found another man at that point. Within three months of meeting John, a construction worker, she married him. Their relationship was extremely intense the first year, but it quickly deteriorated as they confronted the problems of blending their families.

Married previously, John had a six-year-old boy. Although John's contacts with him were irregular, Carol found them threatening. She feared that her husband might return to his former wife, who frequently called him. On the other hand, John resented Jamie's protestations about having to give up sleeping with her mother and about other changes in her maternal relationship. He wanted Carol to draw firmer boundaries. Jamie felt painfully and unfairly displaced. Carol, however, did not notice. She thought she had done her daughter a favor by giving her a "father."

The unplanned birth of Jamie's half-sister a few years later proved to be an insuperable problem. Carol had resisted her husband's demands that she have an abortion. Having lost his job and confidence in his relationship with his wife, John did not want a child at that time. He withdrew for long periods. In response, Carol turned all of her attention to the new baby, Jessie.

Jamie soon became more of a co-parent with her mother than John, which helped satisfy her need for maternal contact. Angry and hurt, John began to look to Jamie for affection. One night Carol discovered him fondling Jamie while she ostensibly slept. Carol angrily threatened to call the police. To her surprise, John precipitously left and never had any more contact with the family. Carol's depression about his leaving overshadowed any concern about her daughter's emotional needs.

Jamie once more came to her mother's aid, emotionally supporting her and continuing to help raise Jessie. Jamie's jealousy of the mothering that her half-sister received, however, exacerbated her underlying feelings of loss. During her pubescent years, she began drifting toward an older group of students in the inner-city school that she attended. They were using drugs, skipping classes, and engaging in other socially marginal behaviors.

Jamie became sexually active by the age of 13. The next year one of her friends, a 17-year-old, persuaded Jamie to join her in a sexual liaison for which they were paid. The two of them continued to prostitute themselves on occasion. Jamie also became involved with a 19-year-old who introduced her to drugs, including heroin. She regarded him as her boyfriend, even after he was imprisoned for drug dealing. It was his baby that Jamie aborted early in her 15th year.

Despite the extent of Jamie's extrafamilial activities, she maintained her parentified role at home. For example, she used the money that she earned sexually to ease her mother's financial burdens. Jamie also often entertained her mother with stories about her various exploits, although she was careful not to reveal the nature of all of her sexual behaviors.

During this period, Jamie's mother met another man, Mr. Frank, who, curiously, befriended her. Had we not introduced ourselves to him in the waiting room of the juvenile court before one of Jamie's hearings, we may never have known of him. The family had said nothing to us about this individual. A businessman who was investing in the restoration of older homes in Carol's neighborhood, he began visiting her regularly. He also helped her financially.

Mr. Frank took an interest in Jamie as well, often giving her money, which she used to buy drugs, and even taking her on business trips. He introduced her as his "daughter." Jamie denied any sexual activity between them, although we were not convinced. It is likely that Carol neither objected to Jamie's relationship with this man nor wanted anyone to know about him, because of her financial and growing emotional dependence on him.

Jamie was referred to us after she violated her probation. She was picked up for soliciting again. Although dubious about Jamie's motivation for treatment, her probation officer added "counseling" as a condition of Jamie's continued probation. A co-therapy team[1] worked with Jamie and her family under my supervision.

At the outset of our work with Jamie and her family, which began about a month before her hearing for violating probation, we were unaware of much of the data that have been discussed so far. Both Jamie and her mother volunteered little information during the initial diagnostic interview. Our early contacts with the probation officer were also uninformative, even though, as we discovered later, she knew about the destructive nature of Jamie's behavior.

Regarding the second soliciting charge, Jamie proclaimed her innocence. "I was just hanging out; I wasn't doing anything wrong," she said. Her mother concurred, adding that she also did not believe that her daughter was guilty of the first charge. That the two of them were extremely enmeshed quickly became apparent.

We were encouraged at this time by Jamie's desire to work. Prompted by our suggestion, her mother, who was not employed at the time, helped her daughter find a job. These developments seemed healthy, possibly laying the groundwork for greater differ-

---

[1]Michael O'Shea, Ph.D., and Marsha Weiss, Ph.D. We also sought the consultation of Carrell Dammann, Ph.D. A portion of our work together on this case is referred to in Jurkovic (1984).

entiation between the two of them. We became concerned, however, upon learning of Jamie's interest in working to help her mother financially—our first clue regarding her parentified status. When she was accused of stealing needle syringes from her place of work, an inner-city health clinic, we also were presented with evidence of a possible addictive disorder. Within that same week, we met Mr. Frank, which further heightened our concern about Jamie's welfare.

INTERVENTION

It rapidly became obvious that we needed to revamp our treatment plan. Thus, we scheduled an emergency meeting with Jamie's probation officer, Ms. Banion, to obtain more information and to coordinate our efforts with those of the court. After we presented her with our concerns about Jamie's family and drug use, she smiled and said, "Don't try to change Jamie; just enjoy her, because there's nothing we can do before she turns 17. Then she'll be out of our hands." She proceeded to tell us cavalierly about Jamie's entertaining qualities, as well as her suspicions about her addiction to heroin and other problematic behaviors (e.g., her abortion and prostitution). She also informed us that she had given some thought to a residential drug rehabilitation program but abandoned the idea in view of the intense competition for a limited number of treatment slots.

My past dealings with this probation officer did not comport with her supervision of this case. She had been instrumental in helping us develop the family treatment program that served Jamie and other court-involved youngsters. Our work with her on previous cases had also gone well. Giving her the benefit of the doubt, I wondered if her gross denial of Jamie's situation stemmed from unresolved issues that this probationer stirred in her or from other external factors. Therefore, although I found her comments unconscionable, I simply said to her, "You may enjoy Jamie now, but I think her days are numbered. In view of the dangerousness of her behaviors, I doubt that she'll be alive on her 17th birthday."

As if told her own death were imminent, she suddenly sobered and asked what she could do. We said that we needed her help in (1) breaking through the mother's denial, (2) confronting Mr. Frank,

(3) mobilizing other resources in Jamie's life (e.g., the minister of the church where her mother was a member), and (4) developing a new course of action, particularly in relation to Jamie's substance abuse and prostitution.

We also suggested that much of this might be accomplished in a network meeting with Jamie's mother, Mr. Frank, and the minister, but questioned how these people could be persuaded to attend. "I'll subpoena them," Ms. Banion said. She unexpectedly took charge, asserting that she would not only call the meeting within 48 hours but would also conduct it with our help.

When we arrived at the meeting, everybody was there, including Mr. Frank in a dark, three-piece suit. Ms. Banion had also invited her clinical supervisor, as well as the nurse at the hospital who had taken a special interest in Jamie at the time of her abortion, and a volunteer from the Big Brother/Big Sister program who had worked with Jamie. After introducing all present and making a few orienting comments, Ms. Banion asked us to begin.

We briefly discussed our futile attempts to help Jamie and her family, our discovery of her likely drug dependence, and our concerns about her sexual behavior. We also alluded to Jamie's parentification in such a way as not to alienate her mother but yet to drawn attention to her desperate need for responsible parenting. We added that unless her mother's needs for support and guidance were appropriately met, perhaps partially through the church, Jamie would remain trapped in her destructively parentified role. To ensure that our comments did not elude Mr. Frank, we wondered aloud about the nature of his involvement with Jamie and her family.

Our remarks also included genuine reservations about whether Jamie could be helped, particularly on an outpatient basis. Placement in a drug rehabilitation program might begin to change the course of Jamie's life, we observed, but only if her family and friends were supportive. As we had communicated to Ms. Banion a few days earlier, we also shared our fears about the lethality of her behaviors. We suggested to everyone present that, at a minimum, if they cared about Jamie, they should express their love, appreciation, and concern for her now, not at her funeral.

Ms. Banion essentially echoed our remarks, emphasizing her concern about Jamie's high-risk behaviors. Ms. Banion's supervisor solemnly spoke next. She thought that both we and the probation officer had underestimated the gravity of the situation, comparing Jamie's behavioral profile to that of another probationer who had died recently of an overdose. She worried that Jamie could suffer the same fate within the next two weeks. We could not have scripted her incisive remarks any better.

Proceeding around the table, it was the nurse's turn to speak. In light of her earlier involvement with Jamie, she was not surprised by what was being said. She too had worried about drug abuse and regretted that she had not raised the issue during Jamie's hospital visit. She volunteered to help in any way possible.

Mr. Frank then addressed the group. To his credit, he seemed alarmed. He confirmed that Jamie was using drugs extensively. According to his account, neither Jamie nor Carol heeded his warnings about the dangers involved. He also underscored the fact that Jamie's mother needed help—not just financial, but also emotional. Sitting next to him with her head down, Carol simply nodded. When asked to comment, she was at a loss for words except to say that she did not know what to do.

At that, the minister exploded, forcefully pushing his chair away from the table and exclaiming:

> I'm in the business of miracles; all this gloom and doom is crap! There's no reason why Jamie can't stay home and get the help she needs. I've known her mama a long time; she's a good woman.

We challenged the minister, saying that it sounded as if he too were denying the seriousness of Jamie's problems. He countered, "Maybe I am; I just don't know about this drug rehab."

We then suggested another meeting in a few days with all the parties present plus Jamie. It was our thought that at the next meeting Jamie could be informed of everyone's concerns and presented with a plan of action. Ms. Banion objected. She announced that the meeting would be held tomorrow, because Jamie could be dead within a matter of days. It was hard to believe that this was the same person who earlier in the week advised us merely to "enjoy" Jamie.

Less than 24 hours later, all of us gathered again at the juvenile court. Also in attendance was Jamie, who reluctantly sat in a chair next to her mother. As Ms. Banion was calling the meeting to order, the minister insistently interrupted, saying that he had something to say. In view of his reactivity the day before, we were concerned that he might subvert the proceedings. His input pleasantly surprised us, however.

Looking directly at us, he talked about how displeased he had been with the initial conference, feeling that many participants had not only overreacted to Jamie's problems but had also suggested untenable treatment responses. He said that, as a result, he had called his own meeting later that night with Carol, the nurse, and Mr. Frank. He had wanted to explore other options with them in preparation for the second meeting. After considerable deliberation, he said they had consensually agreed that Jamie's drug problem was "deadly" serious and warranted residential treatment.

Ms. Banion exclaimed that she and her supervisor had arrived at the same conclusion within 10 minutes after the first meeting. Before leaving work, she said, they had "pulled a lot of strings" to find an opening for Jamie in a state-operated treatment facility. Ms. Banion then turned to Jamie, saying that she wanted what was best for her and could no longer passively watch her "go down the tubes." Everyone else followed suit.

Jamie's initial resistance appeared to soften with each expression of concern. She tentatively admitted that her use of drugs had "gotten out of hand," although she thought that she could overcome her habit on her own. Jamie's denial was immediately met with a spate of dissenting comments. She agreed to allow her mother, the minister, and the probation officer to escort her to the treatment facility immediately after the meeting.

FOLLOW-UP

Although the course of Jamie's treatment continued to be a challenging and sometimes frustrating one, including a serious relapse and a brief stay in detention, the interventions just described appeared to effect a qualitative shift in the treatment system and to initiate changes in her family environment. For example, Mr. Frank disappeared. Fortunately, the minister filled in, providing Carol and the family with ongoing support and guidance.

For several years after her 17th birthday, Jamie visited Ms. Banion on a regular basis. It appeared that she was less enmeshed with her mother and in better health. After completing high school, Jamie married, had a child, and worked part-time. According to her last report, she was staying "clean" and "out of trouble."

DISCUSSION

Our work with Jamie is instructive from an eco-ethical perspective. Perhaps foremost is that pathological parentification and related maladaptive behaviors are often supported by a series of interlocking systems, including treatment settings such as the juvenile court. Consequently, in the face of recalcitrant problems, it is often useful to expand the unit of analysis to include these other systems (Jurkovic & Berger, 1984). For example, although serendipitous, our discovery of the probation officer's role in Jamie's deteriorating behavior immediately pointed us in a new and more productive therapeutic direction.

Consideration should also be given to smaller units of analysis in refractory cases. Had we merely attempted to restructure and ethically rebalance the sociofamilial context of Jamie's problems without directly attending to her addictive behaviors, it is likely that our efforts would have failed. Indeed, they did initially.

On the other hand, just as variables that cause and maintain problem behavior can be found at multiple levels of analysis, so can resources and solutions. For example, as we discovered in our treatment of Jamie, the church and other spiritual groups are rich centers of support in the contexts of many families.

Even systems that are initially part of the problem can become a part of the solution if the therapist is able to draw attention to their unproductive and detrimental involvement while at the same time maintaining an alliance with them. We accomplished this with Jamie's probation officer by indirectly sensitizing her to the probable consequences of her irresponsible interactions with Jamie. She both readily assimilated our input and allied with us to confront what became our common concern.

In ethical terms, we challenged the probation officer and, later, others in Jamie's ecosystem to be accountable for their behavior (cf. Doherty, 1995). As illustrated in our review of the network meetings, it is not necessary to moralize, blame, or judge in order to appeal to people's sense of fairness, responsibility, and caring. Rather, creating a context in which they are confronted with the natural effects of their actions—for example, the possibility of Jamie's dying—is perhaps one of the most efficacious ways to induce a crisis of ethical proportions that demands new thinking and behavior.

When more than one helping agent is involved in the care of multiproblem families, including those with destructively parentified members, accountability is often diffused or avoided. For example, upon learning of the probation officer's initial attitude toward Jamie, we were discouraged. It seemed that neither Jamie's family nor the juvenile court was willing to act responsibly. Important representatives of both denied the gravity of her problems, as did Jamie herself. In fact, early in therapy she had complained to Ms. Banion about our concern regarding her behavior, which doubtless contributed to Ms. Banion's suggestion that we relax our therapeutic efforts. However, rather than give up, which, ipso facto, would have been an abdication of responsibility on our part, we continued to try to help Jamie, albeit in a qualitatively different fashion.

Our decision to remain accountable to Jamie and her family was pivotal. It empowered us to challenge others in her ecosystem to do the same. The fact that we had to make such a decision may raise questions in the minds of some about our professional commitment and ethicality. Is not accountability an assumed part of service delivery, they may ask, particularly on the part of an ethical therapist? I would argue that an assumption of this nature, like many assumptions, is a dangerous one. Deciding to act ethically is not a static event, but, rather an ongoing, self-reflexive process. *It is especially incumbent upon the "ethical" therapist to reexamine his or her own conduct and commitment when working with difficult, public-agency clients with whom therapeutic failure is both expected and easily shared with other helping agents.*

Overtly choosing to be accountable is not only ethical but also often therapeutic, inasmuch as it may galvanize others in the youngster's ecosystem to do the same. We visibly made this choice during our emergency meeting with the probation officer, which laid the groundwork for her asking how she could responsibly help. In the interest of working efficiently, and to guard against further diffusion of responsibility, we suggested that key figures in Jamie's life meet together in a context demanding accountability.

The inherent pressures within the group to account to one another and to the court had a propitious effect on the balance of fairness in this youngster's ecosystem.

CONCLUSIONS

Our work with Jamie was presented to demonstrate one way of generating more responsible actions on the part of family members, agency personnel, and extrafamilial figures who may collusively contribute to highly destructive forms of parentification and related self-injurious behaviors. We emphasize the social network interventions performed early in therapy that acted on both transactional and ethical processes within the larger context of the family. Such interventions can help create a workable therapeutic unit and access extrafamilial resources to break the systemic deadlock in which therapists often find themselves with clients like Jamie.

CHAPTER 7

Parentified Children Grown-Up: Treating Destructive Parentification in Couples

The preceding chapters in Part II of this book have focused on the evaluation and treatment of destructively parentified children and their families. As a result of experiences gained over the years in this area, my sensitivity to parentification in the current relationships and histories of individuals presenting for couple treatment has grown. The unique challenges of treating these couples is the subject of this chapter.

Imbalances in give-and-take are endemic to troubled couples. Individuals who are satisfied with their relationships typically fashion a mutually acceptable quid pro quo. This is not to say that they never assume parental and childlike roles vis-à-vis one another. Indeed, the ability to regress in one's relationship in the service of being soothed, protected, and nurtured or to adopt a parental stance to help structure and organize the maladaptive behaviors of a mate can be therapeutic (Kirschner & Kirschner, 1986). What typically distinguishes dysfunctional from functional relationships is the unilateral, pervasive, chronic, captivating, and ultimately unfair nature of such dynamics.

This chapter, after introducing a case that illustrates a parentifying-parentifed pattern in a couple, discusses various tasks characteristically associated with the beginning (identifying destructive parentification, creating a working therapeutic system), middle (balancing give-and-take, negotiating family–of–origin issues, developing a more secure attachment, addressing the children's needs, resolving sexual problems), and end (promoting trust, facilitating relational choice) of treatment.[1]

By intervening with couples from an ecological-ethical perspective, particularly early in their relationship, it is possible to interdict destructive parentification patterns in their families of origin, as well as in their current and future family relationships. Thus, as we have seen in treating families, couple work can serve as both a treatment and a preventive strategy, effectively interrupting the transgenerational transmission of pathological forms of parentification.

CASE EXAMPLE: CARL AND SHIRLEY

After 12 years of marriage, Carl insisted that his wife, Shirley, attend at least one more couple therapy session as a "last ditch effort" to save their relationship. Shirley passively agreed, although assuming that little could be done to change her feelings. They had seen several therapists in the past five years but had dropped out of each course of therapy after a few sessions. Although Carl had generally found the previous therapists helpful, Shirley complained that they did not offer any concrete suggestions to change their situation. "All they did was talk about how we felt and listen to us argue," she said.

Shirley did, however, remember a different experience with one of the therapists, who told her that she was a "classic co-dependent" and that she "shouldn't do so much" for her husband. Even though

---

[1]As noted in Chapter 5, the link between different therapeutic tasks and stages is not fixed but, rather, variable.

Shirley agreed, she did not know how to stop overfunctioning or what might happen if she did. Carl had misgivings about continuing treatment with this therapist.

My work with Shirley and Carl began inauspiciously as follows:

Therapist: So what brings you here today?

Shirley: (*shrugging her shoulders*) I just don't feel anything for Carl anymore.

Carl: (*obviously hurt and confused*) I don't get it, no offense, but I think there's something wrong with her. We haven't had sex in five years; it's like we don't have a marriage. I don't want us to break up. Look out there (pointing toward the waiting room). We have two beautiful kids. I don't know.

Shirley: I don't want a divorce either, but I guess I'm the one who brought it up.

Carl: Yes, you did! I've been thinking maybe you're right.

Shirley: I don't know what I want.

Therapist: It sounds like both of you agree that the marriage can't continue as it has in the past.

Shirley: I don't feel toward Carl like a wife should. I mean, he's a great guy. I do care about him. But he's more like a little brother than a husband. That isn't right.

Therapist: Little brother?

Shirley: Yes, I feel like I'm always having to take care of him. Like that problem with the telephone bill (*addressing Carl*). Why didn't you....

Carl: (*interrupting*) I didn't know you minded. We both know you're better at taking care of that kind of thing.

Shirley: You didn't even ask if I would do it. You just shoved it in my face and said here, take care of this.

Early in the initial session, signs of destructive parentification were apparent. Indeed, further questioning revealed that Shirley's excessive caretaking in her relationship with Carl mirrored similar behavior in her family of origin. After her parents' divorce when she was seven years of age, she assumed increasing responsibility for her younger brother. Her father, an alcoholic with whom she had sporadic contact before and after the divorce, paid child support irregularly, requiring her mother to work long hours to support the family.

Shirley's brother, who suffered from severe attention deficit and conduct problems, was physically and verbally abusive toward her and often difficult to control. On several occasions he attacked her with a knife, and once he sent her to the hospital with a concussion. No one helped her with him, including her mother. Shirley worked hard to gain her mother's approval by being a "good older sister" and co-parent, but her efforts were seldom recognized. Instead, her mother seemed to notice only when Shirley could not manage her brother's behavior.

For example, once his clothes caught on fire while he was playing with matches in his room. Shirley was in the kitchen preparing supper for the two of them. Screaming and aflame, he bolted from the house. Neighbors quickly came to his aid. Called home from work, Shirley's mother exploded, blaming her daughter for her brother's behavior and injuries and for embarrassing the family in the neighborhood. Both ashamed and guilt-ridden, Shirley withdrew for weeks. Her sense that her mother favored her brother also grew stronger.

After graduation from high school, Shirley continued to live at home while attending a community college in a neighboring town. At this point, she suffered from colitis. She met Carl, also a student at the college. They quickly became involved but, according to Shirley:

> He didn't want to commit. I wanted to have somebody in my life who was stable—a constant. All my life I've felt there's something wrong with me.

She hoped that Carl could correct that feeling, although in retrospect she realized that "everything was just a party to him." He was drinking a lot when they met and was not prepared to commit to a long-term relationship. Within a year, however, they married.

Both dropped out of college. Shirley worked as a secretary and Carl as a sacker in a major grocery store chain.

Observing that he had "no one to go to as a child," Carl said that he learned to keep people at a distance emotionally. Although the thought of marriage "frightened" him, he was infatuated with Shirley and enjoyed "all the fun" they had together "drinking and partying hard." "I really settled down," he said, "after our daughter was born." Carl quit drinking and vigorously pursued advancement on the job, working his way into a managerial position within five years.

Like Shirley's parents, Carl's parents divorced when he was seven years old. His father had abandoned him and his two older sisters and younger brother the previous year. No one in the family has seen him since; all presume that he is dead. Carl's last memory of him was of his arrest for writing bad checks. Carl described his relationships with the rest of the family as being disengaged as well. He physically resembles his father, which he thinks may explain his mother's alienation from him.

In retrospect, Shirley thought her relationship with Carl changed dramatically after their first child, Becky, was born. Although both were exhilarated about the birth and felt extremely close for a few months, Shirley became more and more upset about Carl's unavailability and irresponsibility. Despite Carl's increased commitment to his career and change in his drinking pattern, which pleased her, she found herself burdened with sole responsibility for their newborn.

Shirley also had to increase her time at work to help pay for their mounting bills, caused in part by Carl's "spending sprees." His tendency to "bounce checks" further added to Shirley's stress; she typically took care of them. "I have to or we'd lose our house," she said. Shirley complained, as well, about Carl's response to stress. For example, she observed that when he makes mistakes, he often pounds his head and acts helpless. Shirley noted, "I feel like I have to do all the thinking for him." Carl did perform housework, but usually angrily, complaining about Shirley's "sloppiness."

Shirley seldom voiced her discontent except when extremely frustrated, which Carl tended to handle by withdrawing for days. At one point, however, she was prepared to leave him, only to discover that she had accidentally become pregnant. The birth of their second child, Jimmy, further exacerbated the couple's problems.

Shirley felt that she could not leave Carl at that time. A co-worker recognized Shirley's stress and gave her the name of a therapist.

Interestingly, Carl also recalled feeling close to his wife after their daughter's birth. He did not realize that they had "real problems," however, until they stopped being physically intimate. "I don't get it," Carl asserted. "I was working hard to get promoted; maybe I haven't done as much as I should with the kids, but I wasn't drinking and I brought home a steady paycheck."

Carl also had a different view of their financial problems. He complained about Shirley's "loans" to her brother. Carl observed:

> She's always loaning him money. I doubt if he's paid back one tenth. What a loser. He's unemployed, uses drugs. Been divorced three times, been in jail. It's like her brother and mother are more important than her own family. She's constantly dealing with their problems. No wonder she's a basket case.

BEGINNING PHASE

In the initial stage of therapy with couples in which destructive parentification is a central dynamic, it is important (1) to identify the pattern of parentifying and parentified behaviors in their relationship and (2) to develop a working therapeutic system that is inclusive and fair.

Identifying Patterns of Destructive Parentification

Parameters

The following parameters are important to consider in evaluating the nature and destructiveness of parentification in couples:

1. *Unilateral or bilateral* (Do the partners typically assume the same posture: one parentifying and the other parentified? Or, does each enact a parentified role?)
2. *Instrumental and/or expressive* (Is their parentification pri-

marily instrumental or expressive? Or is it pervasive? That is, do they maintain their respective postures across both domains?)

3. *Chronic* (How long has the pattern characterized their relationship?)

4. *Captivating* (To what extent does the posture of each member represent a functional role, adopted perhaps in response to a crisis, or an ongoing source of personal identity that is enacted compulsively?)

5. *Fair* (Do the partners credit one another's contributions? Do they perceive that the other reciprocates caring? Is the nature of give-and-take in their relationship equitable?)

Concerning the last criterion, it is possible that a couple exhibiting a unilateral, pervasive, chronic, and captivating pattern of give-and-take may, nonetheless, regard their relationship as fair. Closer examination often reveals that one or both harbor thoughts and feelings and behave in ways suggestive of underlying problems. For example, they may not trust each other, display signs of depression and anxiety related to their relationship, suffer from sexual dysfunction, abuse substances, feel resentful, or occasionally explode and verbally or physically mistreat each other. They may be unable to recognize and/or confront the possibility that these problems reflect exploitation and injustice in their relationship because of an undefined sense of self, fear of abandonment, financial dependence, or loyalty to their families of origin. Moreover, because they were destructively parentified as children, many simply do not expect reciprocity. Their internal map of relationships contains only one-way streets.

Jeannie, who consulted me recently about how to handle the advances of a male colleague at work, had a vivid dream, a few days before our first session, of her husband being "held" by one of her friends. Their contact had less of a sexual flavor than of a nurturing one, "as if she were his parent," she observed. Upon saying that, Jeannie suddenly exclaimed: "That's me! I'm the one holding Dan. I'm always taking care of his feelings." When asked whether he reciprocated, she said, "Well, not really, but I don't need much." Her denial of inequities in her marital relationship became apparent upon further analysis of her dream. She recalled that as she watched Dan's being nurtured in the dream, she suddenly "snapped" and told him how "inappropriate" his behavior was. Jeannie also remembered feeling "jealous" of Dan, wishing that she could also be held.

Jeannie's dream helped her comprehend her highly anxious reaction to the flirtatious behaviors of her coworker. "I could easily have an affair with that man—not for the sex but for the attention," she said. Although confused, near the end of the first session she began to talk about how unhappy she felt in her marriage. In subsequent sessions with her husband, Jeannie discovered that she had been unable to confront him because of her long-standing parentified role in her marriage and in her family of origin.

Unilateral Parentification

The five defining properties of parentification in couples often cohere in one of two general ways to form a destructive pattern. The distinction between the two turns on the question of unilaterality. As illustrated in the case of Shirley and Carl, the most obvious pattern involves unilateral parentification, characterized by parentlike functioning by one member of the couple and childlike functioning by the other. At their worst, these functional positions are also pervasive (i.e., both instrumental and expressive), chronic, captivating, and unfair.

The complementary and self-perpetuating dynamics of such couples have been referred to by other theorists as "overfunctioning-underfunctioning" (Bowen, 1978; Guerin, Fay, Burden, & Kautto, 1987), "rescue-indulgent" (Crandall, 1976), "parental-childlike" (Sager, 1981), "co-dependent" (Whitfield, 1991), and "masochistic-narcissistic" (Glickauf-Hughes, 1994).

The presenting complaints and underlying problems of couples who exhibit a destructively unilateral form of parentification are varied, although frequently the parentified member exhibits internalizing symptoms (e.g., depression, anxiety, stress, somatization, self-defeating behaviors), and the parentifier externalizing symptoms (substance abuse, attention deficit, narcissistic traits, and antisocial behaviors, including battering).

One or both partners may also engage in extramarital affairs, although for different reasons. Affairs for the parentifying member often reflect self-indulgent and narcissistic tendencies. One husband dismissed his frequent one-night stands as his way of "having fun" and had little expectation that his extremely loyal and parentified wife would leave him. This pattern also typifies relationships involving spousal/partner abuse (Cotroneo, 1987). In many cases, however, the underfunctioning mate who has become dissatisfied with his or her role may be seeking a more adultlike or mature relationship.

Overfunctioners, on the other hand, are vulnerable to advances by others who promise to attend to their needs in ways that their partners (and perhaps parental figures in the past) have not. This was the case for Jeannie, discussed earlier. Extramarital relationships also allow these individuals to express their hurt and anger to a third party rather than directly to their partners.

Moreover, extramarital affairs of either partner may stem from latent resentment about imbalances in the couple's relationship and long-standing destructive entitlement rooted in the person's family of origin. A conspicuous lack of remorse or guilt often points to such dynamics. One destructively parentified woman, who unexpectedly announced in couple therapy that she had had an affair recently, said to the therapist, "Now maybe he understands how mad I've been at him all these years."

Bilateral Parentification

The other major, although less obvious, pattern of parentification in couples that can assume pathological proportions is bilateral in nature. That is, both partners are excessively self-sacrificing and responsible, but also secretly wanting caretaking. They often vie for who is going to be the parent in the relationship. These "parent-parent partnerships," as Sager (1981) refers to them, may resemble a mature, egalitarian relationship. However, they are inherently unstable, often staid and fraught with boredom.

In the early phase of treatment, both members of one bilaterally parentified-parentifying couple spoke in very measured tones, were overpolite, and compulsively read self-help books on marriage between sessions. They constantly traded tips about how the other could "grow" and realize his or her full potential as an individual and a marital partner. Initially denying my interpretation that their helpful advice to each other might also be a request for "the something" missing in their relationship, which had brought them into therapy, they both eventually acknowledged deep-seated hurts and resentments.

Bilateral parentification in many couples is supported by each partner's (1) unconscious expectation that the other compensate him or her for the previous generation's neglect, yet (2) sense of limitless responsibility for the other's needs, thus perpetuating the cycle of parentification (Crandall, 1976, 1981). Crandall (1976) refers to the first dynamic, which is also captured by Boszormenyi-Nagy and Krasner's (1986) construct of destructive entitlement, as "psychic starvation continuity." Both members of the couple expect their spouses to meet their needs in the same way that they as children helped meet their parents' needs. Acting on their starving mates' demands results in the second dynamic, labeled by Crandall as "nurturant futility." Ironically, as he points out, they are never in a psychic position to receive nurturance, because of their obsessive focus on the partner's pain and needs. Like the husband and wife in O. Henry's (1906/1995) story "The Gift of the Magi," they are unable to benefit from each other's heroic sacrifices.

Often, bilateral parentification appears unilateral in nature, with one spouse regularly overindulging the other. Closer inspection, however, may reveal compulsive caregiving on the part of both. For example, a repetitive sequence frequently reflecting these dynamics involves the "seesawing" of moods: when one is up, the other is down. John and Patty demonstrated this pattern. When Patty felt better, John became depressed. She helped him until his mood lifted, at which point her mood predictably spiraled downward again. He, in turn, extended himself for her. Both explained in therapy, however, that they privately resented having to help the other but felt compelled to, which contributed to their depressive episodes. After several months of therapy, they tentatively risked not helping each other more than they wanted. Rather than becoming disconnected and consumed with guilt, as they had feared, they felt less imprisoned by their relationship and more attracted to each other. They also began giving to each other, spontaneously and authentically.

Individuals who are more parentified than their partners often subtly parentify their mates over time, which leads to bilateral parentification. Having internalized both aspects of the parentifying-parentified dynamic in their roles as parentified children, they may parentify their spouses in the same covert ways in which they were parentified in their families of origin. For instance, a woman whose mother solicited care through suicidal gestures and other insidious means displayed similar behaviors in her marriage. Her husband felt increasingly responsible for her welfare while continuing to depend on her compulsive caretaking.

Creating a Working Therapeutic System

One of the most important considerations at the outset of therapy concerns the unit of treatment. From an ecological and ethical perspective, it includes not only the couple as a whole but also each partner and their respective families of origin and, if applicable, their children and future generations. Although the therapist may not work directly with all available elements of the treatment system, it is incumbent upon him or her (1) to conceptualize their contribution to the couple's problems, (2) to be accountable for the impact of various interventions on them, and (3) to address spousal, parental, and transgenerational ledgers of fairness. For example, as discussed in greater detail later, I anticipated in my work with Shirley and Carl that as their relationship changed, their children would predictably react, particularly the oldest, who had become parentified. Thus, the children were included in the treatment at different points.

As discussed in Chapter 5, an inclusive definition of the unit of treatment also assumes a basic attitude and therapeutic approach involving multidirected partiality (Boszormenyi-Nagy & Krasner, 1986). The technical implications of multidirected partiality, especially during the early phase of treatment of parentification in couples, include (1) resistance to exclusively siding with one partner against the other and (2) discovering and crediting the contributions of each to the relationship, however seemingly inconsequential.

In the case of unilateral parentification, the parentified member characteristically appears to be more functional than his or her mate or, at least, attempts to persuade the therapist to such a view. Shirley, for example, graphically described her husband's incompetence in parenting their children. In addition to criticizing and blaming their partners directly, parentified individuals often present as long suffering and motivated by a strong desire to help. However, in the process of clarifying their good intentions, they may underscore in thinly veiled terms their mates' mulish and reprehensible traits, which, of course, are central to their marital problems.

Parentified individuals may also ask for individual sessions or telephone time between sessions to facilitate the therapist's understanding of their mate. Therapists who accede often find themselves in the next couple session in an untoward coalition. After meeting individually with Shirley, during which time she proffered an in-depth analysis of her husband's character, the following exchange occurred in his presence in a subsequent meeting:

Shirley: We have decided you haven't had any good father models and so that's why you have so much trouble with the kids.

Carl: We?

Shirley: Yes, Greg and I.

Therapist: You know, Shirley, I'm fully aware that you've spent untold time trying to understand and to help your husband. More time than he's probably aware.

Shirley: Yes, you're right.

Therapist: However, by saying "we," suggesting that you and I are in cahoots, like we're co-therapists analyzing your husband, isn't helpful. It'll drive him out of therapy and you, too, eventually.

Carl: Yes, who needs Greg, if you're going to be the shrink here. Maybe I should be paying you instead of him.

Shirley: Maybe you should.

Therapist: Shirley, I think you desperately want Carl to hear you, to appreciate that you may have ideas that might help him. If so, tell him that. You don't have to get me to agree with you, or to make it seem like I do, to have your own ideas.

Shirley: You're right, he doesn't listen to me. I don't know how to get him to listen to me.

Carl: Well, actually, you're probably right about that father business, but …

Shirley: (*interrupting*) I can't believe my ears.

Carl: But when you tell me what you think, it always seems
               like a put-down or like I have to agree with you.

In the event that the therapist becomes part of a coalition, as in
the preceding example, he or she must confront the situation, at
the same time remaining connected to both partners. In the process
of detriangulating myself, I was able to help Shirley and Carl to
begin to differentiate and thus to communicate more effectively
with each other.

Just as parentified, overfunctioning partners can induce therapists to side with them, so can their parentifying, underfunctioning
mates. The latter, for example, often attribute their couple problems to their partners' excessive worrying and controlling tendencies. One husband asked me to help him in his efforts to "chill
out" his wife. Another overdramatized his level of stress to avoid
any responsibility for his partner's marital dissatisfaction. At other
times, he unrealistically assumed complete responsibility.

It is critical that each partner feel understood by the therapist
but in a way that does not imply unidirected partiality. Even careful and judicious attempts at showing partiality, however, are frequently difficult for parentified-parentifying couples to tolerate.
Any display of empathy and understanding by the therapist for
one partner may be interpreted by the other as a snub (Boszormenyi-
Nagy & Krasner, 1986). Of course, this dynamic reflects the lack
of self-other differentiation that characterizes these couples. Thus,
it may be necessary early in therapy for the therapist to reassure
each partner that listening to one is not tantamount to indicting or
disregarding the other.

As Bowen (1978) reminds us, it is also extremely useful to assume that members of couples are operating within the same band
of differentiation. The blatant lack of differentiation of the underfunctioning member of a destructively parentifying-parentified
couple is thus probably a good index of the differentiation level of
his or her overfunctioning cohort. If couples stay in treatment long
enough, the heuristic value of this assumption usually becomes
apparent. For example, as Carl functioned more adaptively vis-à-
vis his children and his wife over the course of therapy, Shirley
became clinically depressed. No longer able to distract herself from

her own unresolved issues and incomplete sense of self by focusing on Carl's shortcomings, she was defenseless. Moreover, the
basis of her attachment to him (i.e., compulsive caretaking) was
threatened.

Multidirected partiality also demands that, as much as possible,
each member of the couple be credited for his or her positive inputs into the relationship. Note, for example, my acknowledgment
of the time Shirley devoted to trying to understand and help her
husband, even within the context of confronting her about forming an unhealthy coalition with me. To credit highly unempathic,
exploitative, boorish, and underfunctioning partners can be challenging. An inability to find any redeeming feature in such individuals may reflect the therapist's unwitting collusion with the
overfunctioning member of the pair. At a minimum, the underfunctioning individual's genogram typically provides the therapist
information (e.g., abuse, neglect) pointing to intrinsic entitlements
that were withheld and that can be productively acknowledged.

Therapists should also be alert to the fact that underfunctioning
partners often attend couple therapy merely to placate their mates
and thus expend little effort in or between sessions to change their
behavior. When confronted with this information, they defensively
point to their participation in treatment as evidence of their caring
and commitment. Certainly, their attendance merits credit. But they
must also be helped to engage more fully in the therapy process.
Exploring the bases of their resistance may reveal apprehension
about being labeled by their partners, and even by the therapist, as
pathological, incompetent, or otherwise undesirable. Their fear or
intolerance of conflict may also be severe, perhaps related to a history of childhood abuse.

Another important consideration in the development of a working therapeutic system is whether the couple presents issues requiring immediate attention. The most common in my experience with
destructively parentified-parentifying partners are substance-use
disorders, battering, and emotional abuse. They must not only be
held accountable for these problems and their consequences, but
also helped to address them. Conjoint couple sessions, therefore,
may have to be supplemented with individual, group, and inpa-
tient interventions, as well as other community-based services (e.g.,
AA, women's shelter). Of course, such interventions are not necessarily incompatible with couple treatment, particularly if they are

conceptualized as part of an inclusive systemic and ethical approach. Indeed, unless services are incorporated into the treatment plan that immediately and effectively impact such issues as substance abuse and domestic violence, conjoint couple therapy is likely to fail. The therapist, moreover, risks placing him- or herself in an ethically untenable position.

MIDDLE PHASE

Throughout the course of treatment, it is important that the therapist actively maintain a working therapeutic system. Resistance and stagnation in therapy often reflect a breakdown in the system or the therapist's failure to lay all of the necessary groundwork (e.g., acknowledging the positive contributions of both partners to their relationship, avoiding triangulation). An inclusive and just therapeutic system is the fulcrum for interventions designed to address (1) the differentiation level of each partner and their interactions with each other and (2) the balance of fairness in their relationship.

The Bowenians propose that individuals with a "solid self" have no *expectations* of reciprocity in relationships. Tolerant of existential separateness, they are able to stand alone, yet also to facilitate their partners to be themselves as fully as possible—unencumbered by norms and shared mores (Kerr & Bowen, 1988; Schnarch, 1991). Thus, focusing on justice in relationships may be seen as misguided from a Bowenian perspective.

In my view, the issue is not expectations per se but rather the manner in which expectations are negotiated and applied in relationships. As individuals' level of basic differentiation increases, so does their understanding and exercise of procedural and distributive justice in relationships, including their ability to hold themselves and others accountable for their actions and to recognize and to act on nonnegotiable principles in the face of contravening pressures (e.g., to interdict a spouse's abusive behavior toward one of their children). In the process of acting fairly, they further their own differentiation process (cf. Boszormenyi-Nagy & Krasner, 1986). *They become not only increasingly tolerant of their existential separateness but also responsibly aware of their existential relatedness.*

The processes involved in both differentiation and fairness, therefore, are integrally related. Just as imbalanced relationships at an ethical level stunt differentiation at an intrapersonal and relational level, so does lack of differentiation constrain the ability of couples to interact in fair ways. For example, parentified partners characteristically point to imbalances in give-and-take in their relationships. Indeed, such imbalances are often strikingly obvious, as in the case of Carl and Shirley. For many couples, however, to attempt to redress these unfair interaction patterns without consideration of differentiation processes ignores the possibility that the exploitative and narcissistic behavior of the "taker" in the relationship reflects an undifferentiated posture and that the "giver," because of his or her own lack of basic differentiation, has actively distorted the ledger of give-and-take by sacrificing and providing too much.

The challenge for the therapist, then, is to facilitate at once both differentiation and justice. In the following paragraphs, some ways of accomplishing this task with parentifying-parentified couples are discussed within the context of issues and problems they commonly present in treatment.

Balancing Give-and-Take

Underscoring Complementarity

Couples struggling with destructive parentification quickly polarize when discussing relational inequalities. Parentified partners' resentment about giving too much is often countered by their mates' indictment of them as martyrs. Indeed, parentified individuals do tend to martyr themselves. Yet, transactionally, their self-sacrificing behavior complements their mates' underfunctioning. Shirley, for instance, worked overtime to ease financial burdens caused partially by her husband's irresponsible spending habits.

It is helpful to sensitize couples to the complementarity of their under- and overfunctioning behaviors. Following the therapist's use of this strategy, a husband, whose wife responded to his nonchalance about pressing problems in their family by worrying excessively, said to her: "Maybe if I worry more, you can worry less." The goal, however, is not merely to redirect the complementary behaviors of members of a couple but to help them to differentiate from their functional positions. They then can increasingly choose their relational response rather than reactively complementing that of their partner (Kerr & Bowen, 1988).

Disrupting Typecasting

Another useful tactic that helps partners to develop a more differentiated view of each other and a greater sense of equity in their relationship is to uncover evidence that is incongruous with their perceived roles (cf. de Shazer, 1991). For example, in Carl's presence, Shirley was assigned the task of carefully noting any behaviors on his part that were "responsible" or "mature." To her surprise, within a week she observed numerous instances of such behavior that were discordant with her typecasting of Carl. The task also motivated Carl, who was self-conscious about his wife's monitoring him, to assume a more responsible posture at home.

Along these lines, prompting parentified individuals to reveal their vulnerabilities and needs can alter their partners' response to them as well. As a result of their overresponsible and self-sufficient public presentation, they may unwittingly convince their mates that they do not expect or need reciprocity and caring. A parentified woman said recently in therapy, "I'd like someone to do nice things for me, like notice when I need new tires." Upon hearing this, her husband responded, "You always seem so independent; I guess I didn't think you wanted much from me."

Parentified individuals, however, may resist expressing their desires directly. Because of their adeptness in intuiting and meeting the needs of their mates, they often think that their mates should be able to do the same. When their mates fail to live up to their expectations, they feel disappointed, hurt, and resentful. Along with pointing out the fallacy of such thinking, it may be helpful to explore other bases for their difficulties in self-expression.

Challenging Unhealthy Attributions and Role Induction Processes

Consider the following exchange between a parentified woman, Kelli, and her therapist:

Therapist: Don't assume your husband can read your mind. Let him know what you want.

Kelli: Why should I? He'll just ignore me like everyone else in my life.

Therapist: Like your mother?

Kelli: If your own mother can't pay attention to your needs, why would anyone else?

In the course of evaluating and challenging interpersonal perceptions in parentifying-parentified couples, the role of unhealthy attributions and induction processes often surfaces.[2] This was evident in the case of Kelli. She attributed qualities associated with her mother (i.e., inattentiveness and lack of caring) to her husband and then unconsciously induced him to behave accordingly by withholding information about her needs. When he did not respond, she accused him of not caring. And when he did appropriately show concern, she questioned his motivation. In effect, she invalidated his love for her and further skewed the balance of fairness in their relationship.

Owing to underlying feelings of worthlessness and unlovability, she could not accept his caring. She lived in fear that he would one day figure out that she was "no good." Kelli benefited from help in differentiating her husband from her mother and claiming her own intrinsic self-worth, regardless of her mother's lack of affirmation. As a result, she became more accepting of her husband's caring.

Her husband, in turn, was challenged to examine his contribution to their problems, particularly his tendency to take too seriously Kelli's attacks on him. "She makes me feel like I'm so selfish; I end up thinking that I can't love her, or anybody else for that matter," he said. In other words, as part of the interpersonal dynamic involved in problematic role inductions, he identified with her attributions because of his own issues. As his own level of

---

[2]These dynamics have been variously discussed in the literature in terms of projection, projective identification, and role induction (see, e.g., Crisp, 1988; Goldstein, 1991; Ogden, 1979, 1982).

differentiation increased, he was less vulnerable to his wife's accusations and able at times to feed them back to her in a form that she found helpful. For instance, when she charged him later in therapy with being such an "idiot" for not empathizing with her about a recent conflict she experienced with her mother, he said:

> For starters, I'm not an idiot, and I don't think you're one either. OK? I really didn't realize how upset you were about that. But now that I've heard more about the situation with your mother, I can really see why you feel so badly.

Shirley and Carl were helped to confront distorted attributions in their relationship as well. Shirley's depiction of her younger brother, for whom she had primary responsibility as a child, closely paralleled her description of her husband. When Shirley was tentatively presented with this fact, she was stunned. "I feel like I've been hit with a ton of bricks," she said. Shirley then began to cry, and for the first time, to reveal the pain and injustice she experienced vis-à-vis her brother and mother.

Interestingly, Carl indignantly objected to his wife's confusing him with her brother, detailing numerous ways in which he differed. She concurred. Carl matured significantly in her eyes at that instant. It was also helpful to explore further why Carl had previously been unable to cope with his wife's attributions differently. Her frequent observations of his irresponsible behavior were difficult for Carl to ignore or to handle effectively because of his own doubts about his fitness as a husband and a father. Carl had no meaningful role models, a fact that he painfully acknowledged.

Highlighting the Effects of Parentifying-Parentified Behaviors

It is often necessary to attack frontally inequities in the relationships of parentifying-parentified couples. Sensitizing them to the effects of their exploitative and self-sacrificing behaviors can point the way to a fairer quid pro quo. Overhelpful behavior is commonly experienced by others as intrusive, infantilizing, controlling, critical, and condescending. When asked to explain to her husband how she experienced his incessant caretaking, one woman said to him, "You don't let me figure out my problems; I feel like a three-year-old around you." Another woman in a similar position commented, "I don't want him fixing my problems all the time; I just want a friend who'll listen to me."

Individuals' excessive taking leaves their mates feeling exploited, used, hurt, and unloved. These feelings are further intensified by criticism of what is given. A wife said to her husband in a couple session, "Not only do I have to take care of you, but I get criticized when I don't do it right."

Fostering Perspective-Taking

Illuminating the effects of partners' behaviors on each other can facilitate mutual perspective-taking, an effective antidote for imbalances in fairness. Reflexive questioning is another intervention that often has the same effect (Rupp & Jurkovic, 1996; Tomm, 1988). Reflexive queries prompt respondents to consider how others view their behavior and can elicit new information and dialogue that reorganize the cognitive substrate of couple relationships. For example, a parentifying woman was asked about her husband's views of her. She said: "I think he thinks I'm too demanding." Her husband was surprised at her insight, which led to a productive dialogue between them. However, such questioning often reveals that parentifying individuals tend not to take their mates' perspectives or, when they do, they derive faulty information, often confusing their self-perceptions with their mates' views. Viewed transactionally, their perceptions also may be incorrect because of their parentified partners' inability or reluctance to self-disclose.

Assertiveness Training

In addition to learning to practice perspective-taking skills, partners working through destructive parentification processes in their relationship may need help asserting their claims for fair treatment (Boszormenyi-Nagy & Krasner, 1986). For severely parentified individuals, however, this is typically a formidable skill to master. Having learned in their families of origin that assertiveness is taboo and evidence of disloyalty, they associate assertive behavior with rudeness, aggressiveness, and selfishness. Moreover, reflecting their lack of self-differentiation and self-worth, they often feel that they do not deserve fairer treatment, are afraid of being abandoned, and have difficulty making clear "I" statements.

At the same time that parentified individuals are being taught assertiveness, their partners must be helped to respond nondefensively. As a result of their own problems in self-differentiation, they tend to interpret assertive statements and behaviors as attacking and mean-spirited. Often, they pressure their mates to be nice and diffident again. As one husband said, "I liked her a whole lot better when she wasn't so damn assertive." Evidence that their mates feel both victimized by and critical of their newly developing assertiveness often induces parentified individuals to abort their efforts to change, unless the therapist helps both members of the couple to endure the growing pains of interacting with one another in a more adult, differentiated, and fair fashion.

After I challenged a parentifying husband not to "wimp out" in the face of his wife's appropriately assertive remarks regarding his self-pitying behavior, during the following session he said:

> Greg, I was really angry at you after our last meeting, and at you too, Robin [his wife], then I got angry at myself for wimping out about a lot of things in my life. I finally said, "Screw it," and decided to feel better and started taking care of things.

Prompting Acknowledgment

Parentified-parentifying partners can also correct imbalances in fairness in their relationships by learning to credit each other to a much greater degree. In most cases, simple acknowledgment of their partners' acts of kindness and giving can make a surprisingly significant difference. Initially, therapists can model such behavior, but increasingly they should encourage their clients to practice this skill. They must, however, be prepared for resistance by the parentified partners. As a consequence of feeling exploited for years by their mates, and possibly by members of their families of origin, they may be unready to perceive, not to mention acknowledge, their partners' contributions until they feel adequately compensated themselves.

Enhancing Self-Giving

Another critical element in equitable relationships is the ability of partners to give to themselves. Both parentified and parentifying individuals need help along these lines. The former are driven to give to others; the latter to take. Often, as a result of early disruptions in the caregiving system of their original families, they failed to learn how to self-soothe, to be alone, and to manage their own anxiety (see Chapter 2). Hence, when part of a bilateral or unilateral parentified-parentifying relationship, they are not only dependent on each other but also inclined to evaluate the balance of give-and-take constantly. Unlike well-functioning couples, they do not assume that the balancing of relational burdens and benefits is an ongoing process that takes time. To wait for acknowledgment and other reciprocal behaviors is emotionally intolerable to them because of their inability to rely on themselves. For the same reason, periods of emotional distance and discord in their relationships are also unbearable. Family-of-origin work is often useful in helping individuals with these issues.

Negotiating Family-of-Origin Issues

Couples' presenting complaints often do not include their families of origin. However, it can be safely assumed that intergenerational processes are at the root of many of their problems and provide a rich source of solutions as well, particularly when destructive parentification is involved. For example, after Shirley realized that she unconsciously classified her husband with her brother and at the same time looked to Carl to be the responsible, nurturing parent she longed for as a child, she was open to interventions designed to help her differentiate from family members and to work through her destructive entitlement.

A pivotal intervention involved challenging her ongoing and captivating sense of responsibility for her brother. It is important in treating parentified individuals such as Shirley to explore whether their relationship problems are exacerbated by compulsive caretaking and competing loyalties in other areas of their lives (e.g., family of origin, friends, and work). Shirley not only stopped lending her brother money, but also processed with her mother her reasons for doing so. She was prepared in therapy for the possibility that her mother might disapprove. To her delight, she discovered that her mother did not expect her to continue taking care of her brother. Her mother also finally acknowledged the burden that Shirley had carried since childhood. Shirley continued to exercise her own voice in future interactions with her mother and brother, which improved her self-concept and increased her appreciation of her husband's unique qualities.

As noted earlier, Carl's ineffectiveness with the children, resulting in his excessive deference to his wife in regard to child rearing, was also traced to his family of origin. Not only did he lack appropriate male role models, but he had never grieved the loss of his father. As I pointed out to him, he had assumed the same absent role as had his father. This observation greatly disturbed Carl, motivating him to stop the intergenerational pattern. Therapy also helped him realize that because of his own destructive entitlement, he expected his wife to meet his childhood needs.

When one partner stridently claims that the other "owes" him or her, one must be careful not to assume that the perceived imbalances in fairness in the relationship are factual. Such claims often reflect not only unpaid debts from the individual's family of origin but also ethical rhetoric born of a lack of self-differentiation. Under such conditions, helping the couple to dialogue about their ethical dilemma to achieve a fairer balance is probably not as useful as holding the claimant accountable for his or her own life and projections from the past, and for resolving the dilemma within the context of his or her family of origin.

Along these lines, simple communication training for parentifying-parentified partners (e.g., teaching them to listen actively or to make "I" statements) without first attending to underlying problems in differentiation and destructive entitlement is also often an exercise in futility. As Shirley and Carl's level of differentiation increased, their communication improved. For example, characteristic of parentified partners, Shirley previously assumed complete responsibility for Carl's feelings. If he was angry at her, she felt at some deep level irrationally culpable, regardless of the circumstances. She, however, would often reactively counterattack to assuage her guilt and feelings of inadequacy. Assisting Shirley to communicate with her husband, particularly in the face of intense emotionality, proceeded much more smoothly after their individual boundaries became clearer.

Developing a More Secure Attachment

Couples whose relationships are undifferentiated and unfairly balanced often display an anxious attachment (Glickauf-Hughes, Foster, & Jurkovic, in press). Indeed, just as many parentified individuals were insecurely attached to parental figures who depended on them for caretaking, so are they insecurely attached to their mates. Although the basis of their partners' attachment may appear more secure, they frequently suffer in this area as well.

Therapists who are sensitive to these issues recognize, then, that their efforts to help couples emotionally separate may meet with resistance. One parentified woman felt that she and her husband had reached a point of diminishing returns in their treatment, until she was helped to understand her underlying fears of losing her relational base, albeit an anxious and conflictual one, if her marriage significantly changed.

As alluded to earlier, parentified individuals may also be reluctant to relinquish the unconscious belief that they can transform their mates to be the parents they never had. Furthermore, through their compulsive caretaking they may mislead their underfunctioning partners into believing that they have found a parental surrogate. Both partners, therefore, must be helped to confront and to grieve their childhood losses, a process that contributes to their reworking of past emotional insults and exploring new relational possibilities in both their families of origin and their partnership.

Within a few months after grieving the loss of his father, Carl called his sister, from whom he had been cut off for years. They discovered that they shared many of the same thoughts and feelings about their childhood and decided to maintain regular contact with each other. In addition, Carl's dependency on and anxious attachment to his wife lessened.

Resolving Sexual Problems

The bedroom is another arena in which battles to differentiate and to seek justice are waged by couples, including parentified-parentifying couples. In many cases, parentified members exhibit low sexual desire, or their mates increasingly find their sexual life boring. These symptoms may reflect parentified individuals' growing disengagement from the relationship after years of unrequited giving. Through their sexual withdrawal or underinvolvement, they may also be unconsciously, if not deliberately, retaliating for the emotionally distant, exploitative, and hurtful behaviors of their mates in other areas of their relationship. Their partners' insensitive and sometimes abusive sexual style and general emotional immaturity are frequently factors as well.

During the course of therapy, Shirley realized that she had become sexually "numb" to Carl. "I feel like he's one of the children," she lamented. "No wonder you don't want to have sex with me," Carl responded. Another parentified woman suddenly found herself attracted to her husband again after he began assuming responsibility for aspects of his life that he previously "whined" about to her.

On the other hand, because of their self-denial and overweening need to please, parentified individuals typically do not feel free to explore their own sexuality, to assert their libidinal desires, or to exercise directly their option of saying no to their partners' sexual advances, thus further corroding their sexual relationship. Their inhibitions and conflicts in this area may also stem from a history of sexual abuse. As indicated earlier, destructive parentification and sexual abuse during childhood are often co-morbid, a possibility that should be considered by therapists working with parentified individuals in couple treatment.

Although sex therapy may be indicated in some cases, the sexual relationship of most parentified-parentifying couples benefits from their being helped to differentiate and to balance fairness (cf. Schnarch, 1991). An added bonus is that as they are able to maintain a greater sense of their individuality within the context of their relationship, their bond becomes less need-based and hence more intimate.

Addressing the Children's Needs

In treating parentified-parentifying partners who have children, success often depends on addressing the younger generation's role in their difficulties. An inclusive and fair therapeutic approach, moreover, demands concern about the needs of the children per se, as well as those of future children. As discussed in earlier chapters, cross-generational coalitions, often between parentified partners and one of their children, are probably most commonly encountered in work with these couples.

Shirley and Carl's oldest child had become overinvolved with her mother. In both family and individual sessions with her, I learned that she closely monitored her parents' conflicts. Assuming that her father was emotionally stronger than her mother, she typically attended to Shirley's needs. It also became evident that Shirley was unwittingly parentifying her.

In the cases of some parentified-parentifying couples, however, the needs of the children are neglected. Because of the parentified individual's consuming concern about his or her partner, the couple relationship may supplant the parent-child subsystem. The therapist who is not sensitive to these dynamics, which are often subtle, risks treating the couple without ever attending to their parental responsibilities.

It is also incumbent upon the therapist to monitor the effects of couple interventions on the children. As Shirley and Carl's relationship improved, Shirley relied less on her daughter to gratify her needs. Even though I had met with their daughter to prepare her for this change, she still had difficulty adjusting to her mother's increasing independence. A precipitous rise in sibling conflict, largely instigated by this daughter, reflected her wish for more parental contact and her anxiety about changes in her role in the family. She was helped to develop a more appropriate relationship with her mother and her father. With a little prompting, she also began to develop her peer network.

ENDING PHASE

Two major issues frequently arise in the later stages of treatment with parentified-parentifying couples: trust and relational choice. Of course, these issues may be prominent earlier in treatment, just as problems highlighted in the preceding section of this chapter may surface later. However, I have found that they are best negotiated after couples have begun to develop a more differentiated and fairer relationship.

Promoting Trust

Trust is an issue frequently mentioned by the overfunctioning member of a couple early in therapy. Shirley, for instance, complained in the first session about her husband's undependability and untrustworthiness. As a result, she often felt like a "single parent," leading her to question the utility of being married. Carl, however, framed his wife's complaints in various ways, ranging from unrealistic demands, signs of personal stress, and attacks on his character, none of which included interpersonal trust. He was simply too well defended, entitled, and undifferentiated at that point to appreciate the meaning and implications of his wife's concerns.

It was thus decided to work on issues discussed earlier to build a foundation for his entering into a purposeful dialogue with Shirley about trust. In doing so, Carl grew psychosocially, becoming increasingly more responsible for himself and his children, as well as sensitive to his wife's concerns; accordingly, at an ethical level, he earned merit. Earning merit through beneficent action is perhaps one of the most effective ways that partners in a relationship can balance fairness and establish themselves as trustworthy (Boszormenyi-Nagy & Krasner, 1986). Beneficence includes behavior that is both other- and self-directed. Parentified individuals, in particular, often view concerted efforts by their partners to address their own issues in therapy as meritorious and grounds for renewed trust in them.

Interestingly, not only was Carl able later in treatment to acknowledge his previous untrustworthiness, but he voiced concerns about his wife's functioning in this area as well. That is, as he discovered in therapy that she had engaged in many behaviors in their relationship merely to placate him, he—like most partners of parentified individuals who come to this realization—questioned her integrity and trustworthiness. Carl naturally began to demand greater honesty from Shirley. Even though this was painful at times, he clearly preferred that she be "aboveboard" rather than that she resentfully pacify him. Not all individuals, however, appreciate the foundational role of integrity in relationships, an indication that they have considerably more therapeutic work to do.

Trust also becomes an issue for most couples after significant changes begin to occur in their relationship. They question the motivation for and temporal stability of the changes. Predictably, especially for highly undifferentiated relationships, early modifications in partners' actions are often superficial, short-lived, and motivated by the wrong reasons. Carl's initial efforts to assume more responsibility at home stemmed from his wish to avoid his wife's censure rather than from a deeper change in his personal and interpersonal functioning. Consequently, his new behaviors were unstable, which further frustrated Shirley.

Nonetheless, individuals' early behavioral changes should be acknowledged. That they may not endure provides opportunities to teach their mates personal qualities, such as patience and supportiveness, associated with a more differentiated stance. Moreover, as members of the couple are helped to invest in their own growth, they become less preoccupied with the other's progress. Of course, relational change typically follows.

Facilitating Relational Choice

Another concern that naturally develops as parentified-parentifying couples become less co-dependent is that they must construct a new relational contract. This issue leads back to the question of attachment. If destructive parentification is no longer central to the couple's relationship, what is the basis for their staying together? As a formerly parentified husband said in therapy recently, "Where do we go from here?"

At this juncture, many couples entertain the idea of separation and divorce more seriously than they have in the past. Such thoughts do not necessarily reflect reactive disengagement on their part or therapeutic failure. To the contrary, they are often a healthy reflection of the couple's growing differentiation. No longer emotionally dependent on their relationship with each other, members of the couple can decide, perhaps for the first time, whether they *want* to remain together. The danger is that they may either regress to avoid the anxiety associated with this choice or precipitously separate before fully processing their options.

At a minimum, they must be helped to complete their "emotional divorce" from the old relationship. Using such language often helps couples to create a psychological graveyard, as it were, for moribund relational patterns. However, some couples seem to need to separate physically, even if only on a short-term basis, to underscore their freedom of choice and to create an overt temporal and spatial boundary between the "old" and the "new" relationship. Those who do physically separate can be encouraged to postpone a final decision about their relationship until they complete in therapy more of the hard work of differentiating and balancing the ethical ledger. It may be useful to frame this option in terms of their respective interests as well as those of their children, if there are any.

If the couple does work through the choice of remaining together and of recommitting to the relationship (or, more accurately for many, of truly committing for the first time), then they must become reacquainted and reconnected in a qualitatively different fashion. In the process of individuating, which disrupts their using each other as targets of projections and destructive entitlement, they characteristically feel estranged. "It's like Carl's a stranger," Shirley commented later in treatment. Couples usually respond to this development with trepidation rather than, as the therapist might suggest, with excitement born of a new relationship.

CONCLUSIONS

Assisting couples to confront and to disable destructive parentification processes in their relationship can be rewarding. Although it is possible to effect changes by working from a limited unilateral theoretical and therapeutic perspective, greater breadth and depth in personal and interpersonal growth and fairness can be achieved through addressing multiple levels of analysis at once. In particular, as emphasized in this chapter, couples who are helped to differentiate and to balance relational fairness are empowered to confront a variety of issues that inhere in relationships generally, and in destructively parentified-parentifying relationships in particular.

As the discussion on treatment thus far has doubtlessly conveyed, working from an ecosystemic and existential-ethical perspective is tremendously demanding of therapists' own capacities to relate in a differentiated and fair manner. Those who have a family history of functioning in a destructively parentified role are particularly challenged. The next chapter, which addresses the concerns of such therapists, may be more important than any of the others for improving one's therapeutic work, not only in the area of parentification but in other areas as well.

CHAPTER 8

Wounded Healer:
From Parentified Child to
Helping Professional

In an earlier chapter, I noted that many helping professionals, including therapists, counselors, and analysts, functioned in a parentified role in their families of origin. Their career choices often have roots in family processes involving various dysfunctional and stressful aspects, such as deprivation, alcoholism, child and spouse abuse, and physical and psychological disorders (Racusin, Abramowitz, & Winter, 1981). Therefore, the concept of the "wounded healer," elaborated by Jung (1966) and others (e.g., Frank & Paris, 1987; Miller & Baldwin, 1987; Whan, 1987), seems an apt description of these therapists.

The filial relationships of parentified children who later pursue therapy as a career are mirrored in their professional relationships. Clients routinely strive to parentify their therapists (Boszormenyi-Nagy & Krasner, 1986). If therapists have a history of destructive parentification that has not been adequately addressed, they are at risk for a variety of professional and ethical problems. Yet, in other ways, the dynamics in their families of origin prepare them well for a career in the therapy field.

Following a discussion of the various professional liabilities and benefits of parentification, this chapter addresses their implications for the person of the therapist and for therapy training. Excerpts from interviews that I conducted with two therapists, Maggie and Daniel, whose backgrounds include parentification, are presented first to set the stage for a discussion of these issues.

MAGGIE

Married and the mother of an eight-year-old girl, Maggie is a marriage and family therapist who has been practicing since 1981. Her parents divorced in her first year of life. After a bitter court battle, her father was awarded custody of Maggie and her two older brothers. For the next two years she saw little of her mother, who was repeatedly hospitalized due to physical illness. Although both of her parents subsequently remarried, they remained emotionally involved with each other through ongoing conflicts about the children.

Interviewer: What was your role in your family?

Maggie: My main concern growing up was trying to help everybody be happy. I wanted everybody to be happy and assumed that I could do that. I thought I had the means and wherewithal, the power to create better feelings.

Interviewer: Why did you think that?

Maggie: Because it seemed to work off and on. I think I became a therapist type early on.

Interviewer: Can you give an example of how you helped?

Maggie: Well, my father was always depressed—always depressed or angry, frustrated continuously. His relationship with my stepmom was tumultuous. He didn't know what she meant, what she needed, so I would tell him. That would resolve many of their fights. And then I could make him feel better afterwards.

Interviewer: How old were you when you started intervening into their conflicts?

Maggie: Four or five.

Interviewer: Did anybody ever acknowledge your role in your family?

Maggie: Well, my Dad does now.

Interviewer: What about then?

Maggie: No, I don't remember anybody acknowledging it.

Interviewer: Were you ever criticized for any of your efforts to help?

Maggie: No. Sometimes I felt like it might not be my place to enter into an argument [between my father and step-mother]. I probably stopped myself. I don't remember ever being stopped by anybody.

Interviewer: What about your mother? Did you try to make her happy?

Maggie: I would try not to get mad at her. I would be upset with her, but I would not let her know. So in that way, I would take care of her.

Interviewer: Do you recall any ways in which your family prompted or induced you to take care of their feelings?

Maggie: No, other than just their continuing depressive behavior. I don't think anybody recognized what I was doing.... I think I got reinforced by their telling me that I was caring ... very compassionate, loving, good—a good girl for caring so much. That kind of thing. I'd get a lot of feedback about being very sensitive as a child, warm.

Interviewer: Were you ever told that you were mature for your age?

Maggie: Oh, yeah! Oh, yeah! I was told I was very advanced and mature.

Interviewer: How did your role in your family affect your development, do you think?

Maggie: Well, first of all I think it didn't allow me to be carefree as a child. I was never very carefree. I was fairly worried and concerned. I carried a load of sorts. I look at children now, and I realize that's not the best way to be a child. My child doesn't seem to have those worries. She has more worries about herself and her issues than about other people's. I grew up with a knot in my stomach. I was so worried about everybody. I would well up in tears at the thought of somebody being upset or wounded in some way. Yet, I was very advanced. I was always trying to figure out ways to help my family. I don't know; it enabled me to be more advanced.

Interviewer: That's interesting. More advanced?

Maggie: More grown-up, responsible, resourceful, sensitive.

Interviewer: Are you still in the same posture vis-à-vis your family of origin?

Maggie: No.

Interviewer: How has your role changed?

Maggie: I don't care to assume that role anymore. I went through a severe depression in my twenties, partially the result, I think, of my family role and realizing that nobody knew my feelings and how bad off I was and that nobody could help me. At that point, I entered therapy.... I learned how my role was destructive for me. In order to survive and be happy as an adult, I needed to change some things about the way I interacted with my family. So I did, and now I pretty much recognize when I'm doing something for somebody and not getting anything in return. And I make a decision about whether I want to be altruistic. I think I have the capacity to still be compassionate, but I can pace myself without becoming drained. And I can establish relationships where there's reciprocity. I don't have to dump my heart and soul in a relationship, feeling like I'm not going to have anything left.

Interviewer: How has your family reacted to these changes?

Maggie: Well, it's kind of ironic. Several things have happened. My mother, for example, has made some efforts to be more maternal. I've been very verbal with her about what I need to do for myself. She tries to understand me and to be maternal, and that's meaningful to me.

Interviewer: Now I'd like to ask you some questions about your career. What factors entered into your decision to become a therapist?

Maggie: I think it was destiny. My career as a therapist began when I was four. I think I was in training at an early age—a long-term residency. I just needed the structure of a formal education to do what I've always been doing. I think it's nice to be paid and recognized for what I do. I think I was drawn to the profession. I've always been doing it, and it seemed to come naturally.

Interviewer: Do you think your family background affected your training as a therapist—your interactions with teachers, supervisors, and so on?

Maggie: Oh, yeah! I was never just an average student. I had to get in with my teachers—to have a personalized relationship. I couldn't be just one in a mass of students. I had to be special and meaningful to them.

Interviewer: Why?

Maggie: That's the way I functioned all the time. My ability to relate to people was based on my being inside their emotional system and helpful to them. But my supervisors nailed me on this. They recognized my style and encouraged me to learn about my tendency to overfunction in relationships. They placed me in a group with a very aggressive therapist. He did role plays in which other group members were instructed to hang on my ankles. He told me to fend them off, while at the same time telling the group members not to let go. I'd try to walk away and very politely say, "Would you please let go of me?" And he'd say, "Now, that's not going to get anybody off your ankles. Kick them off! You have to kick them off!" I learned that I allowed people to take advantage of me. He used to say to me, "You're the biggest teat in the world, and you let everybody suck on you." That group helped me to become an effective therapist. I learned that if I didn't change, I would not be helpful in a therapeutic setting. I would just be meeting my own needs.

Interviewer: Despite the help you received in your training, has your family role as a caretaker affected your functioning as a therapist?

Maggie: Well, I don't always have confidence in my ability to handle boundary issues with my clients. So I seek supervision to determine if what I'm thinking of doing or trying to accomplish in therapy is state of the art or a blurring of boundaries.

Interviewer: How do boundaries tend to blur for you?

Maggie: I have to guard against becoming overinvolved—going above and beyond the call of duty, feeling overly responsible for clients' progress or responding to their neediness in inappropriate ways, for example, feeling pulled to be a friend. A related issue, a major one for me, is burnout, knowing that I have to pace myself. This is not such an issue now that I'm more seasoned. But early on, I really thought ... I had to learn that I couldn't help everybody. The other piece in all of this is that I think my experience in my family of origin helped me to become a better therapist in many ways. I'm very empathic. I'm able to really connect and join with people around painful issues. While sitting in supervision groups, I've realized that other therapists often don't have the same confidence as I do, in their relationship with their clients. My clients, most of them, feel that I really do care about them. They give me that feedback.

Interviewer: Does it ever bother you when your clients don't express sufficient gratitude for your services?

Maggie: Just the opposite. I don't think I have an expectation of recognition, of being well-known, of being respected. It surprises me when I get a referral from somebody who really thinks highly of me. I feel fairly anonymous.

Interviewer: What about concerns of maintaining the approval of clients?

Maggie: I've learned over the years that that is part of the therapeutic process, that clients are going to go through phases of not liking me or raging at me.

Interviewer: Did that used to be a problem for you?

Maggie: Early on I took it very personally. I'd get sick to my stomach if someone didn't like what I did. I'd feel like a failure. I try to predict that now—when's it coming. I try to prepare myself and process it with clients.

Interviewer: Have your loyalties been uncomfortably divided between your current family, your family of origin, and career?

Maggie: Well, there is a sense of existential guilt. My whole family [of origin] is not doing well, and I have made a decision not to help them in the ways I used to. So sometimes I have the feeling that here are these people I could probably help, even though intellectually I know I can't. But the emotional part of me, the little-child part of me, says, "You can do it." And then I make a choice not to; they remain dysfunctional, and I'm left with guilt feelings. I feel guilty for just being here and not taking care of family members.

Interviewer: How do you deal with those feelings?

Maggie: Well, that's my current issue. I'm still trying to deal with it. I struggle with it. I know the problem, but I still have this residual guilt and sadness. I'm here and doing well. Maybe I should be back with all of that and feeling like crap. It's a choice, and I have to deal with it.

It is apparent that Maggie's parentification as a child, especially in the expressive sphere, has challenged her to make some arduous choices as an adult. Whether to continue to assume responsibility for the emotional well-being of her family of origin still haunts her, despite painful self-examination and intensive therapy, including family-of-origin work. Her reflections about personal and professional problems that she has experienced because of her parentified role are echoed in Daniel's comments as well.

DANIEL

Daniel is married and has two children. After completing his doctorate in clinical psychology 13 years ago, he worked in a community mental health center and began seeing clients privately. His practice grew quickly, and within a few years he moved into the private sector on a full-time basis. Currently the director of a successful group practice and an active member of various professional organizations, he sees individuals, families, and couples. As in the case of Maggie, links between Daniel's family background as the firstborn and his career development quickly surfaced in the interview.

Daniel: There were a lot of boundary issues [in my family of origin].... I was probably far more aligned with my mother than with my father. But I was certainly the peacemaker. I remember, I guess I was pretty little, they had a fight, and my father stormed to the front door, and I heard the door slam. He was leaving, and I panicked, and I ran to the front door. I ran down the hallway; and I ran into the living room; and I ran to the front door, and there, tucked away in this alcove, standing by the closed door, was my father going, "Shush"—like *Don't tell your mother I'm still here.*

Interviewer: Can you say a little more about your role as a peace-maker?

Daniel: Because they did so much of this closeness-distance stuff, where they'd get real close, and then they'd have a blowout and be yelling at each other and not talk-ing... I just remember being the one solid, always-there connection.

Interviewer: Solid connection for them.

Daniel: Right, right. And I guess ... I felt I always had to do my best. And so at some level I'm sure I felt a great deal of responsibility. I was responsible for their hap-piness. That was the middle piece.

Interviewer: You were the middle piece.

Daniel: I was. I was their pride and joy. My parents were married seven years before I was born, trying to have a baby the whole time. The birth announcement said, "Seven years in the making. The grand event has fi-nally arrived." I was announced like a movie would be announced, as some grand opening, grand event. And the message I got was that I was the pride and joy of my family.

Interviewer: And you had to deliver, but you didn't know what the parameters were.

Daniel: No, so if I put the maximum energy into everything I do, then I've done my best. But if I haven't, if I've missed something, not quite my best.... To my mother, if I pooped in the potty, it was to be treated like gradu-ation from Harvard. And that was good when I was two. But my sense was that if I do a good job in the bathroom now, I still could get the same accolades.... Every time on the phone as an adult [my father says], "Just promise me you'll drive carefully." "Dad, I'll drive carefully, OK? And if I do, it's not for you." But

I mean, I grew up with this; it is a sense of my responsibility for my parents. Every time when I went to college, every time I left home, I looked in the rearview mirror to get a glimpse of my parents. I was terrified it would be the last time I ever saw them. I did that for nine years prior to finishing graduate school. Every time I visited them and left, I always took that long glance in the rearview mirror.

Interviewer: Help me understand the sense you had of seeing your parents for the last time.

Daniel: I guess it was probably some of the old magical, childhood omnipotence. A piece of that for an adult, a young adult who knew there was nothing I could do but still felt it.

Interviewer: Did your mother ever refer to you as her "little man" or in some related way?

Daniel: "Little man" doesn't feel all that unfamiliar.... There was one phrase my mother would say two different ways. One of them was, "I hope that you have children that do for you what you've done for me." And then, if I screwed up, she would say, "I hope you have children who do to you what you're doing to me!" One word and vocal inflection shift. Those are still really powerful.

Interviewer: Let me switch gears.

Daniel: One more thing about family therapy, being a family healer. As I went off to college, maybe even in high school, I think, I got the feeling that they looked to me not only to perform for them but for help with things. And especially like in graduate school, at that time, I mean here I'm learning this stuff, here's all this craziness in my family, and by that time I had become the family healer.... My sense was that with peers, too, that I always felt a lot of compassion and need to fix.

Interviewer: Let me ask you a big question. Have any of the following issues been a challenge or a problem for you in your practice over the years: professional burnout, savior complex, overinvolvement with or overresponsibility for clients, expectation of gratitude from colleagues or clients?

Daniel: Well, I've always overextended myself.

Interviewer: What about overresponsibility?

Daniel: Now that was the one I resonated to immediately. When I was first seeing patients, even in graduate school, the phrase "I took total care of my patients." I mean, my practice, I'd get a call at home, and I'd get on the phone for an hour or two, no charge, you know ... I still have a hell of a hard time ending a session on time and, as you know, we got started late even this morning, and I'm running over, and I'm holding up somebody else, and that has been an issue always—just overextending, difficulty with boundaries. Overextending with the patients I have had. Any kind of ethical issues—they've always been some form of boundary issue. No flagrant things that people would say, "How could you, you know, you knew you were doing wrong." I didn't know I was doing wrong. I was committed to getting these people well, and I paid lip service to the notion that when they would say, "Oh, you have helped me so much," I would say, "You're the one who did all the work." And I'd be sitting there, thinking "That's a crock." I believe that now. I mean it's really changed, but for years it was me.

Interviewer: It was your role.

Daniel: It really was—the very role. I was responsible for my patients' health, which was measured by their happiness and well-being, and there you are.

Interviewer: A link to your family of origin.

Daniel: A direct link. What were the other questions?

Interviewer: You've touched on several. Balancing professional and
                family responsibilities.

Daniel: Dancing as fast as I can. I want to be home. I'll call
                my wife, and she'll say, "Well, how long are you go-
                ing to be?" And this is nine o'clock at night. On a
                good day I have patients back to back to back to
                back with about a half an hour break, which is never
                a break, because I'm always behind, and I have phone
                calls to make and this and that, and leave. My last
                patient ends usually by about seven o'clock, and it
                was a five-thirty patient, by the time I get started and
                finish checking him or her out.... And then it usually
                takes me an hour and a half to clean up a day that
                has stacked up like this [*pointing above his head*] with
                all my case notes. Make the telephone calls and deal
                with the finances and whatever else. I race home ... I
                can never estimate my time at all. I am so bad about
                that. Packing it in. I asked you, if this was going to
                come up. Here it is. Packing it in, packing it in. You
                know, my favorite line these days is when someone
                says, "How you doing?" "Well, if I take a deep breath,
                I'm a half-hour late."

Interviewer: Do you ever feel like an impostor as a therapist?

Daniel: Well, let me put it this way, when I do work that feels
                really special: right, creative, innovative. You know,
                when I do that, that's a real high for me, and I mean
                I can give a whoop—whoop! That's the way it feels....
                Up until the last couple of years maybe, [I] rarely have
                felt good and competent but have vacillated between
                great and special and totally impostor.

Although perhaps not as obvious, Daniel's parentification in his
family of origin was as personally limiting and captivating as
Maggie's. He came to understand over the years that his parents'
happiness depended on his superior performance and availability
to them as an emotional connector and, finally, as "family healer."

It is apparent that, like Maggie, he is still struggling with the consequences of his parentified role. Both, for example, spoke about ongoing challenges to define themselves differently in relation to their families of origin as well as to their careers. The latter is the subject of the following discussion.

CONSEQUENCES

Therapists who were destructively parentified as children, and perhaps who continue to participate in the process as adults, are at risk of experiencing a number of interrelated problems in their careers. At the same time, however, their parentification may uniquely support their development of skills and sensitivities that enhance their functioning as therapists.

Problems

Boundary Distortions

As Maggie and Daniel noted, maintaining appropriate boundaries in the client-therapist relationship is probably one of the greatest challenges to clinicians with a history of parentification. Maggie, for example, alluded to the pull she experiences to be more than a "therapist" to her clients. Certainly, this pressure inheres in the therapeutic process, contributing to the client's predictable parentification of the therapist. However, clinicians who have routinely responded to the pressing needs of significant others since childhood are at risk of unwittingly "going beyond the call of duty," as Maggie said. Thus, they are susceptible to clients' efforts to transform asymmetries in the therapeutic relationship (e.g., differential disclosure of personal information) into symmetrical elements. The aspect of friendship in the relationship may become paramount and undermine the therapeutic process.

Conversely, asymmetries in the therapist-client relationship may be exaggerated by the parentified clinician as well. He or she, for example, may work longer and harder (often without appropriate financial compensation) than the client. Daniel, for example, mentioned one- and two-hour telephone consultations with clients from his home and difficulty in ending sessions on time. His ethic of assuming "total" patient care required him to overfunction in his role as therapist. The irony is that "therapeutic" overfunctioning contributes to underfunctioning on the part of clients, interfering with their ability to exercise control over their own lives.

Based on her supervision of a third-year resident in psychiatry, Lerner (1988) provides a good example of therapeutic overfunctioning. The supervisee was entangled in a triangle in his family of origin. In response to calls from his father regarding his mother's drinking, he devoted considerable time to assessing the problem and to attempting unsuccessfully to encourage her to enter therapy. In a parallel fashion, Lerner observed that he assumed the role of "rescuer" to depressed women in his practice by providing them with added help (e.g., extra sessions, including telephone calls during his vacations).

Lerner notes that nontherapeutic overfunctioning frequently characterizes male therapists' interactions with female clients. Reflecting differential sex role socialization experiences, the female's helpless self-presentation is confused by the male therapist with her actual and potential competencies. He, therefore, shaped by his masculine image as a doer and overfunctioner, rescues rather than empowers. This process, of course, is especially pronounced, if the therapist has been a rescuer in his family of origin.

In the course of assuming excessive responsibility for clients, especially for the immediately victimized members of a family, therapists also often form unhealthy coalitions with them or are drawn by family members into such coalitions. For example, unilaterally allying with an abused child against his or her parents, although perhaps necessary at different points of therapy, may unnecessarily strain the parent-child relationship—the relationship that must ultimately be healed to serve the best interests of the child. It also ignores the abusing parents' own history of victimization (cf. Boszormenyi-Nagy & Krasner, 1986). Tendencies on the part of parentified therapists to ally excessively with one family member may also lead them to view the rest of the family as an obstacle to treatment, persuading them to favor individual over family-focused therapy modalities (Blumenstein, 1986).

Another dynamic is that just as enmeshed parents unpredictably withdraw from their children or strike out at them when exasperated by and resentful about their overfunctioning in a parental role, so do parentified therapists. Changes in therapist behavior may be subtle but, nevertheless, noticeable to the client who is at risk of feeling abandoned, enraged, or guilty. These feelings may be acted out in various ways (e.g., suicidal gesturing). Unless therapists process their part in the client's reactions, they are likely to blame him or her for being too needy or manipulative; or they may overreact, pouring themselves into the treatment again only to repeat the pattern when engulfed by the client.

Contributing to the problems of many parentified therapists is their difficulty in setting limits with clients or, more accurately, with themselves. I have already mentioned managing time in sessions and telephone contact. Other treatment parameters that are often problematic include handling unpaid fees, scheduling, missed appointments, inappropriate in-session behaviors (e.g., intoxication, destroying property, threatening gestures), and excessive demands (e.g., for extra appointments, longer sessions). Setting limits requires tolerance of client reactivity to discomforting strictures and the ability to function in ways that are not always perceived as caring. If therapists measure their success largely in terms of their clients' happiness, as did both Maggie and Daniel until recent years, then they are likely to stretch therapeutic boundaries and to allow their clients to do the same.

Compulsive Giving

As Waldrip (1993) astutely observed recently, parentified helping professionals are often "involuntary therapists." Recall Maggie's statement: "I think I was drawn to the profession. I've always been doing it, and it seemed to come naturally." Many therapists with Maggie's background do not ply their trade out of choice. Rather, they merely continue to give compulsively as professionals. Reminiscent of their familial script, in which their survival and that of their family depended on them, they are captivated by their clients.

On an ontic level, for many of these therapists, "to exist is to save" (Crandall, 1981, p. 94). Practicing therapy is not a job. It is a way of being that solely defines their identity. Unsuspecting individuals who become involved with therapists who act as saviors may find themselves smothered in caring that is disempowering and possibly disingenuous, entrapping them in a protracted treatment process that neither they nor their co-dependent professional helper can appropriately terminate.

Narcissistic Disturbances

Congruous with patterns in their families of origin, parentified therapists typically experience enormous pressure to be admired by their clients and to perform exceptionally well. Their estimation of their worth as therapists and, often, as persons generally can turn on their perceived competence and approval by clients, supervisors, and colleagues. Unable to regulate their own self-esteem on a consistent basis, they are dependent on feedback from others and their ability to satisfy the overweening demands of parental introjects (Miller, 1979/1981).

Evidence of doing well therapeutically is reason for the parentified therapist to experience an inflated sense of self-worth. On the other hand, suggestions of mere adequacy, not to mention failure, often lead to feelings of incompetence and insignificance. Early in her career, Maggie became "sick" in the face of client disapproval. Self-protectively, she now attempts to anticipate negative feedback in therapy. When accused by clients that they have not done enough, parentified therapists are likely to conclude that they are not "good enough," often spurring them to redouble their efforts to help (cf. Lackie, 1983).

Reflecting pseudo-self processes, these dynamics also contribute to the therapist's feeling that he or she is an impostor (cf. Clance & O'Toole, 1987). Along these lines, Daniel observed: "Up until the last couple of years maybe, [I] rarely have felt good and competent but have vacillated between great and special and totally impostor." An occupational identity that is not fortified by self-acceptance and self-confidence or *solid self,* in Bowenian terms, requires outstanding achievement to conceal feelings of inadequacy. Such therapists are also prone to introject the projections—both good and bad—of their clients, contributing to the cycling of highs and lows of felt competence as a therapist (cf. Ogden, 1982).

Further adding to the feeling of being an imposter experienced by many parentified therapists is the fact that their helping efforts as children typically went unnoticed and seldom, if ever, seemed sufficient to heal or satisfy family members (Welt & Herron, 1990).

Their mature and helpful behavior during childhood and adolescence, therefore, belied underlying doubts about their efficacy as caretakers—doubts that later resurface in their work with clients. Maggie, for example, feels "anonymous" as a therapist and continues to be surprised by recognition and praise from clients.

On the other hand, because of the healing power often attributed to them by members of their families of origin (e.g., "I don't know what I'd do without you"), parentified therapists may overestimate their therapeutic abilities. Their client loads may be unrealistically large and extraordinarily challenging. Witness Daniel's typical workday. It is also frequently difficult for parentified therapists to resist helping in problem areas in which they have limited experience and expertise.

Ethical Violations

Proclivities to cross therapeutic boundaries, to advocate for a particular family member, and to give compulsively, often well beyond their limits, leave parentified therapists at risk for behaving unethically or practicing in ways that raise ethical questions. I suspect that ethical complaints are frequently not lodged against parentified therapists, however, because of their ability to forge intensely loyal therapeutic relationships. Their clients, moreover, may have difficulty attributing the discomfort they experience in therapy to an inappropriate therapeutic relationship. If they recognized this situation, they typically terminate and sometimes resume treatment with another therapist.

The issues about which clients of these therapists do complain frequently pertain to boundary problems. The accused often do not realize that, as Daniel noted, they were "doing wrong." They were "committed" to trying to help. The complainant, however, may argue that the therapist unfairly sided with his or her spouse, children, or other family members, which resulted in divorce, alienation of affection, or loss of custody. This perception sometimes arises because of parentified therapists' ambitious and often controlling efforts to resolve family differences that the family members themselves should handle. To the chagrin of the therapist determined to make everyone happy, these differences may not be immediately, if ever, reconcilable.

Parentified therapists must also guard against tendencies to attempt to rebalance the ledger of fairness between clients and their families of origin (and procreation) in the therapeutic relationship. As Boszormenyi-Nagy and Krasner (1986) remind us, the therapist–client and the family ledgers are separate and nontransferable from an ethical perspective. Although various therapeutic operations (e.g., working through transference reactions, reparenting strategies) at a psychological or transactional level can help, they do not erase the fact of inequities in the parent-client relationship.

Changes in the family ledger necessitate that therapists adopt a different role, one that encourages their clients to engage in a more responsible dialogue with family members (Boszormenyi-Nagy & Krasner, 1986). Through their overinvolvment with clients and associated rescue fantasies involving excessive efforts to help, parentified therapists can greatly interfere in this process.

Moreover, as noted earlier, their unidirected partiality can foster coalitions that compete with and even harm clients' significant relationships. Therapists' biases are often rooted in their own destructive entitlement (Boszormenyi-Nagy & Krasner, 1986). Failure to deal with their parentification places them at risk of unconsciously exploiting clients. For example, they may blame parents in the families they see as a means to avoid confronting their own parents. Thus, they at once preserve family loyalties and symbolically redress past inequities. Clients may also be pulled into co-dependent relationships with them to feed therapists' narcissistic needs and to help, albeit inappropriately, to settle accounts in the therapists' own families. The entitlement that therapists do earn through their work does not alter their own family ledgers. Using clients for that purpose, however unconsciously, undermines trust in the therapist-client relationship and represents a breach of the therapeutic contract.

Divided Loyalties

Most therapists struggle to meet the demands of work and family. Those with a background of parentification, however, are often particularly torn between different commitments. Daniel's marriage, for example, is strained by his long work hours. The partners and children of parentified therapists frequently feel as though they are in competition with clients for time, energy, and commitment. Conversely, in the case of therapists who have yet to extricate themselves from their overfunctioning position in their own families, the clients they see are the unwitting victims of their strained role.

Still keenly aware of the neediness of her family of origin, Maggie feels guilty about not giving to them, as she did before, and about doing well herself. Her plight underscores the difficulty involved in changing parentified role patterns. Modification of surface behaviors does not necessarily alter long-standing, internalized commitments to family members.

Daniel also continues to resist reenacting his role as the "family healer," a role that crystallized during his graduate school years. Family members who had long looked to Daniel to ensure their happiness assumed that his professional training would equip him to be even more helpful to them. It is plausible that he entered the therapy field to meet his family's expectations along these lines. According to Friedman (1987), individuals who obtain a credential to practice therapy may become the "identified therapist" in their families, to the detriment of everyone involved.

Burnout

Like anyone else, therapists can become mentally and physically impaired (Kilburg, Nathan, & Thoreson, 1986). In light of the various problems experienced by parentified therapists in their professional and personal lives, they are at high risk for professional burnout. Drawing from their work with distressed professionals, Kaslow and Schulman (1987) have pointed to some of the early warning signs of this condition: constant complaints about work, sense of "imminent doom," feelings of tedium, increased negative countertransference reactions, extreme irritability and withdrawal at home, frequent illnesses of unknown origin, a desire to "run away," and periodic suicidal ideation (p. 94).

Strengths

Dedicated Empathic Caring

Notwithstanding the compulsivity of many parentified therapists' helping efforts, their clients typically feel cared for and understood by them. Maggie reported that her clients often give her feedback to that effect. Her family experiences have helped her "to really connect and join with people around painful issues."

Of course, the danger here is that therapeutic empathy, sensitivity, and connection may devolve into overidentification and, hence, loss of the sense of self and other. Rather than using the term *empathy*, Buber (1965) prefers to label the ability to experience relationships from the other side without forfeiting one's own perspective and activity as "inclusion." Parentified therapists who have worked to achieve a differentiated sense of themselves are able to empathize with their clients in a deeply meaningful and healing fashion.

Welt and Herron (1990) have also pointed to the "enormous empathic potential" of parentified therapists. They have observed, however, that in seeking to avoid the loss of control and vulnerability they experienced as children in relation to needy parents, these therapists are at risk of overintellectualizing and detaching in their relationship with clients. Consequently, their "available" empathy may be restricted (Welt & Herron, 1990).

Humanness

Perhaps because parentified therapists began practicing long before they were professionally licensed, they often appear less inhibited than their cohorts by the formal structure of the therapy situation. They are freer to be themselves and to engage the person of their clients. Writing about her experience as a client in the book *When Boundaries Betray Us*, Heyward (1993) suggests that therapists who withhold intimacy and authentic emotional relating are as abusive as those who knowingly violate boundaries.

Parentified therapists' ability to humanize the therapeutic relationship helps their charges to break out of the patient role to reclaim their wholeness as human beings (Greenspan, 1993; Laing, 1967). Fostering such person-to-person connections in therapy, moreover, is not incompatible with the treatment approach discussed in previous chapters provided that therapists appreciate that their relationship cannot substitute for authenticity and mutuality in their clients' families. This relationship models what is possible in interhuman relations and establishes a trustworthy and secure base with the therapist from which clients can venture into family interactions in refreshingly new ways.

Clients' hunger for an increasingly authentic bond may threaten professional helpers. As the divide between therapist and client blurs, doubts about the appropriateness of boundaries arise and personal conflicts within the therapist are often provoked (cf. Welt & Herron, 1990). The therapist may then retreat into his or her professional role, supported by the norm of therapeutic neutrality, distance, and objectivity. This process is discombobulating for clients who painfully question the validity of their own perceptions and needs for intimacy (Greenspan, 1993).

Therapists who allow themselves to encounter genuinely the person of their clients rather than merely diagnostic categories, syndromes, interactional patterns, attempted solutions to problems, family ledgers, and so forth, unavoidably push the limits of professionalism as conventionally defined. This is not to gainsay the need for professional boundaries. Indeed, it is critical that therapists closely monitor the nature of their alliance with clients. Maggie, for example, routinely seeks supervision for that purpose.

It is also important to consider, however, the possibility that the professional relationship labors under the same culturally embedded, patriarchal biases that undergird other significant relationships, namely, tendencies to advance an ethic of hierarchy and separation over an ethic of parity and connection (Greenspan, 1993; Gilligan, 1982). Clearly, both ethical orientations have merit, reflecting existential and possibly biologically based proclivities both to distance from and to enter into relation with others (e.g., Gilligan, 1982; Kerr & Bowen, 1988). For Buber (1970), these opposing movements are endemic to mutuality and, I would argue, to responsible caring on the part of professionals (cf. Berry, 1985).

Indeed, as Boszormenyi-Nagy and Krasner point out, clinicians, like responsible parents, structure their clients, facilitating appropriate boundaries in which to relate therapeutically and, ultimately, to let go. Part and parcel of this process is the humanization of the order, procedures, techniques, and special arrangements of the helping situation.

However, a critical measure of the success of the relationship between therapist and client is *not their mutual feelings of affection, attraction, and connection but rather their ultimate "regard for the well being and success of the other"* (Boszormenyi-Nagy & Krasner, 1986, p. 409). This criterion extends beyond the therapeutic context to include all caring and responsible relationships, including those of parents and children, mates, and friends.

Resourcefulness

Prominent in the life stories of parentified individuals are their ingenuity and resourcefulness as children and adolescents in helping their families. Recall the abusive father discussed in the Introduction who during his adolescent years enlisted the help of neighbors in feeding his younger siblings. At the age of four or five, Maggie advised her father on how to resolve conflicts with his wife. Jenny's unusual behaviors (e.g., wearing her coat backward) effectively distracted her depressed mother. Another parentified 10-year-old voluntarily stood in for her absent father as her mother's labor coach during childbirth.

Parentification provides future therapists excellent training in interpersonal problem solving and crisis intervention.[1] As a result, they are often less dependent on techniques learned in their professional schooling than other therapists. Their abilities along these lines are particularly evident during periods of client crisis. Quick to respond, they are able to take charge of the situation and to develop creative and effective intervention strategies.

Maggie, for example, related after the interview an experience she had had with an actively homicidal client who evaded her efforts to hospitalize him. Having also eluded a multistate police dragnet, he later called her from the city in which his intended victim lived. He refused to turn himself in to the authorities, but he did agree to Maggie's request to continue to call her three times daily (morning, noon, and night). During her phone contacts with him, she was able to help him consider alternative ways of dealing with his anger. After returning home several days later, he confided

---

[1]Zahn-Waxler's research team (see Zahn-Waxler & Kochanska, 1988) discovered that five- and six-year-olds—living in high conflict homes with depressed parents—were not only extremely attuned to the problems of others but also able to generate numerous strategies to resolve interpersonal conflicts.

in Maggie that her availability to him and obvious caring helped him to reassess his homicidal intentions. He subsequently began dealing with unresolved family-of-origin issues, which he had previously resisted doing.[2]

Clinical Range

Related to the parentified therapists' resourcefulness are their capacity and willingness to handle severe psychopathology and family dysfunction. The caseloads of both Maggie and Daniel are composed of clients with extremely difficult and clinically demanding problems (e.g., early attachment issues, custody disputes, family violence, sexual abuse). Exquisitely attuned to the pain of their clients, they are able to create a safe, secure, nurturing, and trustworthy therapeutic environment. Clients, moreover, often perceptively recognize or learn in the course of treatment that therapists with a background of parentification and related problems have experienced considerable pain and stress themselves. Having a therapist who has survived and worked through his or her issues increases clients' optimism about their own chances.

IMPLICATIONS

What are the implications of parentified therapists' vulnerabilities and strengths for them as persons and for their training as therapists? Those that have already been touched on (e.g., need to prevent burnout) are further elaborated in this section, along with a number of others.

---

[2]This example may appear to contradict my earlier warnings about parentified therapists' overfunctioning vis-à-vis their clients. Although the line between overfunctioning and responsible, resourceful crisis management is not always clear, I think Maggie's handling of this case is illustrative of the latter. The emergent nature of her client's behavior called for some kind of response, however nonstandard, that would help structure and de-escalate his anger. See Pittman (1984, 1987) and Langsley, Kaplan, Pittman, Machotka, Flomenhaft, and DeYoung (1968) for other examples of unconventional but effective interventions in situations of crisis.

Person-of-the-Therapist

The same sociofamilial and intrapersonal processes that contribute to parentified therapists' giftedness as professional helpers also render them vulnerable, as previously discussed, to numerous difficulties. Like Maggie and Daniel, they typically benefit from therapeutic, supervisory, and personally and professionally enriching activities (e.g., continuing education, consultations).

Enhancing Family-of-Origin Relationships

As noted earlier, the clinical work of therapists who are not attempting to resolve their own destructive entitlement and personal difficulties unavoidably suffers. Their clients are at risk of being exploitatively used and targeted with unwarranted projections. Therefore, it is incumbent upon the responsible therapist, avers Titelman (1987), to "know [oneself] in the context of one's own family" (p. 4).

Yet helpful, intellectual insight into one's family-of-origin relationships is not sufficient. Rather, change involves an in vivo understanding, in which the therapist actually relates to family members in an increasingly differentiated and fair fashion. Changes along these lines usually require therapeutic intervention. Unfortunately, for various reasons (e.g., fear of exposure, narcissism), many therapists are reluctant to seek therapy for themselves and their families (Kaslow & Schulman, 1987).

Of course, a major piece in the family-of-origin work of parentified therapists is their differentiation from a caretaking role. Their credentialing as professional helpers further reifies their "identified-therapist" status in the eyes of family members. Thus, it is critical that they learn to be "just another family member" (Kaslow and Schulman, 1987, p. 83).

Friedman (1987) suggests several techniques to facilitate this process. Verbal and action reversals, for example, involve therapists' saying and doing the opposite of what would be expected of them in their professional role. Friedman's dialogue with his aunt at his mother's 70th birthday party illustrates verbal reversal:

Aunt: Eddie, what do you think of me?

Me: I never analyze my relatives.

Aunt: I have opinions about you.

Me: Well, maybe you can get more distance.

Aunt: You must have some opinions.

Me: Okay, I think you're crazy, but it sure keeps you from being boring. (p. 173)

Although sometimes amusing, and perhaps effective, verbal and action reversals appear merely to substitute one inauthentic and undifferentiated family interaction pattern for another. It is possible to "de-role" in one's family without assuming a counterthera-peutic stance. For example, Friedman might have simply answered his aunt's initial question as another family member would, without concern about changing the way she thought about or related to him.

Keeping the Home Fires Burning

Responsible therapists attend not only to their families of origin but also to their current families. A common problem for therapists, particularly for those with a history of parentification, is their overinvolvment in work relationships (e.g., with clients, supervisees, students, colleagues) and corresponding underinvolvement in their relationships at home (Titelman, 1987). Although family-of-origin work often helps to change this pattern, dissatisfaction and conflict with members of therapists' families of procreation may necessitate professional help as well. Indeed, as a result of their efforts to alter their role in their families of origin, they are often confronted with long-standing inequities and problems in relation to their mates and children. Unless these are attended to, the therapist may regress to his or her previously dysfunctional position vis-à-vis clients and family members.

Remembering "It's Just a Job"

Waldrip (1993), based on personal experience, advises parentified therapists to remember that they probably did not enter their profession voluntarily, but rather were scripted into it as a result of their familial experiences. Coming to grips with this fact is often part of the therapy of parentified therapists and helps them for the first time to choose whether they *want* to continue to pursue their occupation. The conscious choice to do so liberates the therapist. Reflecting on her experience, Waldrip writes:

> Moving ... into a healthier, free place means ... that I don't *have* to "cure" people; I can give them permission to get better or not, and at whatever spced they choose. It means I don't work harder than my clients do in the therapy session. It means that I work at setting appropriate limits with clients and standing firm. It means I'm trying to break the habit of single-handedly taking on any client situation that presents itself, no matter how difficult it is.... I've begun in recent years to taste the fruits of authentic commitment and compassion for my clients, and to see that they come not from compulsion, but from freedom. (p. 7)

Handling Taxing Clients

Waldrip noted that she is now more circumspect about clients she accepts for therapy. It is also advisable that therapists consider handling difficult clientele: (1) by working with a co-therapist, (2) by seeking consultation or supervision, which may involve peer networking, or (3) in the event of an intractable clinical situation, by transferring the client to another therapist (Kaslow & Schulman, 1987). The last may be an impossibility, however, for therapists whose identity and self-esteem are still excessively entwined with their efficacy as caretakers.

Fostering Personal Relationships

In the process of disengaging from their family and professional caretaking roles, parentified therapists rediscover themselves as persons who enjoy not only giving to others but also receiving love and sustenance. Relinquishing their unilateral giving stance, however, is typically a challenge. In meeting the challenge, they are better able to develop personal relationships. Friendships are invaluable to therapists, not merely as counterbalances to the professional relationships, but also as an ingredient in their simply "being human" (Kaslow & Schulman, 1987).

Caring for Oneself

Addressing the various issues discussed thus far can keep parentified therapists from becoming overextended and stressed. Other ways of preventing burnout include attending to physical fitness and health, as well as achieving a reasonable balance between work and play. Scheduling and managing time, Daniel's albatross, are also critical. Moreover, engaging in various professional activities (e.g., teaching, supervising, research, writing) along with clinical practice is stimulating and expands one's professional perspective, social network, and personal outlook on life (Kaslow & Schulman, 1987).

Practicing Ethically

Therapists who actively negotiate the various concerns raised in this discussion are not only less likely to burn out but also subject to fewer complaints about their professional and ethical practices. Predictably, their clinical work reflects a better balancing of therapeutic caring and structure. It is also marked by an inclusive and fair multilaterality on their part, as they attempt to understand and to address the experience of all members of the clients' context. Aspiring to achieve such a multilateral posture exceeds the demands of conventional ethical codes in the helping professions. The ethic of "do no harm," for example, is typically interpreted in terms of the immediate client rather than from the perspective of everyone potentially affected by the therapist's activities. To be accountable on a larger scale is, indeed, a personally and professionally demanding requirement, but one that is necessary in light of the therapeutic community's unavoidable impact, however small, on the solidarity of intergenerational relationships and the humaneness of the social order.

Training

It is my impression that training and education programs for help-ing professionals should be doing considerably more to address the issues raised in this chapter. Although the focus here has been the parentified therapist, many of the points considered are rel-evant to other therapists as well.

Screening Applicants

Interestingly, some (e.g., Racusin, Abramowitz, & Winter, 1981) suggest that questions about family-of-origin experiences be used to assess candidates for therapy training. Having a background of parentification may be an index of an applicant's potential as an empathic, resourceful, and dedicated service provider. Contrari-wise, such a background may portend various problems, as dis-cussed earlier. The willingness of prospective therapists to address the implications of their parentification for their training and future clinical work, therefore, is as important in the screening process as their family history.

Therapy

One way in which students can deal with their parentification is through their own therapy. As seen in the case of Maggie, this played a significant role in her training and laid the groundwork for her to make significant changes in her family role. Not all schools of therapy, however, advocate that therapists seek their own treat-ment. Haley (1987), for instance, recommends skills training in various areas (e.g., in dealing with authoritarian fathers) rather than personal therapy.

   However, therapeutic orientations that emphasize differentiation and justice are more growth oriented than problem oriented. They hinge on the therapist's ability to establish trustworthy, respon-sible, and differentiated relationships with clients and to encour-age them to do the same in their personal and family relationships. Unless the therapist has worked to achieve differentiation, fair-ness, caring, and integrity in his or her interactions with significant others, a process that often requires therapeutic intervention, then he or she inevitably sets limits on the growth potential of clients (Boszormenyi-Nagy & Krasner, 1986; Bowen, 1978).

Supervision

It is incumbent upon supervisors to be aware of parentification in their supervisees and its impact on their therapeutic functioning. The implication is that person-of-the-therapist issues should be part of the supervisory experience. Along these lines, Aponte and Winter (1987) have formulated a systematic "person/practice" model that incorporates guidelines to prevent exploitation of the supervisee. Illustrating the model, Aponte (1994) recently presented excerpts from three training sessions with Elaine, a student therapist. The sessions involved live supervision of Elaine with her client family, discussion with her of the relation of her personal and family life to her clinical work, and an interview by a trainer with Elaine and her mother. Of interest is that in these sessions, she learned that her emotional caretaking of her father and distant relationship with her mother in her family of origin had a direct impact on the way she related to her client family.

Supervisors, however, should be cautious about focusing only on the negative impact of parentification on trainees' therapeutic work. As noted earlier, parentified individuals are often extremely talented therapeutically, a fact that may threaten supervisors and elicit their own countertransference reactions in supervision. These supervisees also challenge their supervisors to help them balance caring and structure in the therapy process. Supervisors whose bias is to encourage hierarchy, neutrality, and distance in the therapeutic relationship may have difficulty with this task, encouraging their trainees to withhold their personhood and to devalue their ability to foster person-to-person connections.

Course Work

Ethics courses in many training sites are organized around extant ethical and legal codes pertaining to the practice of therapy. Consequently, the focus tends to be individualistic rather than multilateral. Although the issue of inclusive, fair multilaterality should be addressed in supervision, it should also be meaningfully incorporated into ethics courses, as well as into other class work that deals with therapy and clinical evaluation.

Other Activities

It is also recommended that other didactic experiences and consciousness-raising activities be included in training programs to address the issues of burnout, the "identified-therapist" phenomenon, differentiation from one's professional role, and family, social, and personal life. How a faculty attends to these matters, of course, provides a powerful example for its students about the nature of healthy life-styles of professional helpers.

CONCLUSIONS

The observations offered in this chapter concerning the common liabilities and strengths of therapists with a history of parentification were drawn largely from my personal experiences, as well as from work with colleagues, students, supervisees, and therapists in therapy. This area is rife with hypotheses and questions that warrant empirical study. The person-of-the-therapist is not only the service provider's primary clinical tool, but also an organic part of the treatment system. It is to the advantage of our clients and trainees that we learn more about the clinician's personhood and ways of more effectively weaving it into the fabric of therapy and therapy training.

CHAPTER 9

Preventing Destructive
Parentification

At the core of the ecological and existential-ethical framework that has organized our discussion of the etiology, maintenance, transgenerational transmission, and treatment of destructive parentification is a concern with the prevention and optimization of human potential. For example, the rights and needs of future generations of children, leveraged by parental responsibility, are the sine qua non of an inclusive and fair multilaterality.

Moreover, consideration of the existential reality of familial relationships points not only to dysfunction, deficits, and pathology but also to residual resources, untapped trustworthiness, and opportunities for family members to help one another and thus to earn constructive entitlement (Boszormenyi-Nagy & Krasner, 1986). Catalyzing the latter represents an essential but, in practice, often ignored dimension in the mental health field, which has been driven by a deficit model over the years (Imber-Black, 1986; Karpel, 1986b).

The deficit model also pervades research and social policy in the field of human development (Bronfenbrenner, 1979). Despite the growth of ecologically and community-based inquiry, researchers, social policymakers, and practitioners continue to orient to deficiencies within persons and their immediate environment. As emphasized in Part I of this book, problems such as destructive parentification extend beyond the child and the family to include society and the larger human context.

Therefore, research and interventions—especially those that have implications for prevention—must address predominant beliefs and social structures within various cultures and subcultures. Indeed, Bronfenbrenner (1979) recommends changing the macrosystem, through "transforming experiments" that systematically alter families, family-community relationships, the workplace, social institutions, and other micro- , meso- , and exosystems that influence children, in an effort (1) to understand eco-processes scientifically and (2) to create a "more human ecology" conducive to psychological growth.

A number of ideas about how to fashion such an ecology in light of the problem of destructive parentification are the focus of this chapter. Following a consideration of the need to broaden the definition of child maltreatment to include extreme forms of pathologically parentifying behaviors, it addresses the nature of a comprehensive prevention approach that incorporates multilevel systemic and multilateral ethical principles discussed earlier. Examples of prevention programming that address destructive parentification are also discussed, followed by consideration of research issues.

ENLARGING THE DEFINITION OF
CHILD MALTREATMENT

A review of the prevention literature reveals that destructive parentification has received scant attention. For example, it is referenced only once in passing ("role reversal") in a recently edited volume on preventing child maltreatment (Willis, Holden, & Rosenberg, 1992). Similarly, priority areas identified in recent years by granting agencies such as the National Center on Child Abuse and Neglect contain no mention of the construct of parentification or related processes. Perhaps this should not be surprising, inasmuch as common definitions of child maltreatment in legal statutes and the professional literature are restricted to physical abuse, neglect, sexual abuse, and emotional or psychological abuse.

Yet, in view of evidence presented in Part I of this book, destructive parentification is often a concomitant of various abusive and neglectful parental practices and appears to constitute a form of child maltreatment in its own right. Although destructively parentified children and adolescents may be classified as psychologically abused, such abuse typically refers to terrorizing, rejecting, ignoring, corrupting, and isolating parental behaviors (Garbarino, Guttmann, & Seeley, 1989). Extreme forms of parentification can also be included in the definition of parental neglect (cf. Buchholz & Haynes, 1983). A case can be made, however, for classifying pathologically parentifying behaviors as a separate category of child maltreatment.

In defining child maltreatment generally, the question of parental intent is frequently raised. Certainly, because many parentifying parents do not intentionally exploit their children in a destructive manner, it may be argued that they are not guilty of maltreatment. Although the issue of intent represents an important piece of the clinical picture of problematic parental behavior, it should not be pivotal in determining whether a child has been maltreated.

These definitional issues notwithstanding, I am concerned that unless the conceptual boundaries of child maltreatment are redrawn to include destructive parentification, it is not likely that this construct will receive the attention it deserves from investigators, social policymakers, practitioners, educators, and prevention programmers. Moreover, to the extent that federal funding of social science research is tied to current definitions of child maltreatment, the database in the area of destructive parentification will continue to develop slowly.

It is fully recognized that enlarging the official definition of child maltreatment to include yet another subcategory may only further add to the ambiguity and controversy involved in defining maltreatment (cf. Giovannoni, 1989). This is particularly likely if the criteria, including the relative seriousness, of destructive parentification are not well developed and operationally clear. Also at risk are parents, who stand to be blamed and labeled with yet another type of parental deficiency by a social system that not only has inadvertently contributed to their problems but also has limited resources to help.

Yet, some means of calling attention to the rights and needs of youngsters—whose childhood is being sacrificed in the interest of their families—are needed. At a minimum, meaningful dialogue about this issue at the county, state, and federal levels would contribute to ongoing efforts to address the plight of increasing numbers of destructively parentified children and their families.

ECOLOGICAL-ETHICAL PREVENTION PROGRAMMING

Just as treatment of destructive parentification benefits from a multilevel systemic and multilateral ethical orientation, so does prevention programming. Indeed, investigators of child maltreatment are increasingly using Bronfenbrenner's model to develop population- and group-based preventive interventions that address risk and protective factors at different points in the child's ecosystem (see Willis, Holden, Rosenberg, 1992; Melton & Barry, 1994). Our efforts to expand ecological theorizing to include an existential-ethical dimension has important implications for the development of prevention programs.

In general, consideration of the larger existential-ethical context of the child's development focuses attention on individual and sociofamilial processes that affect and are affected by intergenerational justice and solidarity, the central dynamic of which is responsible and caring parenting. *Alterations in this dynamic may be one of the most effective ways of transforming the basic blueprint of society at a macrosystemic level.*

It is interesting to note along these lines that a significant antecedent of sweeping political reform may be child-rearing reform. This hypothesis has been the central focus of deMause's (1990) psychohistorical studies over the years. Recent revolutionary changes in the Soviet Union have provided the most dramatic test of deMause's postulation. The physical violence and oppressive policies of czarist and Stalinist Russia mirrored on the sociopolitical plane the widespread abusive child-rearing practices of traditional Russian families. Lenin, for example, was put to bed, during his first few years of life, wrapped in cold towels. Both of Stalin's parents severely beat him (deMause, 1990). Changes in parenting conceptions and practices have contributed significantly, from deMause's perspective, to a new cadre of Russian leaders in recent years whose political orientation incorporates democratic ideals.

As we found in the treatment domain, the practical value of a multilevel, multilateral approach is that different preventive strategies, addressing various layers of the child's ecology and ontology, can be coherently implemented simultaneously. Without an integrated model to serve as a guide, prevention programmers risk developing multifaceted intervention packages that are contradictory, poorly coordinated, and possibly incomplete, thus proving ineffectual or even harmful.

To address the problem of coordination, an increasing number of prevention and early intervention programs are using case managers (see Vourlekis & Greene, 1992). These professionals not only help implement intervention strategies in a coherent fashion but also buttress mesosystemic structures, the instability of which is a key risk factor. That is, case managers help link and reconcile differences between the various microsystems (family, peer group, school, agencies such as the juvenile court and protective services) of the children assigned to them. Teaching parents these skills, collectively referred to earlier as ecological competence, is an important part of our therapy of youngsters being maltreated in various ways and should also be included in the job description of case managers.

Breakdowns in the coordination of different public and private agencies and governing bodies concerned with children at risk for various difficulties are also legion within the larger social system. In a growing number of counties interagency coordination meetings are being held to address this problem.

Curiously, the committee at the federal level appointed to oversee the goals, activities, and initiatives of other congressional committees dealing with children, youth, and families was recently disbanded. Is this reflective of the status accorded children's issues in Congress? Although advocacy for youngsters and families makes for persuasive campaign slogans and rhetoric, candidates soon learn—once elected—that child-related issues do not ultimately build their power base in Washington (cf. Brim, 1975).

That legislation directly related to family life carries little political weight is unfortunate from an existential-ethical perspective, inasmuch as the quality of our lives and, in the final analysis, our survival as a species depend on the priority that we, individually and collectively, give to the nature of the parent-child relationship. Transforming experiments are needed that contribute to macro-systemic change and an increasingly fair and sensitive interpersonal ethic. Some modest examples of such experimentation are presented next.

TRANSFORMING EXPERIMENTS

Home-Visitation Program

The first illustration is taken from the work of Olds and his colleagues (see Olds & Henderson, 1989). Although destructive parentification was not specifically targeted, this project is discussed here in some detail. It contains many of the essential ingredients from an ecological and methodological perspective that are needed in the design and evaluation of prevention programming for parents at risk of not only physically abusing or neglecting their children but also destructively parentifying them.

The project was implemented in a semirural county of New York, which had the highest rates of reported and confirmed cases of child abuse and neglect in the state. Pregnant women (before their 30th week of pregnancy) who had any one of the following risk characteristics were recruited through a variety of public and private educational, health, and human service facilities: (1) less than 19 years of age, (2) single-parent status, and (3) low socioeconomic status. To avoid the stigma associated with programs exclusively for poor and potentially abusive or neglectful parents, anyone bearing a first child was also permitted to enroll.

Using a stratification procedure, the women were randomly assigned to one of four treatment conditions: (1) sensory and developmental screening at the child's 12th and 24th month, (2) screenings plus free transportation to regularly scheduled prenatal and well-child visits, (3) screenings, transportation, and home visitation by a nurse during pregnancy, and (4) screenings, transportation, and home visitation by a nurse during pregnancy and the child's first two years.

The home visitation component was designed to address risk

factors at different levels of analysis associated with child abuse and neglect and to promote the health and well-being of the mothers and children. During the prenatal phase, the nurses focused on the strengths of the women and their families. They also began engaging in three major activities that formed the backbone of the program: (1) parent education, (2) enhancement of informal social support, and (3) linkage with formal services.

The first involved education about fetal and infant development, with an emphasis on (1) improving the health habits of parents (e.g., addressing the use of cigarettes, alcohol, and drugs; exercise, nutrition, personal hygiene), (2) encouraging them to complete their education, find employment, and question having more children, and (3) helping them to understand their infants' temperament and socioemotional, cognitive, and health care needs.

The women's informal social networks were enhanced by recruiting family members and friends to support the mother and, later, to care for the child. For example, close friends and relatives, especially boyfriends and husbands, were encouraged to participate in the home visitation, to reinforce and discuss the nurses' input between visits, and to help with household tasks. The women were also encouraged near the end of their pregnancy to identify a trustworthy friend or relative who could give them additional support and relief if the baby were born with a difficult or challenging temperament.

Finally, the nurses also facilitated the family's connection to other health and human services. The women, for example, were prompted to attend their prenatal and well-child care appointments and to contact the physician's office when problems developed. They were referred when necessary to Planned Parenthood, mental health services, legal aid, and a nutritional supplementation program. The nurses also communicated with the primary health care providers of the mothers and babies, which facilitated their ability to support the recommendations of the physicians.

As their description reflects, the various programmatic elements were implemented in a complementary, integrated fashion. The nurses were also given latitude to tailor their visits and activities to meet the unique needs of the different families. To facilitate their work, they gathered information concerning the following questions (Olds & Henderson, 1989, pp. 732–733):

Does either parent report having experienced a childhood characterized by violence, deprivation, or lack of nurturance?

Do the parents have realistic expectations about the baby and
the demands of child care?

Does either parent appear to have any emotional difficulties,
especially poor impulse control?

Are there any factors in the home that may create later stresses
for parents and undermine their control of impulses (for
example, unemployment, overcrowded housing, marital
problems)?

Do the parents appear to be isolated from sources of support
such as family, friends, and neighbors?

Do the parents' friends, neighbors, and relatives condone violence toward children and substandard caregiving?

Olds and his colleagues gathered data from various sources (maternal reports, children's developmental tests, observations of maternal care giving, and emergency room and department of social
service records) to evaluate the efficacy of their efforts. The pattern
of results suggested that the nurse visitors were effective in preventing child abuse and neglect and other care-giving dysfunction.
Effects were most pronounced for the women at greatest risk of
child maltreatment (poor, unmarried teens).

Unfortunately, the degree of parentification per se was not a
dependent variable. However, in light of the relation of child abuse
and neglect to destructively parentifying behavior, it is likely that
the latter was also reduced. More direct evidence of such an effect
is suggested by the data as well. For example, the women at greatest risk who had been visited by nurses provided their children
with more appropriate play materials than did their counterparts
in the comparison group (conditions 1 and 2 combined). Such child-
centered parental behavior is often inconsistent with a pathologically parentifying orientation.

Preliminary cost-benefit analyses also revealed that reduction in
foster care placements, hospitalizations, emergency-room visits, and
child protective service worker time defrayed program expense.
Other short- and long-term projected savings to the government
and community—related to the women's return to the workforce,
smaller family size, and less involvement in such agencies as the

juvenile court—further point to the cost effectiveness of home visitation.

Children in the Middle

Another less service-intensive but creative approach to preventing exploitation of children has been developed recently by Arbuthnot and Gordon (see Arbuthnot, Segal, Gordon, & Schneider, 1994). It is well documented at this point that children of divorce, whose numbers are continuing to grow at an alarming rate, are at risk for a variety of problems, including declining grades in school, delinquency, substance abuse, withdrawal from friends, and prolonged anger with one or both parents (e.g., Krein & Beller, 1988; Wallerstein & Kelly, 1980).

A common dynamic that insidiously contributes to these problems is the tendency of divorcing or divorced parents to triangulate their children in various ways. For example, they may say (Gordon & Arbuthnot, 1993): "I give money to your mother, get it from her." "Your father's never cared about you as much as I do." "Tell your father you don't want to spend time with him." "Does your father's girlfriend stay overnight when you're there?" As Arbuthnot and Gordon observe, these statements are stress-inducing and hurtful, dividing children's loyalties and forcing them to act as a go-between. I hasten to add that they are also destructively parentifying.

Although therapeutic models have been developed to reduce parentification in families of divorce (e.g., Goldman & Coane, 1977), their large-scale application is limited. In contrast, Arbuthnot and Gordon have developed a multimedia educational intervention, consisting of videotapes and accompanying guidebooks for parents, children, and discussion leaders. For example, the videotape for parents, narrated by a family court judge, portrays common scenes of children caught in the middle and alternative methods of preventing or resolving each situation. The videotapes and guidebooks help parents and children to recognize the triangulation process and to learn communication and problem-solving skills.

The training materials can be used in a variety of contexts, including various public and private social service facilities, school systems, parenting classes, pediatricians' offices, and divorce courts.

Arbuthnot and Gordon's materials are particularly well suited for divorcing parents who are mandated by the court to attend parent training classes. In fact, the program is being used in more than 250 courts in this country, as well as in several in other countries (Mexico, Canada, and Israel). Moreover, as the authors suggest, placing the videotape in local video stores can greatly increase its availability.

Preliminary findings indicate that the education program developed by Arbuthnot and Gordon is effective. In a sample of 21 domestic relations courts that had implemented part or all of the program, 81% of the judges in these courts rated it positively; 100 % of the judges perceived that the parents had benefitted at least somewhat, and 54 percent said that the training had been "extremely helpful" to the parents. There were also indications from the judges' reports that as a result of the program, their decision-making process had become less legalistic, re-litigation had decreased, and the relationship between attorneys and mental health professionals had improved (Arburthnot, Segal, Gordon, & Schneider, 1994).

In a more rigorous evaluative study, Arburthnot, Poole, and Gordon (1996) found that divorcing mothers who received one of the guidebooks, *What About the Children: A Guide for Divorced and Divorcing Parents* (Arburthnot & Gordon, 1992), placed their children in fewer loyalty conflicts and were more supportive of the children's relationship with their father. One year later, in comparison to a nontreatment control group, these parents were found to talk more favorably with their children about the other parent. The nonresidential parents also had more access to their youngsters.

Interestingly, in another study conducted by Kearnes, Gordon, Arbuthnot, and Kurkowski (1994), children who viewed the original tape developed for parents reported at follow-up significantly less divorce-related stress than those randomly placed in a placebo control condition. The authors speculated that the experimental youngsters learned communication skills (e.g., "I" messages) to manage parent-induced stress—such as caused by being placed in the middle—and discovered that their stresses were shared by other children in their position. These data lend support to the suggestion given in Chapter 5 to empower youngsters to manage stressful family interactions, including parentification. In light of these findings, Gordon and Arbuthnot (1994) developed another version of their videotape that more explicitly addresses a child audience.

RESEARCH

The destructive parentification of children has yet be specifically targeted as a significant issue in either the treatment or the prevention field. That is not to say, as noted earlier, that prevention programs, particularly parent education and home visitation approaches (such as the work of Olds and his colleagues), fail to address sociofamilial variables that influence parentifying processes. Unfortunately, parentification is typically not included as a dependent measure.

In addition to collecting data on the effects of different prevention programs on parentification, researchers would be well advised to design interventions that pinpoint this variable. For example, parents could be sensitized, through educational programming, to the various ways in which children become destructively parentified. Arbuthnot and Gordon have focused on one parentifying process. Other processes, such as parents' confiding inappropriately in their children or failing to credit them for their caretaking efforts, warrant attention as well.

Perhaps one of the greatest challenges of educative efforts in this area involves recruitment of at-risk groups. Olds and his colleagues cogently argue that without a home visitation component, many families who need prevention services will not receive them. The parents in their study, for example, lacked self confidence and trust in formal service providers, decreasing the likelihood of their participation in programs, such as parenting classes, outside the home.

On the other hand, if changing or utilizing institutional procedures to foster involvement in prevention programming is part of the research effort, then interventions that are less service-intensive than home visitation may be effective. For example, Arbuthnot and Gordon have productively capitalized on court-mandated parenting classes for divorcing parents to disseminate their educational materials. Mothers' hospital stays following delivery represent other opportune times to intervene in various ways (e.g., education, baby's rooming in).

Yet, as Olds' research team discovered, the ongoing informal support of a home visitor appears necessary for many parents at risk of maltreating their children. Some, moreover, may require even more intensive intervention. Indeed, at follow-up, the rate of maltreatment in the most successful group in the home visitation study was still four percent, pointing to the need for supplemental and rapidly available therapeutic intervention in intractable cases and continuing efforts at the macrosystemic and ethical levels to reduce inequities in social and economic structures (Olds & Henderson, 1989).

Data indicating which parents need more comprehensive and in-depth treatment would be helpful to prevention programmers. Collection of such data will require that researchers increasingly use multivariate models and etiologic theories to understand the origins of child maltreatment, including destructive parentification, and rigorous evaluation methods to identify variables that are predictive of differential outcome for various prevention, intervention, and treatment programs (National Center on Child Abuse and Neglect, 1994; Panel on Research on Child Abuse and Neglect, 1993).

At another level, according to the Panel on Research on Child Abuse and Neglect, we need a research agenda that includes a national science policy on child maltreatment challenging the existing system to accommodate to new viewpoints and discoveries. Data and observations discussed in this book from an eco-ethical view on the nature, scope, treatment, and prevention of destructive parentification promise to contribute importantly to innovative developments in this area.

CONCLUSIONS

It was suggested in this chapter that prevention of destructive parentification proceed on several fronts. The first involves recognition that pathologically parentifying behavior reflects a significant breakdown in the caregiving system in families, falling within the spectrum of child maltreatment. Whether or not destructively parentified children are officially identified as maltreated, they should be increasingly included in the design of prevention and early intervention programs in the area of child abuse and neglect.

Furthermore, it is important that those involved in the direct care of children in medical, child protection, legal, educational, and other helping systems be apprised of the signs and symptoms of destructive parentification and of different prevention and intervention approaches. Further systematic study is needed from an eco-ethical perspective, however, to determine the most effective ways of helping families at risk for destructive parentification. Such investigative activity, particularly if part of a larger research initiative to understand, prevent, and treat child maltreatment, has the potential to transform social policies to reflect a more humane and just perspective.

Constructs Related to the Parentification of Children

INDIVIDUAL AND FAMILY PSYCHODYNAMIC APPROACHES

Unnatural Roles   Severe or protracted marital conflict induces children to assume the role of pawn, confidant, or buffer to compensate for parents' inability to gratify each other's needs (Mahler & Rabinovitch, 1956).

Role Reversal   This process involves a reversal of the dependency role between parents and their small children (Helfer, 1987; Kempe & Helfer, 1972; Kempe & Kempe, 1978; Morris & Gould, 1963, 1979).

Symbiotic Therapist   Therapeutic reconstructions of the childhoods of disturbed patients revealed not only their induction into a caretaking role but also their innate psychotherapeutic strivings to heal fragile parental figures (Searles, 1971, 1973, 1975).

Gifted Child   Miller (1979/1981) described children who are exquisitely attuned to the unconscious roles assigned to them by parents. They are denied their own legitimate narcissistic needs for mirroring, soothing, and empathy.

Selfobject Failure   Infants lacking an empathic and responsive human environment (i.e., selfobjects) may serve as narcissistic extensions of their caretakers or selfobjects for them (Kohut, 1977).

Situations of Horror   Lowen (1983) used this phrase to describe youngsters who are seduced into a special relationship with parents, in which they become privy to and overly stimulated by adult feelings and sexuality.

False Self   Severe impingements of infants' experience because of an unavailable or intrusive caretaker inhibit their spontaneous expression of their "true self" and reinforce a growing "false self" (Winnicott, 1965).

Symbiotic Survival Pattern   Through projective identification, in which parents project introjects onto their spouses or children and induce them to act accordingly, family members become responsible for one another's emotional survival (Slipp, 1973; see also Ogden, 1979, 1982).

FAMILY SYSTEMS THEORY

Family Healer   Another term for the child who acts as peacemaker, go-between, or protector in the family (Ackerman, 1966).

Delegation   In the interest of meeting their own affective, ego, or superego needs, parents may assign their children missions that exploit their loyalties (Stierlin, 1974, 1977).

Family Burden Bearer	This is the one in the family who assumes responsibility for his or her sickly parent, who sometimes protects his or her siblings, and who may support the constellation of family roles (Brody & Spark, 1966).
Well Sibling	Although not an overt caretaker, this sibling indirectly supports his or her family by being overadequate to compensate for symptomatic siblings (Boszormenyi-Nagy & Spark, 1973; Framo, 1965; Friedman, 1964).
Parental Child	To ensure the family's equilibrium, one or more of the children function in an executive capacity (Minuchin, 1974; Minuchin & Fishman, 1981).
Emotional Incest	In highly enmeshed parent-child relationships, the child may be "chosen" to serve as a primary source for emotional support (Love & Robinson, 1990; Mellody, Miller, & Miller, 1989).
Child as Parent or as Mate	Crossgenerational boundary distortions may assume the form of the child's acting in either a parent- or mate-like role vis-à-vis parental figures (Walsh, 1979).
Benevolent Function	Madanes (1981) assumes that the child is often an "active initiator of protective sequences of interaction" (p. 66).
Noble Motivations	Recognition that symptoms may, or appear to, serve a protective function for the family has supported the strategic technique of ascribing "noble" intentions to them (Stanton & Todd, 1979) or "positively connoting" the homeostatic tendencies of families (Pallazolli-Selvini, Boscolo, Cecchin, & Prata, 1978).
Over-functioning	Bowen (1978) and his colleagues (Kerr & Bowen, 1988) have described complementary functioning positions in relational systems, in which one member overfunctions, in direct proportion to which the other underfunctions. This arrange-

ment can exist between parents and children and is supported by an exchange of each member's "pseudo-self," a central piece in functional differentiation. Individuals at higher levels of basic differentiation, and thus possessive of a more "solid self," do not enter into such transactions.

Spousal Replacement

In their discussion of marital schism and skew, Lidz, Cornelison, Fleck, and Terry (1957) observed that parents in disturbed marriages often vie for their children's attention, expecting them to replace the spouse.

Scapegoat

In addition to being assigned overt caretaking roles, children are delegated other roles, such as scapegoat, that help protect family members and stabilize familial functioning (Boszormenyi-Nagy & Spark, 1973).

Family Interpreter

The oldest hearing children of deaf parents often assume this role (Buchino, 1990; Frankenburg, Sloman, & Perry, 1985).

Overburdened Child

Wallerstein (1985) has observed that the pseudo-maturity seen in many children of divorce belies underlying stress.

SOCIOLOGICAL AND ANTHROPOLOGICAL OBSERVATIONS

Unfulfilled Role Function

Echoing the views of many family systems investigators, role theorists (e.g., Tharp, 1965) suggest that inappropriate role functioning on the part of children is prima facie evidence of a breakdown in the parents' organization and fulfillment of family roles.

Junior Partner

Reflecting hierarchical differences in the structure of single-parent and two-parent families, children in the former are more likely to be junior partners in the management of the household (Weiss, 1979).

Cheblakwet   In a community of farm families in Kenya, an older sibling, a *cheblakwet*, is expected to care for infants over four months age. The child's tasks are supervised and clearly defined (Harkness & Super, 1983; Super & Harkness, 1981, 1982).

ADDICTION MODELS

Co-dependence   This term refers to the overly solicitous, controlling, and dependent actions of individuals who are involved with a chemically addicted person. Recently, the definition has been expanded to include such behavior with a dysfunctional person or excessive and distressing focus on the needs of others (Cermak, 1991; Whitfield, 1991).

Family Hero   Wegscheider-Cruse (1985, 1990) differentiates various roles of children in alcoholic families (cf. Satir, 1988). For example, the family hero, who is often the firstborn, assumes parental responsibilities and tends to be an overachiever in school, pseudomature, controlling, approval-seeking, and compulsive.

DEVELOPMENTAL PERSPECTIVES

Spousification   Sroufe and Ward (1980) serendipitously discovered in the course of investigating parental discipline a phenomenon labeled by them as "spousification." When some mothers needed attention or support, they physically overstimulated their children. Their family backgrounds included sexual misuse and deprivation. Subsequently, Sroufe and his colleagues (Jacobvitz, Morgan, Dretchmar, & Morgan, 1992; Sroufe, Jacobvitz, Mangelsdorf, DeAngelo, & Ward, 1985) used the term "boundary dissolution" to refer to a more generalized pattern of boundary problems in parent-child relationships, of which spousification is one form.

Hurried Child	Related to the stress of contemporary adult life and social inconstancies, parents are using their children as surrogate selves, status symbols, partners, and therapists, thus hurrying them to grow up (Elkind, 1981).
Compulsive Caregiving	Bowlby (1979) observed a deviant form of attachment, in which parents fail to respond to the attachment behaviors of their offspring, who prematurely and eventually compulsively caretake as a way of maintaining proximity and of connecting to parental figures.

Parentification Questionnaire

MICHAEL W. SESSIONS, PH.D., AND
GREGORY J. JURKOVIC, PH.D.

The following statements are possible descriptions of experiences you may have had while growing up. If a statement accurately describes some portion of your childhood experience, that is, the time during which you lived at home with your family (including your teenage years), mark the statement true on your answer sheet. If the statement does not accurately describe your experience, mark it false.

1. I rarely found it necessary to do other family members' chores.
2. At times I felt I was the only one my mother/father could turn to.
3. Members of my family hardly ever looked to me for advice.
4. In my family I often felt called upon to do more than my share.

5. I often felt like an outsider in my family.
6. I felt most valuable in my family when someone confided in me.
7. It seemed as though there were enough problems at home without my causing more.
8. In my family I thought it best to let people work out their problems on their own.
9. I often silently resented being asked to do certain kinds of jobs.
10. In my family it seemed that I was usually the one who ended up being responsible for most of what happened.
11. In my mind, the welfare of my family was my first priority.
12. If someone in my family had a problem, I was rarely the one they could turn to for help.
13. I was frequently responsible for the physical care of some member of my family, i.e., washing, feeding, dressing, etc.
14. My family was not the kind in which people took sides.
15. It often seemed that my feelings weren't taken into account in my family.
16. I often found myself feeling down for no particular reason that I could think of.
17. In my family there were certain family members I could handle better than anyone else.
18. I often preferred the company of people older than me.
19. I hardly ever felt let down by members of my family.
20. I hardly ever got involved in conflicts between my parents.
21. I usually felt comfortable telling family members how I felt.
22. I rarely worried about people in my family.
23. As a child I was often described as mature for my age.
24. In my family I often felt like a referee.
25. In my family I initiated most recreational activities.
26. It seemed as though family members were always bringing me their problems.
27. My parents had enough to do without worrying about housework as well.
28. In my family I often made sacrifices that went unnoticed by other family members.
29. My parents were very helpful when I had a problem.
30. If a member of my family was upset, I would almost always become involved in some way.

31. I could usually manage to avoid doing housework.
32. I believe that most people understood me pretty well, particularly members of my family.
33. As a child, I wanted to make everyone in my family happy.
34. My parents rarely disagreed on anything important.
35. I often felt more like an adult than a child in my family.
36. I was more likely to spend time with friends than with family members.
37. Members of my family rarely needed me to take care of them.
38. I was very uncomfortable when things weren't going well at home.
39. All things considered, responsibilities were shared equally in my family.
40. In my house I hardly ever did the cooking.
41. I was very active in the management of my family's financial affairs.
42. I was at my best in times of crisis.

SCORING KEY AND INTERPRETATION

To score the Parentification Questionnaire, tally the number of responses marked "true" to items 2, 4, 5, 6, 7, 9, 10, 11, 13, 15, 16, 17, 18, 23, 24, 25, 26, 27, 28, 30, 33, 35, 38, 41, and 42, and marked "false" to items 1, 3, 8, 12, 14, 19, 20, 21, 22, 29, 31, 32, 34, 36, 37, 39, and 40.

The higher the total score, the greater the degree of parentification. Because this measure was developed for research purposes, a clinical cutoff (based on normative data) has not been established. Investigators who are interested in empirically categorizing individuals' scores relative to their deviation from the mean should refer either to descriptive statistics of the sample from which the individuals' scores were drawn or to locally established norms.

It should also be noted that although extremely low scores on the Parentification Questionnaire suggest an absence of destructive parentification, they may reflect overprotection or infantilization. Therefore, middling scores probably best represent the healthiest scores in terms of responsibilities in one's family of origin. Further research is needed to confirm this impression, however.

Finally, that females may score higher than males on the Parentification Questionnaire should be taken into consideration in the research design and statistical analyses of studies using this measure. See Goglia, Jurkovic, Burt, and Burge-Callaway (1992) for further information on the psychometric properties and utility of the Parentification Questionnaire.

REFERENCES

Achenbach, T. M. (1990). Conceptualization of developmental psychopathology. In M. Lewis & S. M. Miller (Eds.), *Handbook of developmental psychopathology* (pp. 3–4). New York: Plenum.

Ackerman, N. W. (1966). *Treating the troubled family.* New York: Basic Books.

Ackerman, R. J. (1989). *Perfect daughters.* Deerfield Beach, FL: Health Communications.

Adler, T., DeAngelis, T., Moses-Zirkes, S. (1993, June). Clinton budget: Some feast, some famine. *APA Monitor, 1,* 42–44.

Ainsworth, M. D. S. (1989). Attachments beyond infancy. *American Psychologist, 44,* 709–716.

Alexander, P. C. (1992). Application of attachment theory to the study of sexual abuse. *Journal of Consulting and Clinical Psychology, 60,* 185–195.

American Psychiatric Association. (1987). *Diagnostic and statistical manual of mental disorders* (3rd ed., rev.). Washington, DC: Author.
  • (1994). *Diagnostic and statistical manual of mental disorders* (4th ed.). Washington, DC: Author.

Anderson, H., & Goolishian, H. A. (1988). Human systems as linguistic systems: Preliminary and evolving ideas about the implications for clinical theory. *Family Process, 27,* 371–393.

Aponte, H. J. (1994). How personal can training get? *Journal of Marital and Family Therapy, 20,* 3–15.

Aponte, H. J., & Winter, J. E. (1987). The person and practice of the therapist: Treatment and training. *Journal of Psychotherapy and the Family, 3,* 85–111.

Arbuthnot. J., & Gordon, D. A. (1992). *What about the children: A guide for divorced and divorcing parents,* 3rd ed. Athens, OH: Center for Divorce Education.

Arbuthnot. J., Poole, C. J., & Gordon, D. A. (1996). Use of educational materials to modify stressful behaviors in post-divorce parenting. *Journal of Divorce and Remarriage, 25*, 117–137.

Arbuthnot, J., Segal, D., Gordon, D. A., & Schneider, K. (1994). Court–sponsored education programs for divorcing parents: Some guiding thoughts and preliminary data. *Juvenile and Family Court Journal, 45*, 77–84.

Aries, P. (1962). *Centuries of childhood: A social history of family life.* New York: Alfred A. Knopf.

Bacal, H. A. (1989). Winnicott and self-psychology: Remarkable reflections. In D. W. Detrick & S. P. Detrick (Eds.), *Self psychology: Comparisons and contrasts* (pp. 259–271). Hillsdale, NJ: Analytic Press.

Barker, G., & Gump, P. V. (1964). *Big school, small school: High school size and student behavior.* Stanford, CA: Stanford University Press.

Barry, H., III, & Paxson, L. M. (1971). Infancy and early childhood: Cross-cultural codes 2. *Ethnology, 10*, 466–508.

Bateson, G. (1972). *Steps to an ecology of mind.* New York: Ballentine Books.

Bavolek, S. J. (1984). *Handbook for the adult-adolescent parenting inventory (AAPI).* Schaumburg, IL: Family Development Associates.

Belsky, J. (1980). Child maltreatment: An ecological integration. *American Psychologist, 35*, 320–335.

Belsky, J., & Vondra, J. (1989). Lessons from child abuse: The determinants of parenting. In D. Cicchetti & V. Carlson (Eds.), *Child maltreatment: Theory and research on the causes and consequences of child abuse and neglect* (pp. 153–202). New York: Cambridge University Press.

Bentovim, A., & Kinston, W. (1991). Focal family therapy: Joining systems theory with psychodynamic understanding. In A. S. Gurman & D. P. Kniskern (Eds.), *Handbook of family therapy,* Vol. 2 (pp. 284–324). New York: Brunner/Mazel.

Berry, D. L. (1985). *Mutuality: The vision of Martin Buber.* Albany, NY: State University of New York Press.

Blumenstein, H. (1986). Maintaining a family focus: Underlying issues and challenges. *Clinical Social Work Journal, 14*, 238–249.

Boccia, M., & Campos, J. J. (1989). Maternal emotional signals, social referencing, and infants' reactions to strangers. In M. Eisenberg (Ed.), *Empathy and related emotional responses. New directions for child development, No. 44* (pp. 25–49). San Francisco: Jossey-Bass.

Borgman, R. (1984). Problems of sexually abused girls and their treatment. *Social Casework, 65*, 182–186.

Bossard, J. H. S., & Boll, E. S. (1956). *The large family system: An original study in the sociology of family behavior.* Philadelphia: University of Pennsylvania Press.

Boszormenyi-Nagy, I. (1965). A theory of relationships: Experience and transaction. In I. Boszormenyi-Nagy & J. L. Framo (Eds.), *Intensive family therapy: Theoretical and practical aspects* (pp. 38–86). New York: Harper & Row.

- (1987). *Foundations of contextual therapy.* New York: Brunner/Mazel.

Boszormenyi-Nagy, I., & Framo, J. L. (1962). Family concept of hospital treatment of schizophrenia. In J. Masserman (Ed.), *Current psychiatric therapies,* Vol. 2 (pp. 159–166). New York: Grune & Stratton.

Boszormenyi-Nagy, I., & Krasner, B. R. (1986). *Between give and take: A clinical guide to contextual therapy.* New York: Brunner/Mazel.

Boszormenyi-Nagy, I., & Spark, G. M. (1973). *Invisible loyalties: Reciprocity in intergenerational family therapy.* Hagerstown, MD: Harper & Row.

Boszormenyi-Nagy, I., & Ulrich, D. N. (1981). Contextual family therapy. In A. Gurman & D. P. Kniskern (Eds.), *Handbook of family therapy* (pp. 159–186). New York: Brunner/Mazel.

Bowen, M. (1978). *Family therapy in clinical practice.* New York: Aronson.

Bowlby, J. (1973). *Attachment and loss: Separation.* New York: Basic Books.

- (1979). *The making and breaking of affectional bonds.* London: Tavistock.
- (1980). *Attachment and loss: Vol 3. Loss, sadness, and depression.* New York: Basic Books.

Boyd-Franklin, N. (1987). The contribution of family therapy models to the treatment of black families. *Psychotherapy, 24,* 621–629.

Bridgeman, D. L. (1983). Benevolent babies: Emergence of the social self. In D. L. Bridgeman (Ed.), *The nature of prosocial development: Interdisciplinary theories and strategies* (pp. 95–112). New York: Academic Press.

Brim, O. G. (1975). Macro-structural influences on child development and the need for childhood social indicators. *American Journal of Orthopsychiatry, 45,* 516–524.

Brody, E. M., & Spark, G. M. (1966). Institutionalization of the aged. *Family Process, 5,* 76–90.

Bronfenbrenner, U. (1977). Toward an experimental ecology of human development. *American Psychologist, 32,* 513–531.

- (1979). *The ecology of human development: Experiments by nature and design.* Cambridge, MA: Harvard University Press.

Brown, S., & Beletsis, S. (1986). The development of family transference in groups for adult children of alcoholics. *International Journal of Group Psychotherapy, 36,* 97–114.

Buber, M. (1965). *Between man and man.* New York: Macmillan.

- (1970). *I and thou.* (W. Kaufmann, Trans.). New York: Scribner. (Original work published 1923).

Buchholz, E. S., & Haynes, R. (1983). Sometimes I feel like a motherless child: Role reversal as a form of parental neglect. *Dynamic Psychotherapy, 1,* 99–107.

Buchino, J. A. (1990). Hearing children of deaf parents: A counseling challenge. *Elementary School Guidance and Counseling, 24,* 207–212.

Burkett, L. P. (1991). Parenting behaviors of women who were sexually abused as children in their families of origin. *Family Process, 30,* 421–434.

Burt, A. (1992). Generational boundary distortion: Implications for object relations development. *Dissertation Abstracts International, 53,* 4389 (University Microfilms No. 92–35327).

Butler, S. (1978). *Conspiracy of silence: The trauma of incest.* San Francisco: Volcano Press.

Campos, J. J., & Stenberg, C. R. (1981). Perception, appraisal and emotion: The onset of social referencing. In M. E. Lamb & L. R. Sherrod (Eds.), *Infant social cognition: Empirical and theoretical considerations* (pp. 273–314). Hillsdale, NJ: Erlbaum.

Carlson, V., Cicchetti, D., Barnett, D., & Braunwald, K. G. (1989). Finding order in disorganization: Lessons from research on maltreated infants' attachments to their caregivers. In D. Cicchetti & V. Carlson (Eds.), *Child maltreatment: Theory and research on the causes and consequences of child abuse and neglect* (pp. 494–528). New York: Cambridge University Press.

Cermak, T. L. (1986). *Diagnosing and treating co-dependence: A guide for professionals who work with chemical dependents, their spouses, and children.* Minneapolis, MN: Johnson Institute.

- (1990). *Evaluating and treating adult children of alcoholics,* Vol. 1. Minneapolis, MN: Johnson Institute.

Cicchetti, D. (1989). How research on child maltreatment has informed the study of child development: Perspectives from developmental psychopathology. In D. Cicchetti & V. Carlson (Eds.), *Child maltreatment: Theory and research on the causes and consequences of child abuse and neglect* (pp. 377–431). New York: Cambridge University Press.

Cicchetti, D., & Rizley, R. (1981). Developmental perspectives on the etiology, intergenerational transmission, and sequelae of child maltreatment. *New Directions for Child Development, 11,* 31–55.

Clance, P. R., & O'Toole, M. A. (1987). The imposter phenomenon: An internal barrier to empowerment and achievement. *Women in Therapy, 6,* 51–64.

Clark, T., Zalis, T., & Saccho, F. (1982). *Outreach family therapy.* New York: Jason Aronson.

Cohn, J., & Tronick, E. (1983). Three-month-old infants' reaction to simulated maternal depression. *Child Development, 54,* 185–193.

Cook, S. (1979). Parental conceptions of children and childrearing: A study of rural Maine parents. Master's thesis. Tufts University, Medford, MA.

Cotroneo, M. (1987). Women and abuse in the context of the family. *Journal of Psychotherapy and the Family, 3,* 81–96.

Crandall, J. W. (1976). Pathological nurturance: The root of marital discord. *Journal of Family Counseling, 4,* 62–68.

• (1981). A study of pathological nurturance: The marriage of Gustav Mahler. *Clinical Social Work Journal, 9,* 91–100.

Crisp, P. (1988). Projective identification: Clarification in relation to object choice. *Psychoanalytic Psychology, 5,* 389–402.

Cummings, E. M., Zahn-Waxler, C., & Radke-Yarrow, M. (1981). Young children's responses to expressions of anger and affection by others in the family. *Child Development, 52,* 1274–1282.

• (1984). Developmental changes in children's reactions to anger in the home. *Journal of Child Psychology and Psychiatry, 25,* 63–74.

Daniels, D., & Plomin, R. (1985). Differential experience of siblings in the same family. *Developmental Psychology, 21,* 747–760.

Dawson, F. (1980). The parental child in single and dual parent families. Master's thesis. Georgia State University, Atlanta.

Dean, A. L., Malik, M. M., Richards, W., & Stringer, S. A. (1986). Effects of parental maltreatment on children's conceptions of interpersonal relationships. *Developmental Psychology, 22,* 617–626.

deMause, L. (1990). The gentile revolution: Childhood origins of Soviet and East European democratic movements. *Journal of Psychohistory, 17,* 341–352.

de Shazer, S. (1991). *Putting difference to work.* New York: W. W. Norton.

Doherty, W. J. (1995). *Soul searching: Why psychotherapy must promote moral responsibility.* New York: Basic Books.

Elbow, M. (1982). Children of violent marriages: The forgotten victims. *Social Casework, 63,* 465–471.

Elkind, D. (1979). *The child and society: Essays in applied child development.* New York: Oxford University Press.

• (1981). *The hurried child: Growing up too fast.* Reading, MA: Addison-Wesley.

- (1994). *Ties that stress: The new family imbalance.* Cambridge, MA: Harvard University Press.

Ember, C. (1973). Female task assignment and the social behavior of boys. *Ethos, 1,* 424–439.

Erikson, E. (1980). *Identity and the life cycle.* New York: Norton.

Essman, C. S., & Deutsch, F. (1979). Siblings as babysitters: Responses of adolescents to younger siblings in problem situations. *Adolescence, 14,* 411–420.

Feshbach, N. D. (1989). The construct of empathy and the phenomenon of physical maltreatment of children. In D. Cicchetti & V. Carlson (Eds.), *Child maltreatment: Theory and research on the causes and consequences of child abuse and neglect* (pp. 349–373). New York: Cambridge University Press.

Fosson, A., & Lask, B. (1988). Pictorially displayed family patterns as an assessment instrument. *Journal of Family Therapy, 10,* 65–74.

Foster, M. A. (1984). Schools. In M. Berger & G. J. Jurkovic (Eds.), *Practicing family therapy in diverse settings* (pp. 110–141). San Francisco: Jossey-Bass.

Fowler, W. J., & Walberg, H. J. (1991). School size, characteristics, and outcomes. *Educational Evaluation and Policy Analysis, 13,* 189–202.

Framo, J. L. (1965). Systemic research on family dynamics. In I. Boszormenyi-Nagy & J. L. Framo (Eds.), *Intensive family therapy: Theoretical and practical aspects* (pp. 407–462). New York: Harper & Row.

Frank, H., & Paris, J. (1987). Psychological factors in the choice of psychiatry as a career. *Canadian Journal of Psychiatry, 32,* 118–122.

Frankenburg, F. R., Sloman, L., & Perry, A. (1985). Issues in the therapy of hearing children with deaf parents. *Canadian Journal of Psychiatry, 30,* 98–102.

Freud, A. (1965). *Normality and pathology in childhood.* New York: International Universities Press.

Friedman, A. S. (1964). The "well" sibling in the sick family: A contradiction. *International Journal of Social Psychiatry, 2,* 47–53.

Friedman, E. H. (1982). The myth of the shiksa. In M. McGoldrick, J. K. Pearce, & J. Giordano (Eds.), *Ethnicity and family therapy* (pp. 499–526). New York: Guilford Press.

- (1987). The birthday party revisited: Family therapy and the problem of change. In P. Titelman (Ed.), *The therapist's own family: Toward the differentiation of self* (pp. 163–188). Northvale, NJ: Jason Aronson.

Fry, P. S., & Trifiletti, R. J. (1983). An exploration of the adolescent's perspective: Perceptions of major stress dimensions in the single-parent family. *Journal of Psychiatric Treatment and Evaluation, 5,* 101–111.

Fullinwider-Bush, N., & Jacobvitz, D. B. (1993). The transition to young adulthood: Generation boundary dissolution and female identity development. *Family Process, 32,* 87–103.

Gallimore, R., Boggs, J. W., & Jordan, C. (1974). *Culture, behavior, and education: A study of Hawaiian-Americans.* Beverly Hills: Sage.

Garbarino, J. (1977). The human ecology of child maltreatment: A conceptual model for research. *Journal of Marriage and the Family, 39,* 721–727.

- (1980a). What kind of society permits child abuse? *Infant Mental Health Journal, 1,* 270–280.
- (1980b). Some thoughts on school size and its effects on adolescent development. *Journal of Youth and Adolescence, 9,* 19–31.
- (1981). An ecological approach to child maltreatment. In L. H. Pelton (Ed.), *The social context of child abuse and neglect* (pp. 228–267). New York: Human Sciences Press.

Garbarino, J., et al. (1992). *Children and families in the social environment* (2nd ed.). New York: Aldine deGruyter.

Garbarino, J., & Abramowitz, R. H. (1992). Sociocultural risk and opportunity. In J. Garbarino et al. (Eds.), *Children and families in the social environment* (2nd ed., pp. 35–71). New York: Aldine deGruyter.

Garbarino, J., & Crouter, A. (1978). Defining the community correlates of parent-child relations: The correlates of child maltreatment. *Child Development, 49,* 604–616.

Garbarino, J., Gaboury, M. T., Long, F., Grandjean, P., & Asp, E. (1982). Who owns the children?: An ecological perspective on public policy affecting children. *Child and Youth Services, 5,* 43–63.

Garbarino, J., & Garbarino, A. C. (1992). In conclusion: The issue is human quality. In J. Garbarino et al. (Eds.), *Children and families in the social environment* (2nd ed., pp. 304–328). New York: Aldine deGruyter.

Garbarino, J., Guttmann, E., & Seeley, J. W. (1989). *The psychologically battered child.* San Francisco: Jossey-Bass.

Garbarino, J., & Kostelny, K. (1994). Neighborhood-based programs. In G. B. Melton & F. D. Barry (Eds.), *Protecting children from abuse and neglect: Foundations for a new national strategy* (pp. 304–352). New York: Guilford.

Garbarino, J., & Sherman, D. (1980). High risk neighborhoods and high–risk families: The human ecology of maltreatment. *Child Development, 51,* 188–196.

Gilligan, C. (1982). *In a different voice.* Cambridge, MA: Harvard University Press.

Giovannoni, J. (1989). Definitional issues in child maltreatment. In D. Cicchetti & V. Carlson (Eds.), *Child maltreatment: Theory and research on the causes and consequences of child abuse and neglect* (pp. 3–37). New York: Cambridge University Press.

Glickauf-Hughes, C. (1994). Dynamics and treatment of the masochistic-narcissistic couple. *Psychoanalysis and Psychotherapy, 11,* 34–46.

Glickauf-Hughes, C., Foster, M., & Jurkovic, G. J. (in press). Fusion in couples: What Bowenian therapists can learn from their object-relations colleagues. *Journal of Couples Therapy.*

Goglia, L. R. (1982). An exploration of the long-term effects of parentification. Master's thesis. Georgia State University, Atlanta.

Goglia, L. R., Jurkovic, G. J., Burt, A. M., & K. G. Burge-Callaway. (1992). Generational boundary distortions by adult children of alcoholics: Child-as-parent and child-as-mate. *American Journal of Family Therapy, 20,* 291–299.

Goldman, J., & Coane, J. (1977). Family therapy after the divorce: Developing a strategy. *Family Process, 16,* 357–362.

Goldstein, W. N. (1991). Clarification of projective identification. *American Journal of Psychiatry, 148,* 153–161.

Goodnow, J. J. (1988). Children's household work: Its nature and function. *Psychological Bulletin, 103,* 5–26.

Gordon, D. A., & Arbuthnot, J. (1993). *Children in the middle: A parent's and children's guidebook* (2nd ed.). Athens, OH: Center for Divorce Education.

 • (Producers). (1994). *Children in the middle: Children's version* (videotape). Athens, OH: Center for Divorce Education.

Gore, S., Aseltine, R. H., & Colten, M. E. (1993). Gender, social-relational involvement, and depression. *Journal of Research on Adolescence, 3,* 101–125.

Greenspan, M. (1993). On professionalism. In C. Heyward, *When boundaries betray us: Beyond illusions of what is ethical in therapy and life* (pp. 193–205). New York: HarperCollins.

Guerin, Jr., P. J., Fay, L. F., Burden, S. L., & Kautto, J. G. (1987). *The evaluation and treatment of marital conflict: A four-stage approach.* New York: Basic Books.

Gunderson, J. G., Kerr, J., & Englund, D. W. (1980). The families of borderlines. *Archives of General Psychiatry, 37,* 27–33.

Haley, J. (1987). *Problem-solving therapy* (2nd ed.). San Francisco: Jossey-Bass.

Hansen, J. (1992, August 1). A father sees himself in Kenny Hardwick. *The Atlanta Journal–Constitution,* p. 1F.

Hanson, R. A. (1990). Initial parenting attitudes of pregnant adolescents and a comparison with the decision about adoption. *Adolescence, 25,* 629–643.

Hargrave, T. D., & Bomba, A. K. (1993). Further validation of the

Relational Ethics Scale. *Journal of Marital and Family Therapy, 19,* 292–299.

Hargrave, T. D., Jennings, G., & Anderson, W. (1991). The development of a relational ethics scale. *Journal of Marital and Family Therapy, 17,* 145–158.

Harkness, S., & Super, C. M. (1983). The cultural construction of childhood: A framework for the socialization of affect. *Ethos, 11,* 221–231.

Harrison, A. O., Wilson, M. N., Pine, C. J., Chan, S. Q., & Buriel, R. (1990). Family ecologies of ethnic minority children. *Child Development, 61,* 347–362.

Harter, S. (1977). A cognitive-developmental approach to children's expression of conflicting feelings and a technique to facilitate such expression in play therapy. *Journal of Consulting and Clinical Psychology, 45,* 417–432.

Hays, K. F. (1987). The conspiracy of silence revisited: Group therapy with adult survivors of incest. *Journal of Group Psychotherapy, Psychodrama, and Sociometry, 39,* 143–156.

Held, B., & Bellows, D. (1983). A family systems approach to crisis reactions in college students. *Journal of Marital and Family Therapy, 9,* 365–373.

Helfer, R. E. (1987). The developmental basis of child abuse and neglect: An epidemiological approach. In R. E. Helfer & R. S. Kempe (Eds.), *The battered child* (4th ed., pp. 60–80). Chicago: University of Chicago Press.

Henggeler, S. W. (1982). *Delinquency and adolescent psychopathology: A family-ecological systems approach.* Littleton, MA: Wright-PSG.

Henggeler, S. W., Rodick, J. D., Borduin, C. M., Hanson, C. L., Watson, S. M., & Urey, J. R. (1986). Multisystemic treatment of juvenile offenders: Effects on adolescent behavior and family interactions. *Developmental Psychology, 22,* 132–141.

Henry, O. (1995). *The gift of the magi and other stories.* New York: Penguin Books (first published in 1906).

Heyward, C. (1993). *When boundaries betray us: Beyond illusions of what is ethical in therapy and life.* New York: HarperCollins.

Hoffman, L. (1981). *Foundations of family therapy.* New York: Basic Books.

• (1990). Constructing realities: An art of lenses. *Family Process, 29,* 1–12.

Hoffman, M. L. (1976). Empathy, role taking, guilt, and development of altruistic motives. In T. Lickona (Ed.), *Moral development and behavior: Theory, research, and social issues* (pp. 124–143). New York: Holt, Rinehart, & Winston.

- (1982). Development of prosocial motivation: Empathy and guilt. In N. Eisenberg (Ed.), *The development of prosocial behavior* (pp. 281–313). New York: Academic Press.

Hyde, N. (1986). Covert incest in women's lives: Dynamics and directions for healing. *Canadian Journal of Community Mental Health, 5,* 73–83.

Imber-Black, E. (1986). Toward a resource model in systemic family therapy. In M. A. Karpel (Ed.), *Family resources: The hidden partner in family therapy* (pp. 148–174). New York: Guilford Press.

Jacobvitz, D., Fullinwider, N., & Loera, L. (1991, April). Representations of childhood family patterns, the self, and intimacy in romantic relationships. In D. A. Cohn (Chair), *Working models of attachment and couple relationships.* Symposium conducted at the meeting of the Society for Research in Child Development, Seattle, WA.

Jacobvitz, D. B., Morgan, E., Kretchmar, M. D., & Morgan, Y. (1991). The transmission of mother-child boundary disturbances across three generations. *Development and Psychopathology, 3,* 513–527.

Jacobvitz, D., & Sroufe, L. A. (1987). The early caregiver-child relationship and attention-deficit disorder with hyperactivity in kindergarten: A prospective study. *Child Development, 58,* 1496–1504.

Jalali, B. (1982). Iranian families. In M. McGoldrick, J. K. Pearce, & J. Giordano (Eds.), *Ethnicity and family therapy* (pp. 289–309). New York: Guilford Press.

Johnston, J. R., Gonzalez, R., & Campbell, L. E. G. (1987). Ongoing postdivorce conflict and child disturbance. *Journal of Abnormal Child Psychology, 15,* 493–509.

Jones, R. A., & Wells, M. (1996). An empirical study of parentification and personality. *American Journal of Family Therapy, 24,* 145–152.

Jung, C. G. (1966). *The practice of psychotherapy* (2nd ed.). (R. R. C. Hull, Trans.). Princeton, NJ: Princeton University Press.

Jurkovic, G. J. (1980). The juvenile delinquent as a moral philosopher: A structural-developmental perspective. *Psychological Bulletin, 88,* 709–727.

- (1984). Juvenile justice system. In M. Berger & G. J. Jurkovic (Eds.), *Practicing family therapy in diverse settings* (pp. 211–246). San Francisco: Jossey-Bass.

Jurkovic, G. J., & Berger, M. (1984). Conclusions: Implications for practice, training, and social policy. In M. Berger & G. J. Jurkovic (Eds.), *Practicing family therapy in diverse settings* (pp. 332–343). San Francisco: Jossey-Bass.

Jurkovic, G. J., Jessee, E. H., & Goglia, L. R. (1991). Treatment of parental children and their families: Conceptual and technical issues. *American Journal of Family Therapy, 19,* 302–314.

Jurkovic, G. J., & Ulrici, D. (1982). The nature of insight in child psychotherapy: A cognitive-developmental analysis and case study. *Journal of Clinical Child Psychology, 11*, 209–215.

• (1985). Empirical perspectives on adolescents and their families. In L. L'Abate (Ed.), *Handbook of family and psychology and therapy*, Vol. 1 (pp. 215–257). Homewood, IL: Dorsey Press.

Kagan, J. (1989). *Unstable ideas: Temperament, cognition, and self.* Cambridge, MA: Harvard University Press.

Kagan, J., Reznick, J. S., & Snidman, N. (1990). The temperamental qualities of inhibition and lack of inhibition. In M. Lewis & S. M. Miller (Eds.), *Handbook of developmental psychopathology* (pp. 219–226). New York: Plenum.

Karpel, M. A. (1976). Intrapsychic and interpersonal processes in the parentification of children. *Dissertation Abstracts International, 38*, 365. (University Microfilms No. 77-15090.)

• (Ed.). (1986a). *Family resources: The hidden partner in family therapy.* New York: Guilford Press.

• (1986b). Questions, obstacles, contributions. In M. A. Karpel (Ed.), *Family resources: The hidden partner in family therapy* (pp. 3–61). New York: Guilford.

Karpel, M. A., & Strauss, E. S. (1983). *Family evaluation.* Boston: Allyn & Bacon.

Kaslow, F. W., & Schulman, N. (1987). How to be sane and happy as a family therapist or the reciprocal impact of family therapy teaching and practice and therapists' personal lives and mental health. *Journal of Psychotherapy and the Family, 3*, 79–96.

Kazak, A. (1989). Families of chronically ill children: A systems and social ecological model of adaptation and challenge. *Journal of Consulting and Clinical Psychology, 57*, 25–30.

Kearnes, V. A., Gordon, D. A., Arbuthnot, J., & Kurkowski, K. P. (1994, June). *Children in the middle: Reducing the stress of divorce through videotape modeling.* Paper presented at the meeting of the American Association of Applied and Preventive Psychology, Washington, DC.

Keeney, B. P. (1979). Ecosystemic epistemology: An alternative paradigm for diagnosis. *Family Process, 18*, 117–129.

Kempe, C. H. (1978). Sexual abuse, another hidden pediatric problem. *Pediatrics, 62*, 382–389.

Kempe, C. H., & Helfer, R. E. (1972). *Helping the battered child and his family.* Philadelphia: Lippincott.

Kempe, R. S., & Kempe, C. H. (1978). *Child abuse.* Cambridge, MA: Harvard University Press.

Kerr, M. E., & Bowen, M. (1988). *Family evaluation.* New York: Norton.

Kessen, W. (1965). *The child.* New York: John Wiley & Sons.

Kilburg, R. R., Nathan, P. E., & Thoreson, R. W. (Eds.) (1986). *Professionals in distress: Issues, syndromes and solutions in psychology.* Washington, DC: American Psychological Association.

King, A. E. O. (1993). The impact of incarceration on African American families: Implications for practice. *Families in Society: The Journal of Contemporary Human Services, 74,* 145–153.

Kirschner, D. A., & Kirschner, S. (1986). *Comprehensive family therapy: An integration of systemic and psychodynamic treatment models.* New York: Brunner/Mazel.

Kohut, H. (1977). *The restoration of the self.* New York: International Universities Press.

Kreider, D. G., & Motto, J. A. (1974). Parent-child role reversal and suicidal states in adolescence. *Adolescence, 9,* 365–370.

Krein, S. F., & Beller, A. H. (1988). Educational attainment of children from single parent families: Differences by exposure, gender, and race. *Demography, 25,* 221–234.

Kurylo, E. (1993, June 27). Bosnian Muslim family starts anew in Alpharetta. *The Atlanta Journal–Constitution,* pp. 1A, 10A.

Lackie, B. (1983). The families of origin of social workers. *Clinical Social Work Journal, 11,* 309–322.

Laing, R. D. (1967). *The politics of experience.* New York: Pantheon Books.

Landau, J. (1982). Therapy with families in cultural transition. In M. McGoldrick, J. K. Pearce, & J. Giordano (Eds.), *Ethnicity and family therapy* (pp. 552–572). New York: Guilford Press.

Langsley, D., Kaplan, D., Pittman, F., Machotka, P., Flomenhaft, K., & DeYoung, C. (1968). *Treatment of families in crisis.* New York: Grune & Stratton.

Lerner, H. G. (1988). *Women in therapy.* New York: Harper & Row.

Levy, S. R., Jurkovic, G. J., & Spirito, A. (1995). A multisystems analysis of adolescent suicide attempters. *Journal of Abnormal Child Psychology, 23,* 221–234.

Lewis, M. (1990). Models of developmental psychopathology. In M. Lewis & S. M. Miller (Eds.), *Handbook of developmental psychopathology.* New York: Plenum.

Lidz, T., Cornelison, A., Fleck, S., & Terry, D. (1957). The intrafamilial environment of schizophrenic patients: II. Marital schism and marital skew. *American Journal of Psychiatry, 114,* 241–248.

Lightfoot, S. (1992). Loss and privilege: Life journeys of successful African Americans. In *The Annual Report of the Spencer Foundation* (p. 17). Chicago: The Spencer Foundation.

Lopez, F. G. (1986). Family structure and depression: Implications for the counseling of depressed college students. *Journal of Counseling and Development, 64,* 508–511.

Love, P., & Robinson, J. (1990). *The emotional incest syndrome.* New York: Bantam.

Lowen, A. (1983). *Narcissism: Denial of the true self.* New York: Macmillan.

Lusterman, D. (1985). An ecosystemic approach to family-school problems. *American Journal of Family Therapy, 13,* 22–30.

Madanes, C. (1981). *Strategic family therapy.* San Francisco: Jossey-Bass.

Maeder, T. (1989a). *Children of psychiatrists and other psychotherapists.* New York: Harper & Row.

  • (1989b, January). Wounded healers. *Atlantic Monthly,* pp. 37–47.

Mahler, M. (1968). *On human symbiosis and the vicissitudes of individuation.* New York: International Universities Press.

Mahler, M. S., & Rabinovitch, R. (1956). The effects of marital conflict on child development. In V. E. Eisenstein (Ed.), *Neurotic interaction in marriage* (pp. 44–56). New York: Basic Books.

Main, M., & Cassidy, J. (1988). Categories of response to reunion with the parent at age 6: Predictable from infant attachment classifications and stable over a 1-month period. *Developmental Psychology, 24,* 415–426.

Main, M., & Goldwyn, R. (1984). Predicting rejecting of her infant from mother's representation of her own experience: Implications for the abused-abusing intergenerational cycle. *Child Abuse and Neglect, 8,* 203–217.

Main, M., & Hesse, E. (1990). Parents' unresolved traumatic experiences are related to infant disorganized attachment status: Is frightened and/or frightening parental behavior the linking mechanism? In M. Greenberg, D. Cicchetti & M. Cummings (Eds.), *Attachment in the preschool years* (pp. 161–182). Chicago: University of Chicago Press.

Main, M., Kaplan, N., & Cassidy, J. C. (1985). Security in infancy, childhood and adulthood: A move to the level of representation. In I. Bretherton & E. Waters (Eds.), *Growing points of attachment theory and research: Monographs of the Society for Research in Child Development, 50* (Serial No. 209), Nos. 1–2, 66–104.

Main, M., & Solomon, J. (1986). Discovery of an insecure-disorganized attachment pattern. In T. B. Brazelton & M. W. Yogman (Eds.), *Affective development in infancy* (pp. 95–124). Norwood, NJ: Ablix Publishing.

  • (1990). Procedures for identifying infants as disorganized/ disoriented during the Ainsworth strange situation. In M. Greenberg, D. Cicchetti, & M. Cummings (Eds.), *Attach-*

ment in the preschool years (pp. 121–160). Chicago: University of Chicago Press.

Malerstein, A. J., & Ahern, M. M. (1979). Piaget's stages of cognitive development and adult character structure. *American Journal of Psychotherapy, 33,* 107–118.

McAdoo, H. P. (1988). Transgenerational patterns of upward mobility in African American families. In H. P. McAdoo (Ed.), *Black families* (2nd ed., pp. 148–168). Newbury Park, CA: Sage.

McClelland, D. C. (1961). *The achieving society.* Princeton, NJ: Von Nostrand.

McGoldrick, M. (1982). Irish families. In M. McGoldrick, J. K. Pearce, & J. Giordano (Eds.), *Ethnicity and family therapy* (pp. 310–339). New York: Guilford Press.

McRoberts, F. (1993, January 4). At what age can parents safely leave child alone? Illinois case raises troubling questions. *The Atlanta Constitution,* pp. 1A, 6A.

Mead, M. (1961). *Coming of age in Samoa: A psychological study of primitive youth for Western civilization.* New York: Morrow.

Mead, M. (1968). *Growing up in New Guinea: A comparative study of . primitive education.* New York: Dell.

Mellody, P., Miller, A., & Miller, K. (1989). *Facing co-dependence.* San Francisco: Harper & Row.

Melton, G. B., & Barry, F. D. (1994). Neighbors helping neighbors: The vision of the U.S. Advisory Board on Child Abuse and Neglect. In G. B. Melton & F. D. Barry (Eds.), *Protecting children from abuse and neglect: Foundations for a new national strategy* (pp. 1–13). New York: Guilford.

Meyer, R. G., & Karon, B. P. (1967). The schizophrenigenic mother concept and the TAT. *Psychiatry, 30,* 173–179.

Mika, P., Bergner, R. M., & Baum, M. C. (1987). The development of a scale for the assessment of parentification. *Family Therapy, 14,* 229–235.

Miller, A. (1981). *The drama of the gifted child.* (R. Ward, Trans.). New York: Basic Books. (Original work published 1979)

Miller, G. D., & Baldwin, D. C. (1987). Implications of the wounded-healer paradigm for the use of the self in therapy. *Journal of Psychotherapy and the Family, 3,* 139–151.

Minuchin, S. (1974). *Families and family therapy.* Cambridge, MA: Harvard University Press.

Minuchin, S., & Fishman, H. C. (1981). *Family therapy techniques.* Cambridge, MA: Harvard University Press.

Minuchin, S., Montalvo, B., Guerney, B. G., Rosman, B., & Schumer, F. (1967). *Families of the slums.* New York: Basic Books.

Mitchell, G., & Cronson, H. (1987). The celebrity family: A clinical perspective. *American Journal of Family Therapy, 15,* 235–241.

Mitchell, K. M. (1968). An analysis of the schizophrenigenic mother concept by means of the TAT. *Journal of Abnormal Psychology, 73,* 571–574.

Morris, M. G., & Gould, R. W. (1963). Role reversal: A necessary concept in dealing with the "battered child syndrome." *American Journal of Orthopsychiatry, 33,* 298–299.

- (1979). Role reversal: A concept in dealing with the neglected/battered-child syndrome. In *The neglected battered-child syndrome: Role reversal in parents* (pp. 29–49). New York: Child Welfare League of America.

Morrow, L. (1992, December). The ruin of a cat, the ghost of a dog. *Time,* pp. 36–38.

Murdock, G. P., & Provost, C. (1973). Measurement of cultural complexity. *Ethnology, 12,* 379–392.

National Center on Child Abuse and Neglect. (1996). *Child maltreatment: Reports from the States to the National Center on Child Abuse and Neglect.* Washington, DC: U.S. Government Printing Office.

- (1994). Fiscal year 1994. National Center on Child Abuse and Neglect Discretionary Funds Program: Availability of funds and request for applications. *Federal Register, 59,* 12102–12137.

Nelan, B. W. (1992, December). Taking on the thugs. *Time,* pp. 27–29.

Newberger, C. M. (1977). Parental conceptions of children and child-rearing: A structural-developmental analysis. *Dissertation Abstracts International, 38,* 6123. (University Microfilms No. 78-08622.)

- (1980). The cognitive structure of parenthood: The development of a descriptive measure. In R. Selman & R. Yando (Eds.), *Clinical–developmental psychology. New directions for child development, No. 7* (pp. 45–67). San Francisco: Jossey-Bass.

Newberger, C. M., & Cook, S. J. (1983). Parental awareness and child abuse and neglect: A cognitive-developmental analysis of urban and rural samples. *American Journal of Orthopsychiatry, 53,* 512–524.

Newberger, C. M., & White, K. M. (1989). Cognitive foundations for parental care. In D. Cicchetti & V. Carlson (Eds.), *Child maltreatment: Theory and research on the causes and consequences of child abuse and neglect* (pp. 302–316). New York: Cambridge University Press.

O'Connor, M. J., Sigman, M., & Brill, N. (1987). Disorganization of attachment in relation to maternal alcohol consumption. *Journal of Consulting and Clinical Psychology, 55,* 831–836.

Ogden, T. H. (1979). On projective identification. *International Journal of Psycho-Analysis, 60,* 357–373.

- (1982). *Projective identification and psychotherapeutic technique.* New York: Aronson.

Olds, D. L., & Henderson, C. R. (1989). The prevention of maltreatment. In D. Cicchetti & V. Carlson (Eds.), *Child maltreatment: Theory and research on the causes and consequences of child abuse and neglect* (pp. 722–763). New York: Cambridge University Press.

Olson, M., & Gariti, P. (1993). Symbolic loss in horizontal relating: Defining the role of parentification in addictive relationships. *Contemporary Family Therapy, 15,* 197–208.

Palazzoli-Selvini, M., Boscolo, L., Cecchin, G. F., & Prata, G. (1978). *Paradox and counterparadox: A new model in the therapy of the family in schizophrenic transaction.* New York: Aronson.

Panel on Research on Child Abuse and Neglect, Commission on Behavioral and Social Sciences and Education, National Research Council. (1993). *Understanding child abuse and neglect.* Washington, DC: National Academy Press.

Parsons, T., & Bales, R. F. (1955). *Family, socialization and interaction process.* Glencoe, IL: Free Press.

Pelton, L. H. (1994). The role of material factors in child abuse and neglect. In G. B. Melton & F. D. Barry (Eds.), *Protecting children from abuse and neglect: Foundations for a new national strategy* (pp. 131–181). New York: Guilford.

Pittman, F. S. (1984). Wet cocker spaniel therapy: An essay on technique in family therapy. *Family Process, 23,* 1–9.

- (1987). *Turning points: Treating families in transition and crises.* New York: Norton.

Plomin, R., & Dunn, J. (Eds.). (1986). *The study of temperament: Changes, continuities, and challenges.* Hillsdale, NJ: Lawrence Erlbaum.

Racusin, G. R., Abramowitz, S. I., & Winter, W. D. (1981). Becoming a therapist: Family dynamics and career choice. *Professional Psychology, 12,* 271–279.

Radke-Yarrow, M., Cummings, E. M., Kuczynski, L., & Chapman, M. (1985). Patterns of attachment in two and three-year-olds in normal families and families with parental depression. *Child Development, 56,* 884–894.

Reis, H. T. (1986). Levels of interest in the study of interpersonal justice. In H. W. Bierhoff, R. L. Cohen, & J. Greenberg (Eds.), *Justice in social relations* (pp. 187–210). New York: Plenum.

Rheingold, H. L. (1982). Little children's participation in the work of adults: A nascent prosocial behavior. *Child Development, 53,* 114–125.

Rheingold, H. L., Hay, D. F., & West, M. J. (1976). Sharing in the second year of life. *Child Development, 47,* 1148–1158.

Riva, M. (1993). *Marlene Dietrich.* New York: Alfred A. Knopf.

Rosenbaum, M. (1963). Psychological effects on the child raised by an older sibling. *American Journal of Orthopsychiatry, 33,* 515–520.

Rosman, B. L. (1986). Developmental perspectives in family therapy with children. In H. C. Fishman & B. L. Rosman (Eds.), *Evolving models for family change* (pp. 227–233). New York: Guilford Press.

Rupp, G. L., & Jurkovic, G. J. (1996). Familial and individual perspective-taking processes in adolescent females with bulimic symptomatology. *American Journal of Family Therapy, 24,* 75–82.

Russell, D. E. H. (1986). *The secret trauma.* New York: Basic Books.

Sager, C. J. (1981). Couples therapy and marriage contracts. In A. S. Gurman & D. P. Kniskern (Eds.), *Handbook of family therapy* (pp. 85–130). New York: Brunner/Mazel.

Sagi, A., & Hoffman, M. L. (1976). Empathic distress in the newborn. *Developmental Psychology, 12,* 175–176.

Sameroff, A., & Chandler, M. (1975). Reproductive risk and the continuum of caretaking causality. In F. Horowitz (Ed.), *Review of child development research,* Vol. 4 (pp. 187–244). Chicago: University of Chicago Press.

Sampson, E. E. (1986). Justice, ideology and social legitimation: A revised agenda for psychological inquiry. In H. W. Bierhoff, R. L. Cohen, & J. Greenberg (Eds.), *Justice in social relations* (pp. 87–102). New York: Plenum.

Santostefano, S. (1978). *A bio-developmental approach to clinical child psychology.* New York: John Wiley & Sons.

Satir, V. (1988). *The new peoplemaking.* Mt. View, CA: Science & Behavior Books.

Scheflen, A. E. (1980). *Levels of schizophrenia.* New York: Brunner/ Mazel.

Schmideberg, M. (1948). Parents as children. *Psychiatric Quarterly Supplement, 22,* 207–218.

Schnarch, D. M. (1991). *Constructing the sexual crucible: An integration of sexual and marital therapy.* New York: Norton.

Schneider, C., Pollock, C., & Helfer, R. E. (1972). Interviewing the parents. In C. H. Kempe & R. E. Helfer (Eds.), *Helping the battered child and his family* (pp. 271–282). Philadelphia: Lippincott.

Schwartzman, J. (1985). Macrosystemic approaches to family therapy: An overview. In J. Schwartzman (Ed.), *Families and other systems: The macrosystemic context of family therapy* (pp. 1–24). New York: Guilford.

Searles, H. F. (1971). Pathological symbiosis and autism. In B. Landis & E. S. Tauber (Eds.), *In the name of life: Essays in honor of Erich Fromm.* New York: Holt, Rinehart, & Winston.

• (1973). Concerning therapeutic symbiosis. *The Annual of*

Psychoanalysis: A publication of the Chicago Institute for Psychoanalysis, 1, 247–262.

- (1975). The patient as therapist to his analyst. In P. Giovacchini (Ed.), *Tactics and techniques in psychoanalytic therapy: Volume II. Countertransference* (pp. 95–151). New York: Jason Aronson.

Sears, R. R., Maccoby, E. E., & Levin, H. (1957). *Patterns of child rearing.* New York: Row, Peterson.

Selman, R. L. (1980). *The growth of interpersonal understanding: Developmental and clinical analyses.* New York: Academic Press.

Sessions, M. (1986). Influence of parentification on professional role choice and interpersonal style. *Dissertation Abstracts International, 47,* 5066. (University Microfilms No. 87-06815.)

Sessions, M., & Jurkovic, G. J. (1986). *The Parentification Questionnaire.* (Available from Gregory J. Jurkovic, Department of Psychology, Georgia State University, University Plaza, Atlanta, GA 30303.)

Shon, S. P., & Ja, D. Y. (1982). Asian families. In M. McGoldrick, J. K. Pearce, & J. Giordano (Eds.), *Ethnicity and family therapy* (pp. 208–228). New York: Guilford Press.

Slipp, S. (1973). The symbiotic survival pattern: A relational theory of schizophrenia. *Family Process, 12,* 377–398.

Sperry, R. W. (1977). Bridging science and values: A unifying view of mind and brain. *American Psychologist, 32,* 237–245.

Sroufe, L. A., & Fleeson, J. (1986). Attachment and the construction of relationships. In W. Hartup & Z. Rubin (Eds.), *Relationships and development* (pp. 51–72). Hillsdale, NJ: Erlbaum.

Sroufe, L. A., Jacobvitz, D., Mangelsdorf, S., DeAngelo, E., & Ward, M. J. (1985). Generational boundary dissolution between mothers and their preschool children: A relationship systems approach. *Child Development, 56,* 317–332.

Sroufe, L. A., & Rutter, M. (1984). The domain of developmental psychopathology. *Child Development, 55,* 1184–1199.

Sroufe, L. A., & Ward, J. J. (1980). Seductive behavior of mothers of toddlers: Occurrence, correlates, and family origins. *Child Development, 51,* 1222–1229.

Stanton, M. D., & Todd, T. C. (1979). Structured family therapy with drug addicts. In E. Kaufman & P. Kaufman (Eds.), *Family therapy of drug and alcohol abuse* (pp. 55–69). New York: Gardner.

Stern, D. (1985). *The interpersonal world of the infant.* New York: Basic Books.

Stierlin, H. (1974). *Separating parents and adolescents: A perspective on running away, schizophrenia and waywardness.* New York: Quadrangle.

- (1977). *Psychoanalysis and family therapy.* New York: Aronson.

Stipek, D., & McCroskey, J. (1989). Investing in children: Government and workplace policies for parents. *American Psychologist, 44,* 416–423.

Stoneman, Z., Brody, G. H., Davis, C. H., & Crapps, J. M. (1988). Childcare responsibilities, peer relations, and sibling conflict: Older siblings of mentally retarded children. *American Journal of Mental Retardation, 93,* 174–183.

Super, C. M., & Harkness, S. (1981). Figure, ground, and gestalt: The cultural context of the active individual. In R. M. Lerner & N. A. Busch-Rossnagel (Eds.), *Individuals as producers of their development: A life-span perspective* (pp. 69–86). New York: Academic Press.

- (1982). The infant's niche in rural Kenya and metropolitan America. In L. L. Adler (Ed.), *Cross-cultural research at issue* (pp. 47–55). New York: Academic Press.

Sussman, M. B. (1992). *A curious calling: Unconscious motivations for practicing psychotherapy.* Northvale, NJ: Aronson.

Termine, N. T., & Izard, C. E. (1988). Infants' responses to their mothers' expressions of joy and sadness. *Developmental Psychology, 24,* 223–229.

Tharp, R. G. (1965). Marriage roles, child development, and family treatment. *American Journal of Orthopsychiatry, 35,* 351–358.

Thomas, A., & Chess, S. (1977). *Temperament and development.* New York: Brunner/Mazel.

Titelman, P. (1987). The therapist's own family. In P. Titelman (Ed.), *The therapist's own family: Toward the differentiation of self* (pp. 3–42). Northvale, NJ: Jason Aronson.

Toman, W. (1961). *Family constellation.* New York: Springer.

Tomm, K. (1988). Interventive interviewing, Part III: Intending to ask linear, circular, strategic, and reflexive questions. *Family Process, 27,* 1–15.

U. S. Advisory Board on Child Abuse and Neglect. (1993). *Neighbors helping neighbors: A new national strategy for the protection of children.* Washington, DC: U. S. Government Printing Office.

Valleau, M. P., Bergner, R. M., & Horton, C. B. (1995). Parentification and caretaker syndrome: An empirical investigation. *Family Therapy, 22,* 157–164.

Vandenberg, B. (1991). Is epistemology enough? An existential consideration of development. *American Psychologist, 46,* 1278–1286.

VandenBos, G. R., & Karon, B. P. (1971). Pathogenesis: A new therapist personality dimension related to therapeutic effectiveness. *Journal of Personality Assessment, 35,* 252–260.

Vourlekis, B. S., & Greene, R. R. (Eds.). (1992). *Social work case management.* New York: Aldine de Gruyter.

Waldrip, C. C. (1993, Winter). The therapist as a recovering co-dependent. *Georgia Association for Marriage and Family Therapy Newsletter,* pp. 1, 7.

Wallerstein, J. S. (1985). The overburdened child: Some long-term consequences of divorce. *Social Work, 30,* 116–123.

Wallerstein, J. S., & Kelly, J. B. (1980). *Surviving the breakup: How children and parents cope with divorce.* New York: Basic Books.

Walsh, F. W. (1979). Breaching of family generation boundaries by schizophrenics, disturbed, and normals. *International Journal of Family Therapy, 1,* 254–275.

Walsh, J. (1992). Understanding young CoAs. *Adolescent Counselor: Education About Addictions, 5,* 29–33.

Wegscheider-Cruse, S. (1985). *Choicemaking: For co-dependents, adult children and spirituality seekers.* Pompano Beach, FL: Health Communications.

  • (1990). Co-dependency and dysfunctional family systems. In R. C. Engs (Ed.), *Women: Alcohol and other drugs.* Dubuque, IA: Kendall/Hunt.

Weisner, T. S., & Gallimore, R. (1977). My brother's keeper: Child and sibling caretaking. *Current Anthropology, 18,* 169–190.

Weiss, R. S. (1979). Growing up a little faster: The experience of growing up in a single parent household. *Journal of Social Issues, 35,* 97–111.

Welt, S. R., & Herron, W. G. (1990). *Narcissism and the psychotherapist.* New York: Guilford.

Welts, E. P. (1982). Greek families. In M. McGoldrick, J. K. Pearce, & J. Giordano (Eds.), *Ethnicity and family therapy* (pp. 269–288). New York: Guilford Press.

West, M. L., & Keller, A. E. R. (1991). Parentification of the child: A case study of Bowlby's compulsive care-giving attachment pattern. *American Journal of Psychotherapy, 45,* 425–431.

Whan, M. (1987). Chiron's wound: Some reflections on the wounded healer. In N. Schwartz-Salant & M. Stein (Eds.), *Archetypal proces in psychotherapy* (pp. 197–208). Wilmette, IL: Chiron Publishers.

White, M., & Epston, D. (1990). *Narrative means to therapeutic ends.* New York: W. W. Norton.

Whitfield, C. L. (1991). *Co-dependence: Healing the human condition.* Deerfield Beach, FL: Health Communications.

Whiting, B., & Edwards, C. P. (1973). A cross-cultural analysis of sex differences in the behavior of children aged three through eleven. *Journal of Social Psychology, 91,* 171–188.

Wilkerson, I. (1993, April 4). First born, fast grown: The manful life of Nicholas, 10. *The New York Times,* pp. 1Y, 16Y.

Willis, D. J., Holden, E. W., & Rosenberg, M. (Eds.). (1992). *Prevention of child maltreatment: Developmental and ecological perspectives.* New York: John Wiley & Sons.

Winnicott, D. W. (1965). *The maturational processes and the facilitating environment: Studies in the theory of emotional development.* New York: International Universities Press.

Wolkin, J. R. (1984). Childhood parentification: An exploration of long-term effects. *Dissertation Abstracts International, 45,* 2707. (University Microfilms No. 84-24601.)

Zahn-Waxler, C., & Kochanska, G. (1988). The origins of guilt. In R. Dienstbier & R. A. Thompson (Eds.), *Nebraska Symposium on Motivation: Vol. 36. Socioemotional development* (pp. 222–258). Lincoln: University of Nebraska Press.

Zahn-Waxler, C., & Radke-Yarrow, M. (1982). The development of altruism: Alternative research strategies. In N. Eisenberg (Ed.), *The development of prosocial behavior.* New York: Academic Press.

Zahn-Waxler, C., Radke-Yarrow, M., & King, R. A. (1979). Child rearing and children's prosocial initiations towards victims of distress. *Child Development, 50,* 319–330.

Zahn-Waxler, C., Radke-Yarrow, M., Wagner, E., & Chapman, M. (1992). Development of concern for others. *Developmental Psychology, 28,* 126–136.

Zahn-Waxler, C., & Robinson, J. (1995). Empathy and guilt: Early origins of feelings of responsibility. In J. P. Tangney & K. W. Fischer (Eds.), *Self-conscious emotions: The psychology of shame, guilt, embarrassment, and pride* (pp. 143–173). New York: Guilford.

Zeanah, C. H., & Klitzke, M. (1991). Role reversal and the self-effacing solution: Observations from infant-parent psychotherapy. *Psychiatry, 54,* 346–357.

Zeanah, C. H., & Zeanah, P. D. (1989). Intergenerational transmission of maltreatment: Insights from attachment theory and research. *Psychiatry, 52,* 177–196.

Zigler, E., & Hall, N. W. (1989). Physical child abuse in America: Past, present, and future. In D. Cicchetti & V. Carlson (Eds.), *Child maltreatment: Theory and research on the causes and consequences of child abuse and neglect* (pp. 38–75). New York: Cambridge University Press.

NAME INDEX

SUBJECT INDEX